Faulkner's Geographies
FAULKNER AND YOKNAPATAWPHA
2011

Faulkner's Geographies

FAULKNER AND YOKNAPATAWPHA, 2011

EDITED BY
JAY WATSON
AND
ANN J. ABADIE

UNIVERSITY PRESS OF MISSISSIPPI
JACKSON

www.upress.state.ms.us

The University Press of Mississippi is a member
of the Association of American University Presses.

First printing 2015

Library of Congress Cataloging-in-Publication Data

Faulkner and Yoknapatawpha Conference (38th : 2011 : University of Mississippi)
  Faulkner's geographies : Faulkner and Yoknapatawpha, 2011 / edited by Jay Watson,
Ann J. Abadie.
    pages cm. — (Faulkner and Yoknapatawpha series)
  Summary: "The recent spatial turn in social theory and cultural studies opens up exciting new possibilities for the study of William Faulkner's literature. The fictional domains
of Yoknapatawpha County and Jefferson, Mississippi, are not simply imagined communities but imaginative geographies of remarkable complexity and detail, as evidenced by
the maps Faulkner created of his "apocryphal" county. Exploring the diverse functions
of space in Faulkner's artistic vision, the eleven essays in Faulkner's Geographies delve
deep into Yoknapatawpha but also reach beyond it, to uncover unsuspected connections and flows linking local, regional, national, hemispheric, and global geographies in
Faulkner's writings. Individual contributions examine the influence of the plantation as
a land-use regime on Faulkner's imagination of north Mississippi's geography; the emergence of "micro-Souths" as a product of modern migratory patterns in the urban North
of Faulkner's fiction; the enlistment of the author's work in the geopolitics of the cultural
Cold War during the 1950s; the historical and literary affiliations between Faulkner's
Deep South and Greater Mexico; the local and idiosyncratic as alternatives to region and
nation; the unique intersection of regional and metropolitan geographies that Faulkner
encountered as a novice writer immersed in the literary culture of New Orleans; the
uses of feminist geography to trace the interplay of gender, space, and movement; and
the circulation of Caribbean and "Black South" spaces and itineraries through Faulkner's
masterpiece, Absalom, Absalom! By bringing new attention to the function of space,
place, mapping, and movement in his literature, Faulkner's Geographies seeks to redraw
the very boundaries of Faulkner studies"— Provided by publisher.
  Includes bibliographical references and index.
    ISBN 978-1-4968-0227-9 (hardback) — SBN 978-1-4968-0228-6 (ebook) 1.
Faulkner, William, 1897–1962—Criticism and interpretation—Congresses. 2. Yoknapatawpha County (Imaginary place)—Congresses. 3. Geography in literature—
Congresses. 4. Geographical perception in literature—Congresses. 5. Space in
literature—Congresses. 6. Geopolitics in literature—Congresses. I. Watson, Jay, editor.
II. Abadie, Ann J., editor. III. Title.
  PS3511.A86Z78321135 2015
  813'.52—dc23   2014042295

British Library Cataloging-in-Publication Data available

In Memoriam,

Louis Daniel Brodsky
April 17, 1941–June 16, 2014

Betty Zachry Harrington
June 20, 1928–October 22, 2011

Albert Murray
May 12, 1916–August 18, 2013

Stephen M. Ross
November 28, 1943–August 21, 2013

Louis D. Rubin
November 19, 1923–November 16, 2013

Contents

Introduction

"In the beginning," writes Henri Lefebvre, "was the Topos."[1] Lefebvre, perhaps the most influential theorist of space in modern philosophy,[2] did not have William Faulkner in mind when he penned those words, but he certainly could have. Faulkner studies, after all, is highly invested in its own spatially focused origin narrative, in which the creation of a specific topos, the fictional north Mississippi county of Yoknapatawpha, is singled out as the pivotal moment in the authorial ontogenesis of one of the twentieth century's most celebrated writers. Before Yoknapatawpha: a haphazard artistic program ranging from Beardsleyesque line drawings, impressionistic newspaper sketches and caricatures, and earnest but undistinguished lyric sequences and verse plays, to a pair of superficially brilliant but ultimately derivative novels whose physical and social landscapes owed as much to English as to indigenous models. After Yoknapatawpha: a firmly focused and seemingly inexhaustible literary project encompassing fifteen novels and several dozen short stories, in which an intensely realized local world serves as gateway to the eternal verities, "a kind of keystone in the Universe," as Faulkner famously put it.[3] In this narrative, the advent of Yoknapatawpha marks the end of a literary apprenticeship, the birth of literary greatness.[4]

One reason Yoknapatawpha County looms so large in the story of Faulkner's success is that—alone among the numerous global locales he explored in his fiction—he literally mapped it. Twice. Once for the endpapers of *Absalom, Absalom!* in 1936, and then, with important additions, deletions, and variations, for Malcolm Cowley's *Portable Faulkner* volume in 1946. In promoting and interpreting his own work, then, Faulkner intuitively turned to geography's preeminent mode of knowledge production. Geographer Charles S. Aiken suggests that with these acts of cartographic mapping, Faulkner "began to come to grips with the larger geographic setting of his stories," that, in other words, his maps didn't just provide a referential visual schema for an area somehow prior and complete in his imagination but more actively shaped the ways in which he subsequently understood and used that space.[5] To a greater or lesser degree, all maps perform this shaping function, due in part to the principle of selectivity that guides their creation. No more than the textual Yoknapatawpha County could ever encompass the full range of landscape and demographic elements comprising Faulkner's actual county of Lafayette—a point made by Aiken—could a map of Yoknapatawpha hope to capture the entirety of features we find there across Faulkner's oeuvre. In order to be legible at all, "to portray meaningful relationships for a complex . . . world on a flat sheet of paper" without enshrouding "critical information in a fog of detail," maps "must offer a selective, incomplete view of reality."[6] Or, as geographer Mark Monmonier more forcefully puts it, they must lie. Monmonier calls this "the cartographic paradox": maps cannot reveal without concealing, distorting.

What, then, do Faulkner's maps reveal? What do they conceal? Turning briefly to the first question, we could follow Aiken in suggesting that they reveal the workings of an open, fluid, and very contemporary geographic imagination. Yoknapatawpha represents only a tiny section of the globe, 2,400 square miles according to Faulkner's legend, but it is by no means an insular one. As Aiken notes, "Faulkner considered the Tallahatchie and Yoknapatawpha rivers boundaries of his county. But significantly, no boundaries are shown on the two maps of the county that he drew" (55). In this way, the maps signal that the county's residents and visitors "reach toward other areas and operate within a broader spatial context," one that the fictional narratives extend to such places as New Orleans, the Mississippi Delta, Memphis, Chicago, the Appalachian Mountains, Cambridge, the Caribbean, and the battlefields of Europe. Yoknapatawpha may be "a place with a core," as Aiken puts it, "but the county has no isolating walls." It participates actively in a regional, national, and global landscape of mobility, exchange, and flow, what the Martinican novelist and critic Édouard Glissant might have called a *geography* of relation.[7]

And what of the lies these maps tell? We could point to telltale omissions like the puzzling absence of Dewey Dell Bundren from all references on the *Absalom* map to the funeral journey made by "Anse Bundren and his sons" or "Anse Bundren and his boys" to Jefferson.[8] We might also note the absence of much information that would specifically *relate* the county to the other spaces that lie beyond yet traverse its porous borders; there are the neighboring communities of Mottstown to the south and "Memphis Junction" to the north on the *Absalom* map, of course, but little on more distant sites. Moreover, as Scott Romine points out in his contribution to this volume, the maps are at best evasive about historical or geographical formations that lie prior to or beyond the hegemony of the plantation as a land-use regime; even the Chickasaw patent that precedes white settlement in the area is assimilated conceptually to the plantation system, inasmuch as "by 1820" the Indians "had learned to call it 'The Plantation' just like the white men did."[9] Such "cartographic silences," Monmonier observes, amount to "a form of geographic disinformation" that mystifies the historical character of the plantation and ascribes to it instead an elemental, eternal quality as a landscape feature (122).

What Faulkner is doing with these maps, as a reader of his own texts, is more or less the same procedure sketched by Franco Moretti as part of a program of "distant reading" that downplays the idiosyncrasy of textual elements in favor of "a sharper sense of their overall interconnection."[10] Moretti describes this technique as follows:

> You choose a unit—walks, lawsuits, luxury goods, whatever—find its occurrences, place them in space . . . or in other words: you *reduce* the text to a few elements, and *abstract* them from the narrative flow, and construct a new, *artificial* object like the maps that I have been discussing. And with a little luck, these maps will *be more than the sum of their parts*: they will possess "emerging" qualities, which were not visible at the lower level. . . . Not that the map is itself an explanation, of course: but at least, it offers a model of the narrative universe which rearranges its components in a non-trivial way, and may bring some hidden patterns to the surface. (53–54)

It would be intriguing, though beyond the scope of this introduction, to reconstruct the primary "units" of analysis that govern Faulkner's mapmaking projects: homes, farms, and businesses, to be sure, but also, more curiously, sites of death and at least half a dozen crime scenes.[11] For now we can observe that Faulkner shared this cartographic imagination, this mapping impulse, with some of his most memorable characters, who exhibit an intimate feel for and understanding of the spatial contours of their world.

A case in point would be Rider, the African American protagonist of "Pantaloon in Black." If we trace Rider's movements in the aftermath of his wife's death, they suggest that he is himself engaged in a cartographic enterprise, an itinerary that revisits specific places in his quotidian world in order to remap them as sites in a racialized geography of injustice. From a rural graveyard where black funerary customs and the spiritual beliefs they express are destined to go unread at best, disastrously misread at worst, by white observers, and a sawmill skidway where the exploitation of a black labor force meets the corollary despoliation of the area's hardwood forest, Rider proceeds to a white homestead whose bootlegging occupant dispenses racial insults and condescension along with the anodyne the bereaved husband seeks, then to the sawmill again, where the white nightwatchman, Birdsong, runs a crooked dice game that relieves the black mill hands of their pay, and finally, after killing Birdsong, to the jail, where white law enforcement turns a blind eye on the party of Birdsongs who come to lynch the prisoner.[12] Fredric Jameson has referred to the activity in which Rider is engaged as "cognitive mapping," the "practical reconquest" of an alien landscape through acts of physical occupation and point-to-point movement that cumulatively produce a functional sense of spatial orientation.[13] What has rendered Rider's landscape alien is primal loss, the premature death of the young woman whose love gave him purpose and direction, and the racial injustices that his movements expose and limn serve him as social objectifications of the cosmic, existential injustice that has robbed him of his precious Mannie. His spatial imagination thus enables him to reappropriate and remap his earthly territory as the arena for a meta-physical showdown with his true foe, a far more formidable diceman than Birdsong.

One reason that a few thousand square miles of north Mississippi soil undergoing deforestation, organization into plantations, urbaniza-tion, railroad construction, and other modernizing processes could serve Faulkner so effectively as a keystone in the universe is that the lived contours of that universe were themselves undergoing significant trans-formation throughout the author's era. Geographer David Harvey has identified "space-time compression" as a hallmark of the transportation and communications revolutions that attended capitalist development, rendering the globe ever smaller experientially and its peoples ever more proximate and entangled.[14] It can be easy to extrapolate from some of Faulkner's more gothic tales to the false conclusion that Jefferson and Yoknapatawpha are a claustrophobic, stifling domain whose inhabitants are doomed to physical and intellectual immobility, mummified by the dead weight of convention and the past. Emily Grierson, Gail High-tower, and Caroline Compson come immediately to mind in this regard. A far larger group of Faulkner characters, however, embark on broader regional, national, and even international itineraries, taking advantage of the more intimate and accessible global geography created by space-time compression. Such figures as Thomas Sutpen ("Faulkner's first cosmopolite," according to Hortense J. Spillers[15]), Calvin and Nathaniel Burden, Linda Snopes Kohl, Joe Christmas (and his equally "peripa-tetic"[16] father), Caddy Compson, Charles Bon, and the throng of charac-ters pulled from Asia, Africa, North America, and other parts of Europe to the Western Front all experience the world as their village—if not necessarily their oyster. Their peregrinations attest to the demographic porosity Faulkner ascribes to his imagined spaces, and thus to the wis-dom of his refusal to assign closed boundaries to his apocryphal county. Indeed, in this respect, as a site and medium for individual mobility and larger population flows (white settlement, Indian removal, African

American migration, Yankee military occupation, and, later, tourism), Faulkner's fictional domain closely follows his actual one, as can be seen in Don H. Doyle's history of Lafayette County, which posits migration, dynamic social and geographical movement, as the central theme of that history.[17]

At the same time, Faulkner's work offers a rich record of the process Arjun Appadurai has called the production of locality. Appadurai defines locality as "a complex phenomenological quality" that combines the experience of "social immediacy" with the sense of "interactivity" to produce that distinctive "structure of feeling" we live as the local.[18] "The building of houses, the organization of paths and passages, the making and remaking of fields and gardens, the mapping and negotiation of transhuman spaces" are all important aspects of this activity, which "small-scale societies" in particular "do not and cannot take . . . as a given" (180). "Rather," Appadurai adds, small communities "seem to assume that locality is ephemeral unless hard and regular work is undertaken to produce and maintain its materiality" (180–81). Jefferson and Yoknapatawpha are no exceptions. Take the building of houses, for instance, one of the most incessantly and intensively narrativized events in Faulkner. *Absalom, Absalom!* chronicles one such building project, Sutpen's Hundred, as it initially threatens a sense of Yoknapatawpha locality (recall the antagonism that the upstart Sutpen inspires among his Mississippi neighbors) but becomes by Quentin Compson's era a constitutive, if difficult, element of that very locality. This fraught, ambivalent legacy is typical of the other dwellings, great and small, that alternately dot or blanket the local landscape: the Frenchman place, the Compson mile, Rider's rented cabin (where locality is nothing if not a structure of feeling), the Bundren homeplace atop its steep bluff, and so on. Indeed, it is surely significant in this respect that the homestead is the most frequently demarcated landscape element on the *Absalom* map. But roads, trails, and railbeds; cotton stands and pastures; gravestones, graveyards, and Indian mounds; storefronts, porches, and other gathering places; sites of labor and leisure; the hub-like courthouse and the jailhouse in its municipal backwater—all also contribute in fundamental ways to the Yoknapatawpha version of what Appadurai calls the socialization of space (180).

Faulkner's formative years also witnessed another important shift in the modern understanding and experience of space. Citing the work of British geographer Halford J. MacKinder, whose 1904 essay "The Geographical Pivot of History" observed that "the whole of the exotic world available for empire had been mapped" and that there thus remained "no more foreign places to conquer and colonize," along with the realization by Frederick Jackson Turner and other period historians that the frontier era had come to an end on the North American continent, Enda Duffy points to the turn of the nineteenth century as a "paradigm shattering moment when it became clear . . . that global space was finite."[19] What this meant was that capitalist development could no longer turn for what Harvey calls its "spatial fix" to geographical expansion into new territories to absorb excess capital and thus ward off crises of overproduction and overaccumulation at home.[20] Out of this gap, argues Duffy, emerged a new material and cultural emphasis on speed. New and ever-accelerating velocities of production, circulation, consumption, and turnover time allowed the modern economy to exploit a new temporal "fix" in place of the obsolescent spatial one in the pursuit of superprofits, even as speed itself was celebrated as an unprecedented new cultural phenomenon and personal sensation, the one distinctly modern pleasure, "a means to experience space in a new way, at the very moment when there was no more new world space left to organize" (19). For Duffy, the years 1900–1930 mark the pinnacle of this new psychology and geography of speed, and the high modernist period that shares these milestones can be understood in part as a cultural and artistic response to the new phenomenon. Seen in this light, speed becomes "the secret of modernist space" (265).

Duffy's speed era coincides with the years of Faulkner's youth and literary apprenticeship; as a result, perhaps, much of Faulkner's work can be fitted comfortably into a canon of speed literature. From the inaugural Yoknapatawpha novel, *Sartoris*, to the valedictory one, *The Reivers*, Faulkner's fiction turns frequently to scenes in which a diverse array of transportation forms—horses, automobiles, airplanes, even a torpedo boat—are pushed to their limits to yield the raw thrill of speed. Young Bayard Sartoris, *Sanctuary*'s Popeye, the aviators of *Pylon*—all display the need for speed that Duffy cites as a hallmark of modernist affect. Indeed, the new geography of speed even leaves its imprint on *Absalom*'s map of Yoknapatawpha County, at sites like the "church which Thomas Sutpen rode fast to" or the roadside spot "where Old Bayard Sartoris died in Young Bayard's car," victim of a heart attack that attests to speed culture's new demands on the modern body.

Velocity, of course, is a function of space *and* time, a reminder that invites us to consider their interplay in the theoretical reflection that underpins contemporary literary studies. One result of the spatial turn that Edward Soja has examined in recent critical theory is a renewed appreciation for the value of aesthetic reflection and analysis as a complement to social and historical inquiry.[21] Harvey explains the relationship this way:

Social theories . . . typically privilege time over space in their formulations. . . . Aesthetic theory, on the other hand, is deeply concerned with "the spatialization of time." . . . Social theory has always focused on processes of social change, modernization, and revolution (technical, social, political). Progress is its theoretical object, and historical time its primary dimension. Indeed, progress entails the conquest of space, the tearing down of all spatial barriers, and the ultimate "annihilation of space through time." . . . Since modernity is about the experience of progress through modernization, writings on that theme have tended to emphasize temporality, the process of *becoming*, rather than *being* in space and place. . . . Aesthetic theory, on the other hand, seeks out the rules that allow eternal and immutable truths to be conveyed in the midst of the maelstrom of flux and change. . . . Any system of representation, in fact, is a spatialization of sorts which automatically freezes the flow of experience and in so doing distorts what it strives to represent.[22]

These words will resonate with anyone familiar with Faulkner's account of artistic representation as arresting (and thereby spatializing, and thus to some degree falsifying) the motion intrinsic to all life.[23] If Harvey is correct, we need *both* frameworks, aesthetic and social, to unlock the full significance and depth of insight that literature is capable of yielding. "There is much to be learned from aesthetic theory about how different forms of spatialization inhibit or facilitate processes of social change. Conversely, there is much to be learned from social theory concerning the flux and change with which aesthetic theory has to cope" (207). It is imperative, of course, to employ these approaches in an integrated rather than simply oppositional way. The recent volume in this series *Faulkner and Formalism*, which reflects the influence of the so-called New Aesthetic and New Formalist movements in literary studies, suggests that the intellectual adjustment process that Harvey calls for may be under way in Faulkner scholarship.[24] But in order to do full justice to Faulkner's work, we will also need to balance our focus on Faulkner as historian, sociologist, and formal innovator with an equally nuanced attention to Faulkner as geographer. The essays gathered for this volume represent an important step in that direction.

A decade after they opened the influential essay collection *South to a New Place: Region, Literature, Culture* with a pair of essays revisiting the function of place and space in Southern writing *and* Southern literary studies, Barbara Ladd and Scott Romine get the present volume under way with rich reconsiderations of Faulkner's spatial imagination. Ladd's "Local Places/Modern Spaces: The Crossroads Local in Faulkner" explains why Faulkner's writings can be difficult to position within the regionalist projects that dominated the literary scene during his era, since his work points neither to a "reassuring traditionalism" nor to a clearly defined agenda of resistance to nationalizing, modernizing imperatives. Ladd turns instead to the local as a more apt and productive spatial register in which to encounter Faulkner's world—but by "local" she refers not so much to a sanctuary of stable identities and values as to a site of productive *instability* that she associates with the intimate and idiosyncratic, the emergent and supplementary, and the exigencies of the body as the ultimate ground of any sense of place. Ladd's musings on various Yoknapatawpha "locals" from Ike Snopes and Benjy Compson to Rosa Coldfield suggest that reading Faulkner "under the sign of the local rather than under the sign of the South" can help keep us on guard against provincializing the Mississippi writer and his work.

Romine's "Designing Spaces: Sutpen, Snopes, and the Promise of the Plantation" zeroes in on the New World's most durable and pernicious fantasy construction to explore "how . . . the imagined geography of Yoknapatawpha operate[s] relative to the patchy, fluid, confused, and *heterogeneous* grammars of space that exist within it." Noting the plantation's "anxious position in Faulkner's geography," Romine argues that it "epitomizes the paradox of Faulknerian space": by turns bulwark and rupture, scene of aspiration and untenability, "it is both constitutive of, and irreducible to, design," perhaps nowhere more so than in the mutually illuminating careers of Thomas Sutpen and Flem Snopes. Drawing on the work of Michel de Certeau, Romine presents Sutpen as a plantation *strategist* extraordinaire, simple-minded and abstract in the pursuit of his design, and Snopes as a plantation *tactician*, adaptable, opportunistic, improvisational. Sutpen needs money to build a plantation, a place to arrive; Flem uses the plantation that more or less falls into his lap as a way to make money, which he then uses to buy a share in a dingy Jefferson lunch counter (not exactly a typical career move for a member, however briefly, of the Mississippi plantocracy). Their movements toward and through plantation space—each in its own way "inerrant, mechanical, and overdetermined" yet "erratic and anomalous, full of skips and jumps"—return us to the paradox of a spatial poetics "that produces and consolidates spaces even as it fractures and dissolves."

The next two essays take up a pair of metropolitan locales that figure significantly in Faulkner's life and work. In "'My New Orleans Gang': Faulkner's French Quarter Circle," John Shelton Reed examines the motley krewe of "artists, writers, journalists, musicians, poseurs, and hangers-on" who gathered in the Crescent City to pursue the bohemian life in the 1920s. Described by Hamilton Basso as a "Creole version of the Left Bank" and by the WPA guide to Louisiana as a "second Greenwich Village," the movement included many of the "Famous Creoles" lampooned by Faulkner and artist William Spratling in 1926. Fueled by bootleg alcohol from Cuba and the Bahamas, which acted as a social lubricant while underscoring the city's historical and economic links to the Caribbean region, the scene also brought artists and intellectuals together with clubwomen and other society figures from the New Orleans smart set who shared an interest in the cultural revitalization of the Vieux Carré. Though the artist's colony had largely dispersed by 1930 or so, Faulkner's participation in this "Dixie Bohemia" in 1925–1926 was an important moment in his creative and personal development and no doubt part of why New Orleans continued to figure heavily in the geographical imagination at work in his fiction.

Benjamin S. Child's "'No Kind of Place': New York City, Southernness, and Migratory Modernism" places Faulkner alongside Flannery O'Connor and the Harlem Renaissance writer Rudolph Fisher as literary artists exploring Manhattan as a destination for Southern outmigration that harbors vestigial psychic and historical traces of the South even as it invites fantasies of escape from the struggles governing regional and rural life. Fisher's 1925 story "City of Refuge," O'Connor's posthumous tale "Judgement Day," and Faulkner's 1934 story "Pennsylvania Station" all feature male migrants who experience the Northern metropolis as a space that holds out the promise (or threat) of a more modern and progressive social and racial order even as "residue[s] of tradition" troublingly persist, "accretion[s] of cultural memory and experience that a change of venue cannot erase." As "tropes coded 'Southern'"—orality, community, racialized hierarchies of power—resurface despite the "geographic shift northward" in these stories, each tale "jostles both the meanings of Southernness and the shape of the standard migration narrative." "In the urban landscapes of the urban North," Child argues, Southern significations don't disappear but are instead "rerouted and reanimated in unexpected and provocative ways."

The next two essays introduce us to historical geographies arising out of colonialism and empire on the North American continent. In "Jamestown and Jimson Weed: Charting the Autochthonous Claim of William Faulkner's *The Sound and the Fury*," Kita Douglas unearths a fascinating New World ethnobotanical history behind the lowly weed, also known as *Datura stramonium*, that figures subtly but significantly in the interplay between Luster Gibson and Benjy Compson in Faulkner's 1929 novel. "Jimson," as it turns out, is a corruption of "Jamestown weed," linking the plant, and through it Faulkner's text, to a colonial history that includes events like Bacon's Rebellion, where *Datura* played an unlikely role as a hallucinogen ignorantly ingested by English soldiers sent to the Virginia backcountry to put down an interracial insurrection.

Datura becomes *The Sound and the Fury*'s primary way of accessing, from Mississippi ground, a story of national origins in which uprooting Africans from their indigenous world helped English settlers dispossess Native Americans of theirs. The complicated racial interplay between Luster and Benjy, considered in light of the occluded Native American histories that haunt the Compson mile, suggests that Faulkner's world participates in its own way in that ambivalent national legacy. The dense fabric of reference that Douglas weaves around a seemingly unremarkable specimen of local flora helps her pinpoint and develop important historical continuities between the ordeal of colonial Virginia and the aboriginally (and etymologically) "split land" of Yoknapatawpha.

Turning from the nation's eastern seaboard to quite different territory, José E. Limón's "South by Southwest: William Faulkner and Greater Mexico" explores the understudied relationship between Faulkner's South and the history and geography of the region that Américo Paredes christened Greater Mexico, an area encompassing internal Mexico but also large parts of the US West and Southwest "inhabited by people of Mexican culture." As Limón explains, the world of Greater Mexico is the direct historical product of the expansionist US–Mexico War of 1846–1847, a war prompted by nationalist fantasies of Manifest Destiny that were themselves fueled by Southern dreams of a hemispheric slave empire. The Mexican War's catastrophic impact was twofold. North of the border, it intensified the sectional conflict over slavery that eventually led to the US Civil War, whose complex legacy, of course, gave Faulkner his great historical subject. At the same time, the war "destabilized internal Mexico" politically and economically, leading not only to dictatorships and revolution but to widespread emigration to the United States, including the US South—a demographic phenomenon that arguably left its mark on Faulkner's fiction, as evidenced by figures such as Joe Christmas's father in *Light in August*, an itinerant circus worker who is believed by some to be Mexican. Thus it is with a measure of poetic and historical justice that several of the most significant writers to have mapped "the material and moral vicissitudes" of Greater Mexico have turned to Faulkner's work for insight or inspiration, as Limón demonstrates by surveying the careers of Paredes, Rolando Hinajosa, Carlos Fuentes, and Cormac McCarthy.

Three essays examine different aspects of the productive but also problematic engagements with Caribbean geographies in one of Faulkner's greatest novels. In "Thomas Sutpen's Geography Lesson: Environmental Obscurities and Racial Remapping in Faulkner's *Absalom, Absalom!*" Ryan Heryford argues that the "lesson" about the West Indies that propels young Sutpen toward Haiti cannot be confined to a provincial Tidewater schoolhouse in the 1820s but participates instead in a larger, "transgenerational" network of narratives and other representatives that employ "historical demapping" and "figurative remapping" to remove the island from geographical, political, and ecological specificity and ease it toward the timeless condition of myth. Drawing on the rhetoric of apocalypse, disease, and jungle barbarity, and on techniques of spatial and temporal abstraction, this exercise in colonialist cartography is, of course, racially coded as well. Its all too predictable result is to reduce an independent black nation-state and site of "the most important and necessary revolution of the nineteenth century" to "a space of both primordial perversity and capitalist possibility" whose black citizens are refashioned into childlike dependents or "sexual grotesque[s]." Heryford notes that these mapping strategies, which allow Sutpen and the novel's narrators to disavow the "intimate geographies" or "racialized violence" within the United States itself, from Virginia to Mississippi, continue to resonate today, as witnessed by the US response to the terrible Haitian earthquake of 2010.

If Heryford foregrounds the pedagogy that maps the Caribbean *for* Sutpen, Valérie Loichot catalogues the discursive strategies that map the Caribbean *on* Sutpen and other figures whose transnational itineraries take them through the region on their way to US destinations. In "Faulkner's Caribbean Geographies in *Absalom, Absalom!*" Loichot acknowledges that accounts of actual Caribbean locations like Martinique and Haiti remain vague, repressed, or "skewed" in the novel but that the "multifarious presence" of the region nonetheless emerges "through an incarnation of the landscape in the characters' bodies." Sutpen's sunburned skin, feverish complexion, and aura of amorality upon his arrival in Yoknapatawpha County function as metonyms for the tropics, the torrid zones of the colonial imaginary. Sutpen's "wild negroes," demonized and bestialized by the uncomprehending locals; the French architect, with his dandified ways and racially ambiguous "Latinness"; voiceless, bodiless Eulalia Bon, conspicuous in her absencing by the narrators; and the miscegenated and miscegenating cosmopolitan Charles Bon, whose entry onto the Mississippi scene edges the Sutpen genealogy toward the "extended-family style" Glissant associates with the Antilles—all round out the gallery of figures in and through whom buried Caribbean content resurfaces. And inasmuch as the Caribbean ever attains the status of place, a distinct, credible geographical location, in the novel, that place is probably the city of New Orleans traversed by so many of the novel's characters, embodying the Caribbean on US soil via its traditions of *métissage* and its nineteenth-century institutionalization of *plaçage*. As Loichot concludes by demonstrating, Faulkner's awareness of how New World spaces become Caribbeanized "through the intrusion of unruly blood into the land" is one important reason why his work speaks so powerfully to (other) Caribbean writers such as Aimé Césaire, Wilson Harris, Maryse Condé, and, of course, Glissant.

In "A Daughter's Geography: William Faulkner, Zora Neale Hurston, and a New Mapping of 'The Black South,'" Farah Jasmine Griffin focuses on Faulkner as a formative figure for a different group of writers, one engaged in tracing the contours of the transnational region she calls "The Black South," "a cultural, economic, and political space made up of the United States South, the Caribbean, and parts of Central America." These writers, who include Toni Morrison, Katherine Dunham, Nellie Rosario, Marlon Ross, Erna Brodber, Edwidge Danticat, Gloria Naylor, and Isabel Allende, have responded powerfully to the combined legacy of Faulkner and his contemporary Zora Neale Hurston, both of whom connected Deep South spaces with the cosmopolitan city of New Orleans and the Caribbean world beyond, as represented above all by Haiti. Faulkner explicitly traces a Black South migratory pathway from Haiti to New Orleans in *Absalom, Absalom!*, going on to link both spaces with Mississippi. At the same time, Hurston's work of the 1930s traces an elaborate circuit of African cultural energies linking Florida to New Orleans (via the fieldworker's travels in *Mules and Men*), New Orleans to Haiti (via the anthropological explorations of hoodoo and voodoo in *Mules* and *Tell My Horse*), and Haiti back to Florida (via the character of Janie Woods in *Their Eyes Were Watching God*, a figure modeled in part on the Vodou goddess Erzulie). The movement of figures like Charles and Eulalia Bon, Janie Woods, and Hurston herself through, across, and between these spaces delineates a Black South geography that continues to inform the work of contemporary writers of color in the hemisphere.

Harilaos Stecopoulos turns to the defining geopolitical crisis of Faulkner's late career in "William Faulkner and the Problem of Cold War Modernism." Noting that "no other US writer of the era played so active a role in the cultural Cold War," Stecopoulos gauges Faulkner's complex attitudes toward "the Cold War state and its relationship to literary culture." Stecopoulos focuses on "Faulkner's most difficult experience with US cultural diplomacy," his participation in Eisenhower's People-to-People (PTP) program in 1956, and on his 1959 novel *The Mansion*, which offers a "wry narrative commentary on the very idea of Cold War modernism." As Stecopoulos reveals, Faulkner's cover letter as cochair of the PTP writers' committee is a cagy modernist document in its own right, offering "a provocative riposte" to the prospect of "enlisting modernists in . . . a decidedly middlebrow project" of cultural exchange. In *The Mansion*, however, V. K. Ratliff's encounters with high modernist art objects created by Barton Kohl, husband of Linda Snopes Kohl and communist veteran of the Spanish Civil War, and by the Russian tie designer Myra Allanovna—abstract works that "resist easy figural interpretation"—hint at a different role in the Cold War moment for a modernism that "challenges the viewer not only to forge his or her own response to a difficult artwork and thus to assert individualism, but also to use that moment as an opportunity to . . . recognize the importance of community and collectivity," promoting what we could call a people-to-people agenda. Faulkner's Cold War writings and diplomatic experiences thus suggest that "literary modernism had the capacity to bind together different peoples," to underwrite "another sort of internationalism" whose "energies exceeded the grasp of any state, East or West."

The Mansion also figures significantly in Lorie Watkins's "Woman in Motion: Escaping Yoknapatawpha," which draws on the work of feminist geographers to detail the way women experience and use space in Faulkner's writings. Citing the examples of Lena Grove, Caddy Compson, Temple Drake, Drusilla Hawk, and others, Watkins notes how throughout Faulkner's work geographic movement through space affords women a degree of freedom from patriarchal strictures that typically pursue female disempowerment through physical immobilization. She then devotes extended discussions to the mother-daughter duo of Eula Varner Snopes and Linda Snopes Kohl. Watkins finds Eula to be "Faulkner's most fully contained natural woman," conflated with land and denied mobility from first to last. Even Eula's geographic relocation from Frenchman's Bend to Jefferson "ultimately comes to naught," as she is unable to free herself from her husband's manipulations by any stratagem short of suicide. It is sadly appropriate, then, that the objects most closely associated with Eula's memory are a cemetery monument and a postwar subdivision, Eula Acres; to the end, her fate is to be tied down, affixed to landscape. By contrast, Linda's totem object, the new Jaguar that takes her away from Jefferson in the wake of her father's murder, attests to her control over physical geography. Commanding a freedom of movement denied to her mother, Linda, according to Watkins, actively shapes and reshapes her environment, "construct[ing] new fictionalized geographic spaces through motion"—the quintessential Faulknerian woman on the loose.

Individually and collectively, these essays demonstrate the exciting potential of social and historical geography as a window onto Faulkner's work. As such, they bear out the interest of professional geographers like Charles Aiken in Faulkner's writings, and indeed in literature more generally. As Yi-Fu Tuan, another eminent figure in the field, has written, "Many places, profoundly significant to particular individuals and groups

. . . are known viscerally, as it were, and not through the discerning eye or mind." So it falls to "literary art" to "illuminate the inconspicuous fields of human care such as a Midwestern town, a Mississippi county, a big-city neighborhood, or an Appalachian hollow."[25] Can readers of this volume have any doubt about the Mississippi county Tuan had in mind?

Jay Watson
University of Mississippi

NOTES

1. Henri Lefebvre, *The Production of Space*, trans. Donald Nicholson-Smith (1974; Malden, Mass.: Blackwell, 1991), 174.

2. Geographer Edward W. Soja calls Lefebvre "the original and foremost historical and geographical materialist." See Soja, *Postmodern Geographies: The Reassertion of Space in Critical Social Theory* (New York: Verso, 1989), 42.

3. William Faulkner, *Lion in the Garden: Interviews with William Faulkner, 1926–1962*, ed. James B. Meriwether and Michael Millgate (1968; Lincoln: University of Nebraska Press, 1980), 255.

4. For some representative examples of Faulkner scholarship, ranging over several decades, that offer variations on this theme, see Richard P. Adams, "The Apprenticeship of William Faulkner," *Tulane Studies in English* 12 (1962): 113–56, and Max Putzel, *Genius of Place: William Faulkner's Triumphant Beginnings* (Baton Rouge: Louisiana State University Press, 1985). For a contrary view focusing on the formative role of Jefferson, not Yoknapatawpha County per se, in Faulkner's Mississippi imagination, see Thomas L. McHaney, "First Is Jefferson: Faulkner Shapes His Domain," *Mississippi Quarterly* 57.4 (2004): 511–34. On Yoknapatawpha as a primarily (inter)textual rather than topographical phenomenon, see Martin Kreiswirth, "'Paradoxical and Outrageous Discrepancy': Transgression, Auto-Intertextuality, and Faulkner's Yoknapatawpha," in *Faulkner and the Artist: Faulkner and Yoknapatawpha, 1993*, ed. Donald M. Kartiganer and Ann J. Abadie (Jackson: University Press of Mississippi, 1996), 161–80.

5. Charles S. Aiken, *William Faulkner and the Southern Landscape* (Athens: University of Georgia Press, 2009), 26. See also McHaney, "First Is Jefferson."

6. Mark Monmonier, *How to Lie with Maps*, 2nd ed. (Chicago: University of Chicago Press, 1996), 1. "Not only is it easy to lie with maps," he writes, "it's essential."

7. Here I am taking liberties with the key concept developed in Glissant's book *Poetics of Relation*, trans. Betsy Wing (Ann Arbor: University of Michigan Press, 1997).

8. William Faulkner, *Absalom, Absalom!* The Corrected Text (1986; New York: Vintage International, 1990), 314–15.

9. William Faulkner, *The Portable Faulkner*, rev. ed., ed. Malcolm Cowley (1967; New York: Penguin, 2003), n.p.

10. Franco Moretti, *Graphs, Maps, Trees: Abstract Models for Literary History* (New York: Verso, 2005), 1.

11. For an interesting foray in precisely this direction—an effort to determine the principle that governs "what is mapped in Yoknapatawpha" that ultimately "informs the cartography"—see Joseph R. Urgo, "The Yoknapatawpha Project: The Map of a Deeper Existence," *Mississippi Quarterly* 57.4 (2004): 639–55.

12. William Faulkner, *Go Down, Moses* (1942; New York: Vintage International, 1990), 131–32, 138–42, 142–43, 146–49, 152–54.

13. Fredric Jameson, *Postmodernism, or the Cultural Logic of Late Capitalism* (1991; Durham: Duke University Press, 1993), 51–52.

14. See David Harvey, *The Condition of Postmodernity: An Enquiry into the Origins of Cultural Change* (Cambridge, Mass.: Blackwell, 1990), 147.

15. Hortense J. Spillers, *Black, White, and in Color* (Chicago: University of Chicago Press, 2003), 32.

16. See Leigh Anne Duck, "Peripatetic Modernism, or, Joe Christmas' Father," *Philological Quarterly* 90.2–3 (2011): 255–80.

17. Don H. Doyle, *Faulkner's County: The Historical Roots of Yoknapatawpha* (Chapel Hill: University of North Carolina Press, 2001), 374.

18. Arjun Appadurai, *Modernity at Large: Cultural Dimensions of Globalization* (Minneapolis: University of Minnesota Press, 1996), 178, 181. Compare Appadurai's model with Yi-Fu Tuan's account of the conversion of "amorphous space" into place, "articulated geography." "When space feels thoroughly familiar to us, it has become place." See Tuan, *Space and Place: The Perspective of Experience* (1977; Minneapolis: University of Minnesota Press, 2011), 83, 73.

19. Enda Duffy, *The Speed Handbook: Velocity, Pleasure, Modernism* (Durham: Duke University Press, 2009), 267, 19.

20. Harvey, 183.

21. See Soja, 59–60.

22. Harvey, 205–6.

23. Faulkner, *Lion in the Garden*, 253.

24. See *Faulkner and Formalism: Returns of the Text: Faulkner and Yoknapatawpha, 2008*, ed. Annette Trefzer and Ann J. Abadie (Jackson: University of Mississippi Press, 2012).

25. Tuan, 162.

Note on the Conference

The thirty-seventh Faulkner and Yoknapatawpha Conference sponsored by the University of Mississippi in Oxford took place July 17–21, 2011, with nearly two hundred of the author's admirers in attendance. Eleven presentations on the theme "Faulkner and Geographies" are collected as essays in this volume. Brief mention is made here of activities that took place during the five-day conference.

The program began on Sunday with lectures "Local Places/Modern Spaces: The Crossroads Local in Faulkner" by Barbara Ladd and "Designing Spaces: Sutpen, Snopes, and the Promises of the Plantation" by Scott Romine. Following a buffet supper at the home of Dr. M. B. Howorth Jr., Daniel W. Jones, chancellor of the University of Mississippi, and George "Pat" Patterson, mayor of Oxford, welcomed participants, and Jay Watson, Howry Professor of Faulkner Studies and president of the William Faulkner Society, announced winners of the 2011 John W. Hunt Scholarships. These scholarships, awarded to young scholars selected to present conference papers, are funded by the Faulkner Society, the *Faulkner Journal*, gifts from Greg Perkins and Penelope Cooper, and donations in memory of John W. Hunt, Faulkner scholar and emeritus professor of literature at Lehigh University. Ted Ownby, director of the Center for the Study of Southern Culture, presented the twenty-fifth annual Eudora Welty Awards in Creative Writing. Kate Thompson, a graduate of the Mississippi School of Math and Science in Columbus, won first prize, $500, for her poem "Mama's Hands." Anna Adorno, a graduate of the Mississippi School for the Arts in Brookhaven, won second prize, $250, for her poem "Thunder." Both winners are from Picayune. The late Frances Patterson of Tupelo, a longtime member of the Center Advisory Committee, established and endowed the awards, which are selected through a competition held in high schools throughout Mississippi.

The Sunday evening program explored the conference theme with a special panel, "The Curators of Rowan Oak," focusing on the antebellum home where Faulkner lived and wrote from 1930 to his death in 1962. Four curators of Rowan Oak spanning the years from 1980 to the present—Howard Bahr, Keith Fudge, Cynthia Shearer, and William Griffith—traced the history of the home from its building in the early 1840s and its restoration and modernization by Faulkner over the

years to its current status as a National Historic Landmark that annually attracts hundreds of visitors from around the world. The curators
also told about their own experiences in managing what is perhaps the
most famous literary home in the United States. Donald M. Kartiganer,
Howry Professor of Faulkner Studies Emeritus and longtime director of
the conference, moderated the session.

Monday's program opened with Charles A. Peek and Terrell L.
Tebbetts discussing "Boundaries: Reading Faulkner, Reading Geography" during the first of three "Teaching Faulkner" sessions. Presentations during the first of four panels featuring short papers selected
through an annual call for papers were "'No Kind of Place: New York
City, Southernness, and Migratory Modernism" by Benjamin S. Child,
"The Proper Frontier in Late Faulkner" by Peter Alan Froehlich, and
"Faulkner's Animal Geographies" by Bart Welling. Seth Berner, a book
dealer from Portland, Maine, offered advice in his presentation "Col-
lecting Faulkner" and José E. Limón presented "South by Southwest:
William Faulkner and Greater Mexico." Papers read during the second
panel of scholars were "'Each in His Ordered Place': The Spatiality
of Suffering in Faulkner's *The Sound and the Fury*" by Eric Matthew
Bledsoe, "Jamestown and Jimson Weed: Charting the Autochthonous
Claim of William Faulkner's *The Sound and the Fury*" by Kita Douglas,
and "Woman in Motion: Escaping Yoknapatawa" by Lorie Watkins. The
day ended with Colby Kullman moderating the twelfth annual Faulkner
on the Fringe Festival, an open-mike evening at Southside Gallery on
the Oxford Square. Among the highlights of the evening were readings
of excerpts from interviews, letters, and the novel *A Fable* during the
"Faulkner in His Own Words" presentation by Oxford actor George
Kehoe and Betty Harrington, widow of conference cofounder Evans
Harrington and longtime participant in *Voices from Yoknapatawpha*
sessions at the conference.

Tuesday's program began with James B. Carothers and Theresa M.
Towner conducting the second "Teaching Faulkner" session, which
focused on the topic "Teaching Intertextually: Faulkner's Map of Yokna-
patawpha." Farah Jasmine Griffin's lecture "A Daughter's Geography:
William Faulkner, Zora Neale Hurston, and a New Mapping of 'The
Black South'" was followed by John Shelton Reed's "'My New Orleans
Gang': Faulkner's French Quarter Circle." Panel presentations were
"Decaying Spaces: Faulkner's Gothic and the Construction of the
National Real" by Lisa Klarr, "Undisclosed Origins: A Retelling of the
Story of Charles Bon in Faulkner's *Absalom, Absalom!*" by Jenna Grace
Sciuto, and "'Not Only Beyond the Town but Beneath It': The Geogra-
phy of Abjection and Sutpen's Design in *Absalom, Absalom!*" by Erin

Sweeney. Colby Kullman and his neighbors Harold and Dinah Clark hosted an afternoon party at Tyler Place.

Wednesday's program included three lectures: "Geographies of White Deviance: The Eugenic Family Studies, *Buck v. Bell*, and William Faulkner, 1930–1931" by Jay Watson, "Faulkner's Caribbean Geographies in *Absalom, Absalom!*" by Valérie Loichot, and "Thomas Sutpen's Geography Lesson: Environmental Obscurities and Racial Remapping in Faulkner's *Absalom, Absalom!*" by Ryan Heryford. There was also a panel with scholarly papers by Patrick Mooney ("Horse Trade, Mule Trade, Woman Trade: Comparative Geographies in Faulkner's Snopes Trilogy"), Scott Ortolano ("Off the Psychological Map: Darl and Gavin Stevens's Homeless Minds"), and Stefan Solomon ("Detecting the Great Migration"). Attendees gathered for the annual afternoon picnic at Faulkner's home, Rowan Oak, and ended the day with a discussion of teaching and reading Faulkner. Guided tours of North Mississippi, the Delta, and Memphis took place on Thursday, and the conference ended with a party at Off Square Books.

Four exhibitions were available throughout the conference. The University Museum hosted *Faulkner's Geographies: A Photographic Journey*, which included photographs of Faulkner and the surrounding environs from several collections in the Southern Media Archive of the University's John Davis Williams Library—principally the Cofield and Dain collections—as well as the Museum's newly acquired images of Faulkner by Henri Cartier-Bresson. The Department of Archives and Special Collections at the Williams Library displayed Faulkner portraits and various materials related to the author's life and work. *Southern Crossings: Where Geography and Photography Meet* by David Zurick was on exhibit at Barnard Observatory's Gammill Gallery. The University Press of Mississippi exhibited books about Faulkner and the South published by university presses throughout the United States.

The conference planners are grateful to all the individuals and organizations that support the Faulkner and Yoknapatawpha Conference annually. In addition to those mentioned above, we thank Square Books, Southside Gallery, the City of Oxford, and the Oxford Convention and Visitors Bureau.

Faulkner's Geographies

Local Places/Modern Spaces:
The Crossroads Local in Faulkner

BARBARA LADD

Faulkner's relationships with geography were complex. Depending on whom you ask, he is or is not a "Southern" writer. He once wrote that "I'm inclined to think that my material, the South, is not very important to me. I just happen to know it, and dont have time in one life to learn another one and write at the same time."[1] Although he wrote very perceptively about the South, few would call him a regionalist, because that is a minoritizing term in US literary history, and very few would call Faulkner a minor writer. This is not so much the case in Latin America, where regionalism carries different associations and stronger political inflections, but here in the United States regionalist writing, at least until fairly recently, has been largely understood to be limited, bounded, descriptive of life within a distinct region—sometimes a matter of "local color" composed, in the words of Carl Van Doren (who was obviously thinking of late nineteenth- and early twentieth-century regionalism) of "skimpy moods analyzed with a delicate competence of touch" and leading to what he famously called "a revolt from the village" in the writing of men like Sinclair Lewis.[2] Of course, there is no one regionalism. In addition to the local color of which Van Doren was writing, there is the work of the Southwestern humorists of the 1830s through the 1850s, which no one would describe as possessing anything resembling a "delicate competence of touch." Mississippi was certainly at the very center of the old Southwest, and there have been numerous discussions of the influence of Southwestern humor on Faulkner's work, a lot of them focusing on *The Hamlet*.[3] Also of relevance to Faulkner, and less often acknowledged, is the regionalism of those twentieth-century writers of the long 1930s, broadly aligned with movements in architecture and art led by Frank Lloyd Wright and Grant Wood, the latter of whom published a manifesto of sorts entitled, in a jab at Van Doren, "Revolt against the City." There are still other "regionalisms" as well. It is tempting to speculate that there is, at present, something akin to the local color of the late nineteenth century in what we might call a "global local color" project, and it might be interesting to compare the regionalist publishing agenda of the late nineteenth and early twentieth centuries to that of contemporary publishing in the area of "global fiction," but this is not my purpose here.[4]

In any event, most academics within the US academy understand "Southern literature" (which, of course, Faulkner is assumed to transcend) as a regionalist form, although I have heard that contested by those who say that the US South—unlike the Northeast, Midwest, or West—has produced a major literature distinct from mainstream American literature and is therefore something other than "regional." Personally, I would rather tackle the matter from the other side and say that American literature is so varied that to speak of a mainstream confuses more than it clarifies. More to the point, the predominance of "regionalism" as paradigm for the recognition of the importance of place in US literary studies has sometimes distorted, more than it has clarified, the nature and the significance of place in US imaginative writing, because what "regionalism" does, given its history in the United States, is to subordinate the engagement with place to other, more privileged, discourses like literary nationalism, class, gender, urbanity, or cosmopolitanism. Seeing regionalisms in terms of resistance does not change that logic.

If Faulkner as regionalist is a hard sell, most readers readily accept that he is a modernist writer, but the fact remains that Faulkner has seldom been as fully incorporated into broad studies of US literary modernism as his work warrants.[5] No doubt literary modernism's traditional association with the urban has something to do with this—with some exceptions, Faulkner's work is engaged with rural and small town life. It may also be the case that the location of Faulkner's work (and Faulkner himself) in what so many US literary and cultural historians think of as the "problem South"—a South perceived as fundamentally different from and, therefore, unrepresentative of the United States mainstream—means that Faulkner's modernism has been much more likely to be discussed by students of international and, more recently, global modernisms than by those students of US modernism who are not specifically Faulknerians. Pascale Casanova, for example, French author of *The World Republic of Letters*, considers Faulkner to be one of the two great twentieth-century revolutionaries in literature. She writes:

> William Faulkner, no less than Joyce, was responsible for one of the greatest revolutions in the world of letters, comparable in its extent, and in the depth of the changes it introduced in the novel, to the naturalist revolution of the late nineteenth century. But while in the centers, and especially in Paris, the technical innovations of the American novelist were understood and valued

only as formalistic devices, in the outlying countries of the literary world they were welcomed as tools of liberation. Faulkner's work, more than that of any other writer, henceforth belonged to the explicit repertoire of international writers in dominated literary spaces who sought to escape the imposition of national rules, for he had found a solution to a commonly experienced political, aesthetic, and literary impasse.[6]

That impasse, for Casanova, is the great gulf that lay between center and periphery, and this is a paradigm that underwrites the idea of regionalism. Faulkner, she observes, gave us "characters, landscapes, ways of thinking, and stories that exactly coincided with the reality of all those countries said to lie in the 'South'—a rural and archaic world prey to magical styles of thought and trapped in the closed life of families and villages."[7] She goes on to contrast (somewhat problematically) Faulkner's literary fortune with that of James Joyce, who has been "annexed by critics in the centers and so thoroughly dehistoricized that deprived writers, bowing to the monopoly power of the capitals over literary consecration, tend to overlook the subversive dimension of his work." On the other hand, Faulkner, "in putting an end to the curse of backwardness that lay over these regions, by offering the novelists of the poorest countries the possibility of giving acceptable literary form to the most repugnant realities of the margins of the world . . . has been a formidable force for accelerating literary time."[8]

I have to admit to being a little put off by Casanova's sense of the "world"—her acceptance of the paradigm of "center" and "periphery" in a world in which, it seems to me, "centers" and "peripheries" are themselves shifting, in which so much of what the modern, secular subject took for granted a few decades ago is challenged;[9] her sense of Faulkner's "South" as "exactly coinciding" with an actual South "closed" and "trapped"; and her certainty that there is only one "literary time" when in fact literary temporalities proliferate in our unstable world. Literary modernism itself was less the product of a fully realized modernity than a record of conflict between modernities and what preceded, coexisted with, and emerged alongside them. Casanova may be right that Faulkner was appreciated in Paris and London and New York and Boston for his technical innovations primarily—the Faulkner I studied at the University of North Carolina at Chapel Hill in the 1970s and at the University of Texas in the 1980s was certainly that writer, the one so often discussed in terms of technical innovation, specifically "stream of consciousness." I did not read him that way, however. For me, Faulkner spoke of home and world in the cadences of home inseparable from world (or center). So I want to make some remarks about modernity and modernism, region and the local, place and space as they figure in Faulkner's work.[10]

The Hamlet appeared in 1940, during a period in which place had once again acquired a particular significance in US culture, and, again, it coincided with an upsurge of nationalist feeling. When Alfred Kazin, in *On Native Grounds*, describes these years in terms of a "thundering flood of national consciousness and self-celebration," he is speaking of a "new nationalism" that arose in response to the Great Depression and the rise of fascism in Europe. "Suddenly," he observes, "American writing became a swelling chorus of national affirmation and praise. Suddenly all the debunkers of the past [the American Left and others] . . . became the special objects of revulsion and contempt [and] . . . the country once more became, as Jefferson had long ago foreseen, 'this government: the world's best hope.'"[11]

Certainly Faulkner wrote some stories in the spirit of the times: "Shingles for the Lord" (published in the *Saturday Evening Post* in 1943), for example, and "The Tall Men" (also in the *Saturday Evening Post*, 1941). Both celebrate the American spirit in the form of Southern farmers whose sense of independence and "Americanness" is challenged by the new intrusiveness of the state. (Recall that in some circles the New Deal was seen as a step toward communism or, for some, toward fascism.) In "Shingles for the Lord," Solon tries to regularize the volunteer labor his fellow farmers put in on reroofing a church by plotting it all out in "work units" and "man hours," which Pap Grier just can't assimilate. At the end of the story—after numerous plot twists having to do with a dog trade and events that lead to the church being accidentally burned to the ground by Pap—the old man, finally lying down that night, says in exasperation, "Work units. Dog units. And now arsonist. I Godfrey, what a day!"[12] In "The Tall Men," the self-reliant farmers of Yoknapatawpha County just cannot quite meet mind to mind with the government man come to arrest two boys for failing to register for the draft. They don't understand the difference between registering for the draft and enlisting, and the government investigator doesn't understand the pride and sense of honor that would preclude them from trying to shirk any patriotic duty. This is the time, we know, when former radicals on the Left, like Max Eastman and Robert Cantwell, began to turn toward the center, or the right in some cases. Malcolm Cowley, who had not been one of Faulkner's fans during the early 1930s, would find in him something very valuable, and quintessentially American, by the middle of the 1940s when Cowley published *The Portable Faulkner*.

Best sellers in fiction during these years tended to exhibit a kind of celebratory or reformist regionalism and included Pearl Buck's *The Good Earth* (1931), Erskine Caldwell's *God's Little Acre* (1933), Margaret Mitchell's *Gone with the Wind* (1936), and John Steinbeck's *The Grapes of Wrath* (1939).[13] But the Works Progress Administration (WPA) state guides say as much about life in the decade as the best sellers, and much more about local life. As we know, in order to put writers and photographers to work, and also to capitalize on the "new nationalism" of the moment, the federal government hired writers to collect oral histories and research local histories and photographers to document ordinary scenes and ordinary people. State guides appeared that covered everything from natural resources to history to folklore and literary and artistic traditions. This work has provided us with a huge compendium of material about life in that decade. Despite its framing as part of the regionalism of the time, it has also challenged some of the most deeply held myths of America.

For Robert Cantwell, "the America revealed in the state guides was a chronicle not of the traditional sobriety and industry and down-to-earth business wit of the American race" but constituted "a grand, melancholy, formless, democratic anthology of frustration and idiosyncrasy, a majestic roll call of national failure, a terrible yet engaging corrective to the success stories that dominate our literature." It gave us an America of "cockalorum demi-gods." And it provided writers of the period with "a whole world of marvels . . . to possess . . . a world of rivers and scenes, of folklore . . . , of a heroic tradition to reclaim and forgotten heroes to follow."[14] Unlike the mythical heroes of other countries, Max Eastman said, ours were "born in laughter, consciously preposterous. That is the natively American thing—not that her primitive humor is exaggerative, but that her primitive exaggerations were humorous."[15]

The Hamlet may be the work in Faulkner's corpus most responsive to this wilder register in American literary culture. Here we find the "traditional sobriety and industry and down-to-earth business wit of the American race" exemplified in Flem Snopes, one of the most grotesquely exaggerated creations in all of Faulkner. To be sure, the grotesque is not always a figure to scorn, but in this case the depth of Faulkner's distaste can be seen in his description of Flem as "that squat reticent figure in the steadily-soiling white shirts and the minute invulnerable bow, which in those abeyant days lurked among the ultimate shadows of the deserted and rich-odored interior with a good deal of the quality of a spider of that bulbous blond omnivorous though non-poisonous species" (64–65). Note the subtle association of Flem not only with the spider but with defecation (the figure is "squat," there is a reference to "soiling," and to "odor"). This is hardly part of Kazin's "swelling chorus of national affirmation and praise," although *The Hamlet* might well be described in Cantwell's terms as "a grand, melancholy, formless, democratic anthology of frustration and idiosyncrasy." And it certainly gives us a "world of marvels," "scenes," and "folklore," its "heroic tradition" about as "preposterous"—indeed as grotesque—an appropriation of classical myth and pastoral as can possibly be imagined. For example, the twelve-year-old Eula Varner is introduced to us as "bigger than most grown women," a girl whose "entire appearance suggested some symbology out of the old Dionysic times—honey in sunlight and bursting grapes, the writhen bleeding of the crushed fecundated vine beneath the hard rapacious trampling goat-hoof" (105). And writing of Ike Snopes, the "idiot" of the family (although all of them are deficient in some way or another), Faulkner waxes poetic: "Then he would see her; the bright thin horns of morning, of sun, would blow the mist away and reveal her, planted, blond, dew-pearled, standing in the parted water of the ford, blowing into the water the thick, warm, heavy, milk-laden breath; and lying in the drenched grasses, his eyes now blind with sun, he would wallow faintly from thigh to thigh, making a faint, thick, hoarse moaning sound" (183). The bucolic swain indeed, in love not with Eula (although the description reminds one of her) but with a cow, his mouth "slobbering" and "hanging" (95)!

The experience of place in US literary studies has been, for the most part, mediated by regionalism, and, as interesting as regionalism is and as relevant to literary history, this is unfortunate. Certainly modernity's flight from place has something to do with it. One very fundamental characteristic of modernity has been the discursive displacement of place in favor of "space": the devaluation of discourse based on ideas of differentiation and qualification in preference for discourses based on ideas of quantification and standardization—and "regions," like "nations," are imagined in terms of a pretty high degree of internal coherence.[16] Modernity, we might say, has a "normalizing"/"standardizing" agenda: is it normal or not, we ask; can we get a replacement part if it breaks? If it isn't "normal," if it isn't "standardized," it is either extraordinarily valuable or useless or both—and this applies as much to natural and human resources as to aesthetic objects.

    Alfred North Whitehead, in *Science and the Modern World*, argued that this modern emptying of place into "space" amounts to the erasure of the agency of the human body in structuring perception. The body, he writes, "is the organism whose states regulate our cognizance of the world."[17] In other words, it is the body upon which our sense of place depends—we cannot know what is up or down, in front or in back, inside or outside, except through the body. In the words of Edward S. Casey, the body "possesses a unique efficacy that allows it to reach out to all places from within its own implacement."[18]

The Hamlet, like many other novels and stories by Faulkner, is deeply placed and profoundly and grotesquely embodied. Before delivering this talk, I sent a query to the Faulkner listserv, asking who is the most grotesque character in Faulkner. I included some statements on the nature of the grotesque. John Ruskin, in *The Stones of Venice*, described it as exhibiting both the "ludicrous" and the "fearful."[19] It has been associated with "distortion," especially of the human form. In *Rabelais and His World*, Mikhail Bakhtin describes the grotesque body as one that is "unfinished," a body that "outgrows itself, transgresses its own limits," a body where "the emphasis is on the apertures or the convexities, or on various ramifications and offshoots: the open mouth, the genital organs, the breasts, the phallus, the potbelly, the nose," a body "copulat[ing], preg[nant], giving birth, dying, eating, drinking, or defecat[ing]," and thus "not a closed, completed unit." It is "ever unfinished, ever creating."[20]

Among the many characters named, the ones who most often came up were Popeye, various members of the Snopes family (Clarence, Mink, Ike, "Byron's little Indian Snopeses"), Eula Varner, Benjy Compson, Emily Grierson, Addie Bundren, and Anse Bundren.

Faulkner is a genius at evoking the grotesque through "some modification of the human form." In *Absalom, Absalom!* Rosa Coldfield is introduced to us sitting "so bolt upright in the straight hard chair that was so tall for her that her legs hung straight and rigid as if she had iron shinbones and ankles, clear of the floor with that air of impotent and static rage like children's feet."[21] Thomas Sutpen is (as Quentin pictures him) "man-horse-demon."[22] Popeye Vitelli: "under size," a man whose "face had a queer bloodless color, as though seen by electric light; against the sunny silence . . . he had that vicious depthless quality of stamped tin."[23] The old man, deaf and nearly blind, perhaps Lee Goodwin's father, in *Sanctuary*, seen by Temple: "between [his eye]lids two objects like dirty yellowish clay marbles." Later, Temple "watche[s] the old man go down the hall at a wide-legged shuffling trot, the stick in one hand and the other elbow cocked at an acute angle."[24] In *The Town* Byron Snopes's four little Indian kids, when they get off the train in Jefferson, come to stay, "didn't look like people. They looked like snakes." The description of Clarence Snopes from the same book emphasizes the "grayish pasty look to his flesh, which looked as if it would not flow blood from a wound but instead a pallid fluid like thin oatmeal."[25]

None of these bodies is especially "regional." They may be deviant, anachronistic, idiosyncratic, but not in any discernible "Southern" way. By the way, the "idios" in "idiosyncratic" (from which we get "idiom" and "idiot") signifies the "private," the "personal," and the "local." It should be no surprise that "idiom," "idiolect," and "idiot" are derived from "idios" and embedded in "idiosyncratic"—the local is associated with feeble-mindedness and disability, with preverbal, prenational, or extranational forms of speech, with the grotesque.

Over the past few years I have become less interested in the idea of the Southern and increasingly interested in the local, in the traces, in literary and cultural discourses, of lives lived according to the rhythms of place and body. In popular culture, the local is oedipal, focusing on family stories and generational narratives that are conventionalized, scripted according to received ideas of what a family is, what it does, and what in it is most or least conducive to the reproduction of the modern subject. The matriarchs, the strong man regimes of the good ole boys' networks, secreted crimes and codes of silence, the violations that are not abstract but concrete, personal, bodily, the deformations that are equally of the body—all must be confronted and bested or, at the least, contained in order for the modern light of day to steal into the scene. Of late, stories of intergenerational haunting—the feeding of one generation upon another, so often eroticized—in the form of vampire tales are very popular, especially among adolescents and young adults. The local can be quite deviant: lawless, extravagant, and subversive or revolutionary, alternately conformist and repressive, violent, destructive, creative. It connotes, as Whitehead and Casey argue, something on the margins, or just beyond the margins, of the normalizing institutions and discourses of the regional, the national, the international. It often connotes something against which modernity defines itself and establishes its own authority.

Alternately the local can be something to embrace for its idiosyncrasies and its alternative temporalities. W. B. Yeats employs locale in terms relevant to my argument when he writes of an old Irish priest: "nobody had been to hell or heaven in his time. . . . The dead stayed where they had lived, or near it, sought no abstract region of blessing or punishment but retreated, as it were, into the hidden character of the neighborhood."[26] Yeats's old priest, despite his identity as the agent of a Church that tells us that people, when they die, go to heaven or hell, is very local, subversively so. His world lies only partially under the authority of the Church; he is Irish too. And his perspective on the local is not unlike one presented by Faulkner on numerous occasions. It is reminiscent of Cass Edmonds's idea of "return" in Faulkner's "The Old People," where he tries to reassure the young Ike McCaslin that he believes that Ike has seen the Spirit Buck.[27] "Why not?" Edmonds asks.

> "Think of all that has happened here, on this earth. All the blood hot and strong for living, pleasuring, that has soaked back into it. For grieving and suffering too, of course. . . . But you cant be alive forever, and you always wear out life long before you have exhausted the possibilities of living. And all that must be somewhere; all that could not have been invented and created just to be thrown away. And the earth is shallow; there is not a great deal of it before you come to the rock. And the earth dont want to just keep things, hoard them; it wants to use them again. Look at the seed, the acorns, at what happens even to carrion when you try to bury it: it refuses too, seethes and struggles too until it reaches light and air again, hunting the sun still."[28]

In short, the perceived deviance of the local can come as much from its feeding of the emergent (in Raymond Williams's definition of the word) as from its anachronisms.[29] Faulkner's bodies are local in that they speak not to (or of) an already mapped "region" (such as the "South" as regionalism has imagined it) but to a place much wilder—to a deeply historical, unevenly developed, deviant, anachronistic, idiosyncratic place that extends, both in temporal and spatial dimensions, well beyond anything envisioned by literary regionalism.

I want to call this a "crossroads local": "What we need . . . is a global sense of the local, a global sense of place," Doreen Massey has said.[30] And, as Arjun Appadurai has argued, "globalization is itself a deeply historical, uneven, and . . . localizing process. . . . There is nothing mere," he adds, "about the local."[31]

The local has always been relatively unstable, relatively fluid—much more so than the regional—and it is a site both of discovery and potentiality and of anxiety and violence. The varied spatiotemporalities of the crossroads local permit us to discover other (prenational, extranational, international, transnational, and global) legacies and possibilities within a "place." Michael Woods writes usefully of local lives as "hybrid assemblages of human and nonhuman entities, knitted-together intersections of networks and flows that are never wholly fixed or contained at the local scale."[32] The claim that this is a *new* "local," the result of a relatively new reality produced by contemporary globalization, has been discredited by any number of students of modernity and globalization: the kinds of encounters we associate with globalization today have defined many cultures throughout history.[33] Think of the varied encounters associated with Sutpen's Hundred, the encounters (across time as well as space) among voices hailing from West Virginia, Virginia, Haiti, New Orleans,

Martinique, and New England. Think about the names: "hamlet" (a cluster of dwellings around a mill, a habitation not large enough for a church), Old Frenchman Place, Sutpen's Hundred (a reminder of the Berkeley Hundred, in the Virginia colony, granted to Richard Berkeley in 1618—the economic and cultural pattern for Thomas Sutpen's "design"), Jefferson, Yoknapatawpha County with its Native American origins.

In short, the local as I am conceptualizing it suggests a crossroads repressed almost as much in most regionalist as in nationalist discourses, and it can continue to designate what has been repressed or marginalized for as long as it retains something of an oppositional force with reference to "regionalism" and "nationalism."[34] It can inscribe—differently than the word "regional" does—the anachronistic, the marginal remainder, the not fully interpellated, the something left over after the assimilationist project, because, importantly, it also carries the potential for inscribing the emergent. It invokes a locatedness that looks beyond a regionalizing or nationalizing agenda.

What does looking at Faulkner's world under the sign of "the local" rather than under the sign of "the South" enable us to see? Of Faulkner's idiots, for instance? Isn't it after all Benjy Compson, the first narrator to whom we are introduced in *The Sound and the Fury*, who creates "place" for us in the novel in the most corporeal and intimate of ways, as a site of intense loves and anxieties, a world that is opaque to most readers on first (and second and third) readings? I don't think Benjy is especially "Southern." His is a very "local," private place. (Quentin's place is "Southern." Jason's, I have always thought, is mid-American, small town.) Ike Snopes is not especially "Southern"; he is intensely local—radically deviant, preverbal, and atavistic. He has as much relevance to classical precedent as to any narrative of regional or national identity—he cannot be assimilated, he can only be (like Benjy) contained, constrained, prevented from reproducing.

Nothing is more local, or localizing, in this sense, than the "touch of flesh with flesh," as Faulkner put it in *Absalom, Absalom!*, or the "marriage of speaking and hearing" from the same novel.[35] These are two of the most revealing lines in Faulkner's corpus, not only (or even chiefly) of the sensibility of the characters but of Faulkner's ethical and aesthetic commitments to the potential of proximity, even among the displaced (Benjy, Ike Snopes, Quentin Compson, and Shreve McCannon), to create place, however fleetingly.

What does looking at Faulkner's Yoknapatawpha County in this way enable us to see? Rosa Coldfield—with her feet that do not touch the floor, with her ignorance about so much (she knows so little about Sutpen, about Charles Bon; remember that she never even sees Charles Bon), with her rationale for calling Quentin Compson to visit her (because he is going to Harvard, because someday he can write the story down for the magazines, which, of course, he never does)—is a figure of deterritorialization.[36] By that I mean that she is a figure who decontextualizes. It is Jason Compson, Quentin Compson, and Shreve McCannon who try to make sense of the story of Thomas Sutpen in terms of *Southern* history, in terms of its racial decorum, to construct an understanding of why Henry Sutpen kills Charles Bon that is consistent with a regional history of segregation. On the other hand, Rosa's most significant cross-racial encounter is inconsistent with that history. As she tries to climb the stairs out at Sutpen's place, because she wants to see the body of Bon, Clytie calls her "Rosa." Like the *Southern* white woman she is, Rosa is outraged. (Clytie is supposed to call her "Miss Rosa.") But for a moment, however brief, in this book in which virtually all the speakers are involved in the project of creating a narrative that is consistent with the South's continuing commitment to segregation, Rosa and Clytie touch:

> Because there is something in the touch of flesh with flesh which abrogates, cuts sharp and straight across the devious intricate channels of decorous ordering, which enemies as well as lovers know because it makes them both:—touch and touch of that which is the citadel of the central I-Am's private own: not spirit, soul; the liquorish and ungirdled mind is anyone's to take in any darkened hallway of this earthly tenement. But let flesh touch with flesh, and watch the fall of all the eggshell shibboleth of caste and color too.[37]

Here it is Rosa—as it is Bon elsewhere in *Absalom, Absalom!* and Ike Snopes, along with Eula Varner, in *The Hamlet*—who (for a moment) is lifted out of the normative regionalism of "the South." This is momentary; elsewhere Rosa is nothing if not a spokeswoman for "the South," one of its commemorative poets who will not let the past go. But hers is nevertheless, in this one moment, a response to Clytie's touch that is local and placed, both ephemeral and generative.

NOTES

I want to thank Anne Goodwyn Jones and Jay Watson for their comments on an earlier draft of this essay.

1. Faulkner to Malcolm Cowley, November 1944, in *Selected Letters of William Faulkner*, ed. Joseph Blotner (New York: Vintage, 1978), 185.

2. Carl Van Doren, *Contemporary American Novelists, 1900–1920* (New York: Macmillan, 1922), 16.

3. Quotations from *The Hamlet*, hereafter cited parenthetically, are from the first Vintage International Edition (New York, 1991). See William Van O'Connor, *The Tangled Fire of William Faulkner* (Minneapolis: University of Minnesota Press, 1954), 116–17; Richard Gray, *The Life of William Faulkner* (Cambridge, Mass.: Blackwell Publishers, 1994), 49–51; Daniel Hoffman, *Faulkner's Country Matters: Folklore and Fable in Yoknapatawpha* (Baton Rouge: Louisiana State University Press, 1989), 71–106; Thomas L. McHaney, "What Faulkner Learned from the Tall Tale," in *Faulkner and Humor: Faulkner and Yoknapatawpha, 1984*, ed. Doreen Fowler and Ann J. Abadie (Jackson: University Press of Mississippi, 1986), 110–35; and Peter Alan Froehlich, "Faulkner and the Frontier Grotesque: *The Hamlet* as Southwestern Humor," in *Faulkner in Cultural Context: Faulkner and Yoknapatawpha, 1995*, ed. Donald M. Kartiganer and Ann J. Abadie (Jackson: University Press of Mississippi, 1997), 218–40.

4. Although regionalisms are numerous and complex, the local color writers of the late nineteenth and early twentieth centuries come most readily to mind for the majority of students of American literature, and much of the work on US regionalism focuses on those writers. We see evidence of the minoritizing of this work in the classic traditional studies, from Jay Martin's *Harvests of Change: American Literature, 1865–1914* (Englewood Cliffs, N.J.: Prentice-Hall, 1967) to Larzer Ziff's *The American 1890s: Life and Times of a Lost Generation* (Lincoln: University of Nebraska Press, 1967), both of which read late nineteenth-century regionalism as escapist, to Richard Brodhead's *Cultures of Letters: Scenes of Reading and Writing in Nineteenth-Century America* (Chicago: University of Chicago Press, 1993), which sees the regionalism of that era as the product of a touristic impulse, to Amy Kaplan's "Nation, Region, and Empire," in *The Columbia History of the American Novel*, ed. Emory Elliott (New York: Columbia University Press, 1991), 240–66, and Stephanie Foote's *Regional Fictions: Culture and Identity in Nineteenth-Century American Literature* (Madison: University of Wisconsin Press, 2001), both of which associate late nineteenth-century regionalism with resistance. Southwestern humor has also received some attention. See, in particular, Kenneth S. Lynn, *Mark Twain and Southwestern Humor* (Boston: Little, Brown, 1959); M. Thomas Inge, ed., *The Frontier Humorists: Critical Views* (Hamden, Conn.: Archon, 1975); M. Thomas Inge and Edward J. Piacentino, eds., *The Humor of the Old South* (Lexington: University Press of Kentucky, 2001); and James H. Justus, *Fetching the Old Southwest: Humorous Writing from Longstreet to Twain* (Columbia: University of Missouri Press, 2004). Arguably this literature has not received the attention it deserves—and it is significant that anthologies and critical work on Southwestern humor have appeared chiefly from smaller and regional presses. The regionalism of the 1930s is less studied and most often represented as nativist and even fascist in the scholarship that does exist. One of the earliest treatments of this idea is Carey McWilliams's *The New Regionalism in American Literature* (Seattle: University of Washington Press, 1930). See also Walter Benn Michaels, *Our America: Nativism, Modernism, and Pluralism* (Durham: Duke University Press, 1995). Complicating this picture of early twentieth-century regionalism is Michael C. Steiner's "Regionalism in the Great Depression," *Geographical Review* 73.4 (October 1983): 430–46.

5. Faulkner is usually mentioned, sometimes dealt with in a page or two, but, given his preeminence in studies of international modernisms, it is surprising that his work is so seldom centered in studies of US modernism.

6. Pascale Casanova, *The World Republic of Letters*, trans. M. B. DeBevoise (Cambridge: Harvard University Press, 2004), 336.

7. Ibid., 337.

8. Ibid. Casanova's assessment of the scholarship on James Joyce seems somewhat out of date. Recent studies, like Declan Kiberd's *Inventing Ireland: The Literature of the Modern Nation* (London: Jonathan Cape, 1995) and Nicholas Allen's *Modernism, Ireland, and Civil War* (Cambridge: Cambridge University Press, 2009), reclaim Joyce for the Ireland of his time.

9. As Stuart Hall has observed, the "cultural empowerment of the marginal and the local" has undermined the very idea of center and periphery. See Hall, "The Local and the Global: Globalization and Ethnicity," in *Culture, Globalization, and the World-System: Contemporary Conditions for the Representation of Identity*, ed. Anthony D. King (Binghamton: State University of New York Press, 1991), 33.

10. Casanova's perspective is representative of a metropolitan elitism that still predominates at many of the most prestigious academic institutions in the United States and abroad, but it is also increasingly challenged by some of the most innovative work in the field of modernist studies. Raymond Williams's classic "Metropolitan Perceptions and the Emergence of Modernism," in *The Politics of Modernism: Against the New Conformists* (London: Verso, 1989), 37–48, is well worth reading for its critique of the metropolitan stance. We have seen the development of this critique in collections like *The Geography of Identity*, ed. Patricia Yaeger (Ann Arbor: University of Michigan Press, 1996); *Geographies of Modernism: Literatures, Cultures, Spaces*, ed. Peter Brooker and Andrew Thacker (New York: Routledge, 2005); and *Geomodernisms: Race, Modernism, Modernity*, ed. Laura Doyle and Laura Winkiel (Bloomington: Indiana University Press, 2005). Leigh Anne Duck's *The Nation's Region: Southern Modernism, Segregation, and U.S. Nationalism* (Athens: University of Georgia Press, 2006) is exemplary of this development in Southern literary studies. John Duvall predicts that "twenty years from now . . . what we mean by the regional will be more fully a part of the modern, and our modernity will be unknowable apart from the various regions of identity represented by American literature." See Duvall, "Regionalism in American Modernism," in *The Cambridge Companion to American Modernism*, ed. Walter Kalaidjian (New York: Cambridge University Press, 2005), 259.

11. Alfred Kazin, *On Native Grounds: An Interpretation of Modern American Prose Literature* (New York: Harcourt Brace, 1942), 502–3. For further examples of the link with nationalism, see Robert Cantwell, "America and the Writers' Project," *New Republic* (April 26, 1939). Donald Davidson provides a Southern angle on the subject in "Regionalism and Nationalism," in *"Still Rebels, Still Yankees" and Other Essays* (Baton Rouge: Louisiana State University Press, 1957), 270–71. Scholarly treatments of the subject include Michael C. Steiner, "Regionalism in the Great Depression," *Geographical Review* 73.4 (October 1983): 430–46, and Lauren Coats and Nihad M. Farooq, "Regionalism in the Era of the New Deal," in *A Companion to the Regional Literatures of America*, ed. Charles L. Crow (Malden, Mass.: Blackwell Publishing Ltd., 2003), 72–91.

12. William Faulkner, "Shingles for the Lord," in *Collected Stories of William Faulkner* (New York: Vintage, 1977), 43.

13. Of all the novels Faulkner published, maybe the relatively late *Intruder in the Dust* best exemplifies the reformist agenda of "regionalist" writing in the early to mid-twentieth century.

14. Cantwell, 324, 323.

15. Max Eastman, *Enjoyment of Laughter* (New York: Simon and Schuster, 1936), 168.

16. Edward S. Casey has written at length about this modern tendency in *The Fate of Place: A Philosophical History* (Berkeley: University of California Press, 1997).

17. Alfred North Whitehead, *Science and the Modern World* (New York: Free Press, 1953), 91.

18. Casey, 214.

19. John Ruskin, *The Stones of Venice* (New York: Da Capo, 2003), 165.

20. Mikhail Bakhtin, *Rabelais and His World*, trans. Hélène Iswolsky (Bloomington: Indiana University Press, 1984), 26.

21. William Faulkner, *Absalom, Absalom!* The Corrected Text (New York: Vintage, 2010), 3.

22. Ibid., 4.

23. William Faulkner, *Sanctuary:* The Corrected Text (New York: Vintage, 1993), 4.

24. Ibid., 43, 51.

25. William Faulkner, *Novels 1957–1962* (New York: Library of America, 1999), 316, 323.

26. W. B. Yeats, *The Collected Works of W. B. Yeats*, vol. 5, ed. William H. O'Donnell (New York: Charles Scribner's Sons, 1994), 210. Written in 1937 as an introduction to the never-published "Dublin Edition" of Yeats's works, the essay was published in *Essays and Introductions* (1961) as "A General Introduction for My Work."

27. See Cleanth Brooks, "Faulkner and W. B. Yeats," in *Toward Yoknapatawpha and Beyond* (New Haven: Yale University Press, 1968), 330.

28. William Faulkner, *Go Down, Moses* (New York: Vintage, 1991), 179.

29. See Raymond Williams, *Marxism and Literature* (Oxford: Oxford University Press, 1978), 121–27.

30. Doreen Massey, "A Global Sense of Place," in *Reading Human Geography: The Poetics and Politics of Inquiry*, ed. Trevor Barnes and Derek Gregory (London: Arnold, 1997), 315.

31. Arjun Appadurai, *Modernity at Large: Cultural Dimensions of Globalization* (Minneapolis: University of Minnesota Press, 1996), 17–18.

32. Michael Woods, "Engaging the Global Countryside: Globalization, Hybridity, and the Reconstitution of Rural Place," *Progress in Human Geography* 31.4 (2007): 499.

33. Doreen Massey writes that "the local is always already a product in part of 'global' forces, where global in this context refers not necessarily to the planetary scale, but to the geographical beyond, the world beyond the place itself." See Massey, "Places and Their Pasts," *History Workshop Journal* 39 (1995): 184.

34. Even though this essay focuses on the local in Faulkner and takes the "Southern" as its oppositional discourse, there is nothing necessarily "Southern" about the concept. We can find instances of a comparable fluidity of boundaries in opposition to regionalisms and nationalisms elsewhere in the United States as well, in Maine, Washington State, Nevada, Montana, California, and elsewhere, wherever we can locate life in more of its historical, temporal, spatial complexity than either "nationalism" or "regionalism" permits.

35. Faulkner, *Absalom, Absalom!*, 111 (emphasis removed), 253.

36. See Gilles Deleuze and Felix Guattari's work on deterritorialization and reterritorialization, specifically *A Thousand Plateaus: Capitalism and Schizophrenia*, trans. Brian Massumi (Minneapolis: University of Minnesota Press, 1987).

37. Faulkner, *Absalom, Absalom!*,111–12 (emphasis removed).

Designing Spaces: Sutpen, Snopes, and the Promise of the Plantation

SCOTT ROMINE

In 1936 William Faulkner marked graphically for the first time the limits of Yoknapatawpha. But in the foldout map of Yoknapatawpha County included in *Absalom, Absalom!* Faulkner indulged in an authorial conceit that would fail to be borne out by the critical record. In designing a fictional territory of which he claimed to be "sole owner," Faulkner was, to put it mildly, kicking against the pricks: readers and critics ever since have been redrawing, reimagining, and repositioning what Faulkner once called his "postage stamp of native soil." In stamping Faulkner's fictional letter to the world, however, Yoknapatawpha served a useful function—one that Faulkner marks covertly in his 1936 map, where he appropriates for himself a role not only as sole owner but as *proprietor* as well. Like its 1945 counterpart "surveyed and mapped" for Malcolm Cowley's *Portable Faulkner* (1946), Faulkner's map constituted shrewd marketing of a literary property.[1] At the most basic level, and despite the symbolic complexities that they generate (more on this momentarily), these maps performed the work of spatial organization, and thus provided a kind of readerly handle on a body of work that had, in manifold and obvious ways, proven hard to grasp. This logic holds, I think, for most of the paratexts Faulkner generated during his career, including *Absalom, Absalom!*'s Chronology and Genealogy, and, most famously, the Compson Appendix, which provided a genealogy and character glosses for one of Yoknapatawpha's leading families. Of the Compson Appendix, Faulkner wrote to Cowley, "I should have done this when I wrote the book. Then the whole thing would have fallen into pattern like a jigsaw puzzle when the magician's wand touched it."[2] Whatever the aesthetic desirability of such wand work, it is hard not to hear in Faulkner's belated enthusiasm the memory of *The Sound and the Fury*'s poor sales figures.

Like all maps, and perhaps all fictions of property, Faulkner's representations of Yoknapatawpha enact a violence on the spaces they represent, representing from a single and authoritative perspective—that of an eye in the sky, or of a sole owner and proprietor—"a homogenization and reification," to use David Harvey's language, "of the rich diversity

of spatial itineraries and spatial stories."[3] Faulkner's texts are themselves
rich in such diversity, singularly scarce in single perspectives and homo-
geneous spaces. Yoknapatawpha itself was, as Thomas McHaney has
shown, a relatively late phenomenon (both lexically and conceptually) in
Faulkner's career.[4] In *The Hamlet* Ab Snopes is described as defending
"the entire honor and pride of the science and pastime of horse-trading
in Yoknapatawpha County" in his ill-fated trade with Pat Stamper, but
such moments wherein Yoknapatawpha per se spatially organizes a collective identity are rare.[5] Even granting that the post-*Portable* novels
increasingly anchored Faulkner's fiction in his postage stamp, how, then,
does the imagined geography of Yoknapatawpha operate relative to the
patchy, fluid, confused, and *heterogeneous* grammars of space that exist
within it? As I hope to show, the homogenizing work of Faulkner's mapping is not merely crude or irrelevant to his fiction, but rather *sympto-
matic* of fantasies of stable geographies and coherent fictions of space
that operate within it, especially as such fantasies and fictions accumu-
late around the figure of the plantation. Through a comparative reading
of Thomas Sutpen and Flem Snopes, I explore two modes of "falling into
pattern" relative to that space and the social order in which it is positioned. Both Sutpen and Snopes imagine the plantation as adjunctive
to their respective designs, although the forms of social mobility they
entail acquire qualitatively different properties. In attempting to subject
space to intention, Sutpen aligns the plantation with property and status,
while Snopes uses it in a regime of commodity and contract. In both
instances, however, the plantation—and more particularly, the plantation house—resists consolidation into a protected space of social position
and psychological shelter. In this sense, the plantation epitomizes the
paradox of Faulknerian space: it is both constitutive of, and irreducible
to, design.

Given its historical prominence, it is little wonder that the plantation figures significantly in Faulkner's mapping, orienting both the 1936
and 1945 maps. Besides the southwest quadrant of Yoknapatawpha, a
mostly blank space wherein Faulkner inscribes his sole ownership in
1936 and simply names the location in 1945, the other three quadrants
are anchored by plantations, at least in the latter instance. Besides Sutpen's Hundred and the Old Frenchman Place in the northwest and
southeast respectively, "McCaslin Edmonds" (which hadn't really existed
prior to the 1942 publication of *Go Down, Moses*) anchors the north-
east sector. But more interesting, for my purposes, is the marking of
Yoknapatawpha's northwest quadrant as "ISSETIBBEHA'S CHICKA-
SAW PATENT, Where by 1820 his people had learned to call it 'The
Plantation' just like the white men did." This points to another paradox

surrounding Faulkner's plantation: namely, that while the plantation appears as a historical phenomenon—a space subject to the temporal grammars of past, present, and future tense—there is no space on Faulkner's map marked as historically prior to it.

Nor is there any space fully subsequent to it. If one of the organizing chronologies of early Faulkner studies was the transition from the planter class to poor white, from the genteel Compsons to the horse-trading Snopeses, it is worth observing that Compson's Mile is marked in the 1945 map as originating from a horse trade between Ikkemotubbe and Jason I. In *The Mansion* (1959), horse trading of a different sort leads to the final portion of the "original family holding" passing from Compson hands. There, Jason IV, who falsely advertises the land as the future site of a military air-training field, is bested in a land deal by Flem Snopes, who lets Jason "over-reach himself out of his ancestral acres" because he knows that their boundary line, derived from the 1821 Chickasaw grant, will be used as the survey line for a new highway.[6] In the interim, Jason IV returns to cotton in *The Sound and the Fury* (1929)—not as a planter, but as a spectacularly inept speculator, the plantation proper having have long since passed. Its residues, however, persist. Jason remains firmly entangled in a postplantation household and fanatically committed to the memory of *his* people owning slaves when "you all" (his epithet for an imagined public) "were running little shirt tail country stores and farming land no nigger would look at on shares."[7] Jason's error in overlaying two discontinuous moments—when his people owned slaves, and when "you all" competed against "niggers" in the postbellum economy of tenant farming—suggests the persistence of the plantation in his imagined geography. The plantation abides as a kind of ghostly barracks—structurally haunting, if materially absent.

On the map, it is always, already there—not as an original, but as a copy: a way Issetibbeha's people have learned from the white man to call space. Neither, however, does the white man—at least any single white man—have original, authoritative access to the space so designated. To speak generally, Faulkner's plantation is a peculiarly *imagined* space, an object of aspiration or disavowal more than a habitus. Alternatively, it is a distinctive instance of Philip Weinstein's insight that "habitus does not prosper: Faulkner's protagonists typically shatter, and are shattered by, habitus."[8] Either way, it is never quite inhabitable, never available to everyday practices of routine and ritual or to normative modes of cultural transmission. It constitutes a desired space from which one is blocked— a scenario that initiates the careers of Sutpen and Snopes—or an object of longing consigned to an irretrievable past. Even in *Go Down, Moses* (1942), the novel in which it is imagined and visually presented as most intact, the plantation will not bear intention or inheritance. In a passage from "The Bear" notable for its singularity, McCaslin Edmonds gestures

> not even toward the ledgers: so that, as the stereopticon condenses into one instantaneous field the myriad minutia of its scope, so did that slight and rapid gesture establish in the small cramped and cluttered twilit room not only the ledgers but the whole plantation in its mazed and intricate entirety—the land, the fields . . . that whole edifice intricate and complex and founded upon injustice and erected by ruthless rapacity and carried on even yet with at times downright savagery not only to the human beings but the valuable animals too, yet solvent and efficient and, more than that: not only still intact but enlarged, increased.[9]

The moment is unusual in Faulkner's visual presentation of the plantation, which tends to follow the logic of what Tara McPherson calls lenticular vision, an "economy of visibility" that prevents an understanding of how images are joined.[10] Faulkner's style tends, in a pattern with a history dating back to the antebellum plantation novel, to see, first and foremost, the plantation house and then, if at all, the fields and the quarters through a visual ellipsis that disconnects the spatial continuum. Here, by sharp contrast, the plantation comes into focus "in its mazed and intricate entirety," instantaneously visible as a totality, intact in space and time. The reason for this, I suggest, is the intention orienting the view: Ike McCaslin is leaving the plantation, or trying to. But the plantation door proves as difficult for Ike to exit as it does for Sutpen and Snopes to enter. As Edouard Glissant says, "In Faulkner's world, the 'impossibility' of establishing a territorial foundation is also the impossibility of foreseeing, making plans, and projecting into the future."[11] In Ike's case, it is almost as if the plantation's territorial integration exists only so that Ike, in trying to push from it, finds that he cannot—that he is condemned to inhabit spaces (the big woods, rapidly giving way to capitalist invasion; his house in town, which is never a home) whose foundations and futures are equally condemned. For Ike, too, the plantation resists design.

Even so, the plantation's marks and traces are everywhere. *The Hamlet* begins with an image of a house and a place. "Hill-cradled and remote, definite yet without boundaries, straddling into two counties and owning allegiance to neither," Frenchman's Bend

> had been the original grant and site of a tremendous pre–Civil War plantation, the ruins of which—the gutted shell of an enormous house with its fallen stables and slave quarters and overgrown gardens and brick terraces and promenades—were still known as the Old Frenchman place, although the original

boundaries now existed only on old faded records in the Chancery Clerk's office in the county court house in Jefferson, and even some of the once-fertile fields had long since reverted to the cane-and-cypress jungle from which their first master had hewed them. (731)

As a matter of mapping, there is not much precision here: boundaries are either disavowed (Frenchman's Bend has none, despite being a "definite" place) or vestigial, as with the plantation boundaries that exist in records not only old, but faded too. Although the Yoknapatawpha County courthouse keeps those boundaries, nature does not, and an unspecified county line bisects the unbounded and unpledged community to which the plantation lends its name. As for the name itself, it is not certain that a Frenchman was involved, although the "first master" had "quite possibly been a foreigner" and, for the "people who had come after him and had almost obliterated all trace of his sojourn," anyone with a funny accent would have been deemed a Frenchman (731). Never mind that the "people who had come after him" never heard him speak, nor that those who did, and who lived as neighbors to the largest planter in the area, apparently never determined his actual origin to pass down to posterity.

As an organizing center, then, the Old Frenchman place barely holds. As James A. Snead observes, the "unsettled facts at the heart of the Frenchman's Bend 'setting'" work to "make the unreal seem unquestionable."[12] And yet hold it does because it continues to mark and organize space. The maybe–maybe not Frenchman's most legible trace in Yoknapatawpha—indeed, "all that remained of him" other than the "skeleton of the tremendous house"—is the "river bed which his slaves had straightened for almost ten miles to keep his land from flooding" (731). Marked neither linguistically ("Frenchman's Bend" seems to suggest the opposite) nor cartographically (neither map shows a straightened river), the straightened river signals the imposition of spatial order often associated with Yoknapatawpha's plantations.[13] Like Wallace Steven's jar, the skeleton ruin of the Frenchman's house makes the slovenly wilderness surround it, even after the slovenly wilderness (in the form of a "cane-and-cypress jungle") reclaims the fertile fields once hewed out of it by the Frenchman, their "first master." By at least implying the existence of subsequent masters, that phrase in turn suggests how the Old Frenchman place occupies the position that it does: occupying the Old Frenchman place signifies territorial mastery. *The Hamlet* begins with a shift in masters. First, it is Will Varner who habitually reclines in his makeshift throne, a flour barrel modified by his blacksmith, amidst the ruins of the Old Frenchman place, "inviting no company, against his background of fallen baronial splendor" (734). But by the end the novel's first section, it is Flem Snopes who occupies the flour barrel; he is on his way up, and the Old Frenchman place will facilitate his ascent.

Early in *The Hamlet*, V. K. Ratliff searches for goats to sell to a Northerner who formulated a long-distance plan for a goat-ranch. Ratliff explains that Northerners "does things different from us":

> "If a fellow in this country was to set up a goat-ranch, he would do it purely and simply because he had too many goats already. . . . But a northerner dont do it that way. . . . He dont start off with goats or a piece of land either. He starts off with a piece of paper and a pencil and measures it all down setting in the library—so many goats to so many acres and so much fence to hold them." (804)

As regards his own and this Northerner's particular relations to space, Ratliff's characterization is sound. As an "itinerant sewing-machine agent" (734), his livelihood depends on watching for and seizing opportunities on the wing. For Ratliff, territory means not property, but a field of tactical improvisation. By contrast, the Northerner assumes a highly abstracted and circumscribed space in which a design might be effected, practical questions—the number of available goats, for instance—be damned. What is scandalous, however, is the larger imagined geography produced by Ratliff's characterization, which imagines that only Northerners operate space in this way. Perhaps Ratliff hasn't noticed lately the Old Frenchman place, where Will Varner reclines in order, he explains, to imagine "what it must have felt like to be the fool that would need all this . . . just to eat and sleep in" (734). Never mind that Thomas Sutpen, another "fellow in this country," hardly sets up his cotton ranch because he happens to have a few slaves on his hands and nothing to do with them. Rosa Coldfield is explicit on the point, noting that Sutpen was "no younger son sent out from some old quiet country like Virginia or Carolina with the surplus negroes to take up new land."[14]

Lacking either land or a surplus that would make it profitable, Sutpen's design depends upon a highly abstracted and future-oriented use of space. In comparing the forms of social mobility entailed in Sutpen's project with those of Flem Snopes and his shiftier negotiations, I draw upon Michel de Certeau's differentiation between what he calls *strategies* and *tactics*. A strategy, according to Certeau, is a "calculus of force-relationships which becomes possible when a subject of will and power . . . can be isolated from an 'environment' [and which] assumes a place that can be circumscribed as proper and thus serve as a basis for generating relations with an exterior distinct from it." Depending on a "view of the whole" and its attendant visual logics, strategies "privilege spatial relationships," depend on the theoretical elaboration of place by means of "systems and totalizing discourses capable of articulating an ensemble of physical places in which forces are distributed," and materially realize those places as "proper." The tactic, conversely, is a "calculus which cannot count on a 'proper' (a spatial or institutional localization), nor . . . on a borderline," and which thus must assume a protean, improvisational character as it responds to the contingencies available at a given moment. "Lacking its own place, lacking a view of the whole," tactics require "a creativity as persistent as it is subtle, tireless, ready for every opportunity, scattered over the terrain of the dominant order . . . founded on established rights and property."[15] Although Sutpen and Snopes can be fairly aligned with the strategy and tactic, respectively, neither moves toward the plantation (as both material and social reality) in a uniform way. Rather, Faulkner's two greatest narratives of social ascent describe movements that are coded simultaneously as erratic and anomalous, full of skips and jumps, but also as inerrant, mechanical, and overdetermined—a paradox that depends, as I have suggested earlier, on a poetics that produces and consolidates spaces even as it fractures and dissolves.

"I had a design," Thomas Sutpen explains to General Compson. "To accomplish it I should require money, a house, a plantation, slaves, a family—incidentally of course, a wife" (218). He might have ended with the first item on his checklist, since his career effectively demonstrates that the subsequent items, with the possible exception of the incidental wife, can basically be purchased. But he doesn't, and his syntax suggests why: the items on the list are, to use Sutpen's language, "adjunctive or incremental" to his design, not constitutive of it. At its core, the design is an image of "tak[ing] that boy in where he would never again need to stand on the outside of a white door and knock at it . . . so that that boy . . . could shut that door himself forever behind him" and look ahead to descendants who "waited to be born without even having to know that they had once been riven forever free from brutehood" (216). Although the distinction is relatively fine, it is crucial to recognize that the design terminates not in possession of a house, plantation, and so forth, but in a cognitive, imaginative use of them: a fantasy. As Fredric Jameson observes, fantasies are not "available at any time or place for the taking of the thought"; certain "material preconditions must exist" in order for the "subject successfully to tell itself this particular daydream."[16] Not just any door will do; the door-to-door arc of Sutpen's design depends on a culturally specific articulation of spatial and institutional localizations that will, as Certeau says, "serve as a basis for generating relations with an exterior distinct from it." As Sutpen moves toward the fantasy of being inside, not outside, the white door, he secures certain spatial fictions and disrupts others.

The door at issue, of course, derives from the traumatic encounter in Sutpen's childhood at the Tidewater plantation to which his family has moved. Hailing from an ahistorical, prelapsarian Appalachia wherein he had "never even heard of, never imagined, a place, a land divided neatly up and actually owned by men" (183), Sutpen is more or less bound to make such a breach of spatial etiquette. Directed by the "monkey nigger" to "go around to the back before he could even state the business" (193), Sutpen comes to regard the regime of property as defining the threshold of animal and human. He understands how "the rich man (not the nigger) must have been seeing them all the time—as cattle, creatures heavy and without grace, brutely evacuated into a world without hope or purpose" (194), and he comes to see his family's labor as "brutish and stupidly out of all proportion to its reward: the very primary essence of labor, toil, reduced to its crude absolute which only a beast could and would endure" (195).

Sutpen envisions a social totality organized by the division between human and brute, and by the spatial configuration of plantation-house-door as the boundary separating the one domain from the other. In this way, the plantation enables a separation *of space* (protected inside from unprotected outside) by means of positioning *in space*, which is to say, social position within a proper. Rosa Coldfield is thus essentially correct (however extreme her insinuations) to characterize Sutpen as "hid[ing]" or "conceal[ing] himself behind respectability, behind that hundred miles of land" (13, 12) and to imagine that "choos[ing] respectability to hide behind" indicates that "what he fled from must have been some opposite of respectability too dark to talk about" (13). In condemning "Yoknapatawpha County" for "suppl[ying]" Sutpen with a "place to hide himself" (11), Rosa ticks off several items on the design checklist, including the land (as concealing buffer) and the incidental wife—"the shield of a virtuous woman," as Rosa puts it, required to secure "respectability" and "to make his position impregnable." Her language of barrier is spot-on.

Yet even as she gives the demon his due in securing an impregnable respectability, Rosa registers the community's resistance to Sutpen, who does not merely build a plantation, but, as Quentin glosses his arrival, *"came out of nowhere and without warning upon the land with a band of strange niggers and built a plantation—(Tore violently a plantation, Miss Rosa Coldfield says)—tore violently"* (6). Rosa's correction codes

Sutpen's Hundred as a rupture, a rent in space, dependent upon the historically dubious premise of an established planter class culturally and spatially continuous with the plantation cultures of Virginia and Carolina from which, she notes, Sutpen conspicuously does not come. Quentin imagines that rupture as "tranquil and astonished earth" being "overrun" as Sutpen and his slaves "drag house and formal gardens violently out of the soundless Nothing . . . creating the Sutpen's Hundred, the *Be Sutpen's Hundred* like the oldentime *Be Light*" (6). If the deviance here is marked by excessive originality—a plantation that comes out of nowhere—an alternative coding of Sutpen marks him as excessively imitative, a copy of the real thing. Consonant with Sutpen's own understanding of his design as combat by imitation—after his confrontation at the plantation door, he understands that "to combat them you have got to have what they have. . . . You got to have land and niggers and a fine house to combat them with" (197)—this reading of Sutpen positions him as "underbred" (37), a proto–Jed Clampett hailing from the mountains and newly installed in a fancy domicile but never truly accepted by the local Drysdales. After relating the community's revulsion at Sutpen's acquisition of furniture, an affront by imagined felony "born of the town's realization that he was getting it involved with himself" (35), Mr. Compson explains that Sutpen "was like John L. Sullivan having taught himself painfully and tediously to do the schottische, having drilled himself and drilled himself in secret until he now believed it no longer necessary to count the music's beat, say" (37).

Even as it supplies Sutpen with a field for his design and its adjuncts, Yoknapatawpha County (to borrow Rosa Coldfield's reification) cannot understand his plantation as fitting neatly inside of it. Sutpen's combat by imitation relentlessly decodes the social fictions to which the plantation order is committed. Even as he builds the edifice that will separate him from the brutes, Sutpen brutalizes himself, foregoing the trappings of civilization as he labors "stark naked save for a coating of dried mud" (28) alongside his "wild niggers like beasts half tamed to walk upright like men" (6). (The latter's association with the animal world is a consistent textual feature.) He will save the clothes, Rosa surmises, for his "last assault" on respectability: his courtship of Ellen (30). Rosa's martial metaphor is apt; the imitation is truly combative. As John T. Matthews delightfully puts it, Sutpen is "the clumsiest plantation grandee you ever saw. . . . It's difficult to think of a single step in his climb to becoming the county's biggest plantation master that he doesn't do badly. . . . In order for a collective fantasy to work, you can't have someone walking around rehearsing in front of the audience, muffing lines, and declaiming the stage directions."[17] The irony, of course, is that Sutpen makes it work, inserting himself in the town's social order regardless of what scorn, arrests, or "clods of dirt and vegetable refuse" (46–47) might come his way. He hardly puts a foot *wrong*, becoming the county's largest planter "by the same tactics with which he had built his house— the same singleminded unflagging effort and utter disregard of how his actions . . . might look" (59). In multiple passages of this kind, Sutpen's effort to establish his plantation is textually coded as an inerrant trajectory, a straight-line march dependent on a deep knowledge of how social forces are distributed and materially arrayed. However he might muff his lines in Yoknapatawpha, he possesses a deep fluency in its social and spatial grammars: his checklist is, at its core, spot-on. He understands the lay of the land and buys his way in. A few years after being pelted at his wedding, and despite the persistence of those "who believed that the plantation was just a blind to his actual dark avocation," Sutpen "was accepted; he obviously had too much money now to be rejected or even seriously annoyed" (59). Property renders propriety a moot point, and Sutpen knows it.

Sutpen's competence also threatens Yoknapatawpha's broader plantation geographies. In marking Sutpen's lack of connection with the plantation cultures of Virginia and Carolina, Rosa Coldfield elides the existence of the plantation culture with which he is intimately related and in which, as a logical matter, his competence must have been developed. The narrative is emphatic on the point of Sutpen's merely tactical maneuverings in Haiti. Having recognized that to accomplish his design, he would "need first of all and above all things money in considerable quantities" (201), Sutpen recalls his schoolhouse lesson on the West Indies as a place "to which poor men went in ships and became rich, it didn't matter how, so long as that man was clever and courageous: the latter of which I believed that I possessed, the former of which I believed that, if it were to be learned by energy and will in the school of endeavor and experience, I should learn" (200). Improvising on the basis of sheer ignorance, he does not even know that a different language is spoken.

One of the intriguing questions of *Absalom, Absalom!*—intriguing precisely because the narrative is so ambiguous on the point—is whether Sutpen imagines that his design might be executed in full in Haiti. Is a plantation *like* Pettibone's available there, or merely the wealth that will enable the design to be articulated back in the States? Although we might pause over that fact that Sutpen acquires not just wealth, but a wife in Haiti—the checklist begins to be ticked off overseas— the locals in Yoknapatawpha, I suggest, read the design as capable only of local articulation. General Compson initiates the logic, immediately transitioning from Haiti's status as the "place where money was to be had quick if you were courageous and shrewd" to its status as a place of absolute difference and total violence (206–7). In Haiti, General Compson explains, "the sheen on the dollars was not from gold but from blood"; the whole place is a "theatre for violence and injustice and bloodshed and all the satanic lusts of human greed and cruelty" (207). Sutpen's design is made to serve the imagined geographies of the locals in Yoknapatawapha, which, as John Matthews acutely observes, depend on a disavowal, a "knowing not-knowing" that represses even as it registers "the whole history of the new-world plantation that makes Sutpen's career from Haiti to Jefferson entirely legible as a story of colonial crime."[18] Here, the limit of Yoknapatawpha fictitiously marks a boundary inside of which the social fact of disavowal differentiates *our* kind of plantation (secure, civilized) from the kind in Haiti (volcanic, barbaric). Whatever Sutpen's own intentions, local propriety requires the configuration of the West Indies as but a stop on a path to Yoknapatawpha, where Sutpen will need to travel in order to acquire a real plantation, even if, once there, he can only simulate the authentic copies of the original back in the Tidewater. To connect Sutpen's Hundred with Haiti would be to recognize that Yoknapatawpha's money, too, is sheened with blood.

If money permits Sutpen's design to hold for a time, it is, of course, doomed to failure for reasons altogether overdetermined: Sutpen's particular fantasy, which will require his son Henry to shut the gate to the brute trying to get in lest the design deteriorate into a "mockery and a betrayal of that little boy who approached that door fifty years ago" (226); history (or God, as Rosa Coldfield has it), which will destroy the institution on which the design is founded; Sutpen's crude failures to improvise in the postwar terrain. As Glissant observes, the impossibility of territorial foundations in Faulkner correlates with an inability to foresee and protect against contingency. To this rule, however, Glissant offers an exception, noting that "Only the Snopeses can see ahead."[19] In turning to Flem Snopes and his plantation maneuverings, I begin by noting the parallels between him and Sutpen, which, although long recognized, have not always been appreciated for their specificity. Both sagas involve a protagonist who obtains a plantation house imagined as a barrier to the outside world and as positioned "respectably" within it. Both are treated as intruders by the social order that they successfully invade, and in both cases the intrusion is marked as imitation: while Flem consistently apes the clothing of his betters, the planter's hat he eventually dons is never credited as belonging to him. Both Sutpen and Snopes acquire (and honor with fine gravestones) wives who are merely "adjunctive" to their respective designs and who function as units of exchange in an economy in which money and "respectability" are uneasily yoked. Both are subjected to multiple narrators, at least some of whom deploy a theory of "innocence" to explain their perplexing subjects.

Yet for all their similarities, I want to begin by suggesting that Glissant is essentially wrong in his characterization. Sutpen sees—or at least looks—much farther ahead than does Flem Snopes. Sutpen's design is intact from the beginning: his understanding of plantation culture appears as a paradigm shift—a gestalt—that dictates his strategy "all at once." Thus, he acquires his wife because he needs one; his acquisition is determined by a view of the total social structure organizing the position toward which he moves. Flem's movement, by contrast, is temporally impoverished and essentially tactical in nature. He seizes opportunities on the wing, acquiring Eula not because he needs a wife (or a wife like her), but because she is available and useful to him at a specific moment. She is adjunctive, but also nearly accidental. She also comes with a plantation.

Flem's differentiation from Sutpen begins with his ambiguous positioning (as the shadowy brother of "Barn Burning") in the originating trauma of the Snopes saga: the confrontation at Major de Spain's door. Where Sutpen's cognate experience is immediate and direct, Flem recedes into the background as the crisis of class and property is filtered through the perspective of his younger brother. Still, the parallels are significant. Installed in a tenant house ("identical almost with the dozen others") that his "bovine" sisters declare "ain't fitten for hawgs," Sarty associates, as does Sutpen, his family's female labor with brutishness.[20] Like Sutpen, who realizes that his father's "whupp[ing] one of Pettibone's niggers" is only to strike at "a child's toy balloon with a face painted on it" (*Absalom*, 191, 190), Sarty imagines the property is impervious to his father's violence. The De Spain mansion, *"big as a courthouse,"* confers immunity: *They are safe from him. People whose lives are a part of this peace and dignity are beyond his touch"* ("Barn Burning," 10). They are not, however, beyond Ab's footprint, which he has smeared in fresh horse droppings and used to despoil De Spain's French rug. Where Sutpen is paralyzed by the "monkey-dressed nigger" at Pettibone's (*Absalom*, 221), Ab walks right through De Spain's servant, similarly attired in broadcloth and linen, who tries to deny him entry until he wipes his feet. Nor is the plantation safe from Ab's torch; Sarty's fantasy that *"even the barns"* are *"impervious to the puny flames he might contrive"* will eventually go up in smoke ("Barn Burning," 10).

Flem is not, however, his father's son. (If anything, Mink is the Snopes heir to Ab's tribal ethos and propensity for physical retribution—an inheritance that will lead to Flem's demise.) Upon the family's arrival in Frenchman's Bend, Flem *trades* on Ab's reputation as a barn burner. Jody Varner hopes to use this reputation as blackmail to drive the Snopes family away just as their crop is harvested, mistakenly framing the scenario in terms of social status. He imagines that the Snopeses cannot bear the stigma and that "a man that's got habits that way will just have to suffer the disadvantages of them" (*Hamlet*, 739). Flem's sharp dealing depends on a different calculus that values material property more than social capital. He recognizes that Varner values his barns more than the Snopeses value their reputation; indeed, the latter—dependent on a view of the social totality that measures and defines status—is mostly irrelevant to Flem's itinerant clan. Flem moves in a purely tactical and fluid way, improvising on the fly to take advantage of circumstances. Negotiating from a position of material and social disadvantage, he changes Jody's joke and slips the yoke, securing a position in Varner's store and quickly displacing Jody within the economy Will Varner commands. He adheres rigidly and scrupulously to the logic of contract whereby he might surmount the deficits of social status. Unlike Will Varner, who encourages sloppy bookkeeping because he can afford to, and because the social deck is stacked in his favor—even his customers know that "they would pay interest for that which on its face looked like generosity and open-handedness" (782)—Flem insists upon exactitude, never making "mistakes in any matter pertaining to money" (782). At least initially, Flem's social mobility depends on being severed from propriety and property—except insofar as the latter can be reduced to a pure unit of exchange. As Charles Mallison explains in *The Town*, Flem deals not in monuments, but in footprints: "A monument only says *At least I got this far* while a footprint says *This is where I was when I moved again.*"[21]

Unlike his father, whose footprints violate the social order, Flem steps at the edges of property and the plantation: he doesn't want to move in, he wants to move up. Although he comes to "possess" the Old Frenchman place—at least to be able to sell it—he, like Thoreau, never has his fingers burned by actual possession. Rather, the plantation is but a commodity to be exploited, which Flem does by following the exact practice of Pat Stamper in his celebrated horse trade with Ab Snopes: he resells the same object after adding the illusion of value. The swindle is, however, far from straightforward, and its complexities suggest the ambiguous values attached to the plantation even in ruins. Surely the most perplexing feature of Flem's "swindle" is the belated recognition of its evidence. When Ratliff finally examines the coins with which Flem has "salted" the Old Frenchman place, he determines that they are from the 1870s and thus could not be the antebellum treasure buried, according to local folklore, by the Frenchman. When merely looking at them would have settled the question, why does Ratliff assume that the silver dollars are "all coined before 1861" as he does prior to negotiating with Flem (*Hamlet*, 1057)? Clearly Ratliff is predisposed to believe that they are, but why does that predisposition cause him to overlook clear evidence to the contrary? A partial answer, I suggest, is provided when Flem asks him why he wants the Old Frenchman place. Ratliff's response—"To start a goat-ranch" (1063)—hits closer than Ratliff perhaps realizes, since his project is as abstract and ungrounded as the Northerner's he has earlier satirized. He believes that money will spring from the ground (an old plantation mythology), and his evidence is that cotton hasn't, despite that "Will Varner could have raised cotton or corn either in it so tall he would have to gather it on horseback just by putting the seed in the ground" (1051). In short, Ratliff attributes value to the Old Frenchman place because Varner *hasn't* profited from it. Ratliff's "pragmatism" causes him to distrust Varner's characterization of the plantation as his "one mistake"—the "only thing I ever bought in my life I couldn't sell to nobody" (734)—just as it leads him to accept Varner's characterization of the Frenchman as the "fool that would need all this . . . just to eat and sleep in" (734). But Varner's language here is subtle, and we might well read his stated desire to try "to find out what it must have felt like" to be that fool as a literal effort to enter into the excessive imagination of his predecessor. If the Frenchman didn't need "all this," we should pause to consider that neither does Varner: he can afford *not* to grow horse-high cotton (when he could) and to recline publicly in his barrel in what amounts to a display of conspicuous leisure. As Brannon Costello observes, the "wasteful gestures" historically associated with plantation paternalism help to "organiz[e] the white social structure" by representing "the pinnacle of achievement in the economic arena: they simultaneously signify financial superiority and disinterest in the process of 'cajolery,' 'trickery,' 'threat,' and 'force' that characterizes the economic struggles of lesser men."[22] The art of Flem's deal, I suggest, derives from his understanding of that surplus value—that is, the gap between the social capital signaled by waste and the economic value of the plantation—and his knowledge that Ratliff will misread it in an excruciatingly literal way as "buried" treasure.[23] A more careful man would "salt" with a few antebellum coins, but Flem knows his dupe.

In making the deal that will propel him toward Jefferson, Flem remains mired in the lesser economic world of trickery and the horse trade; he is still moving by footprint. Once in town, however, he begins his long transition toward "respectability" and the monuments to which it adheres. Unlike Sutpen, who, following his traumatic insult, determines in short order what he "would have to do . . . about it in order to live with himself for the rest of his life" (*Absalom*, 193), Snopes belatedly recognizes respectability as the "one thing he would have to have if there was to be any meaning to his life or even peace in it" (*Town*, 227). But as Ratliff explains, this recognition is no less traumatic for a "a feller that come—came up from where he did," assuming that "money would buy anything he could or would ever want," only to discover "maybe too late" that he had thrown it away (227). Once recognized, however, the signs of respectability prove not so hard to purchase. As Noel Polk observes, Flem's power is that he "profoundly understands the human longing to possess the signs that certify and affirm a person's place in the culture"; he also understands which signs perform that function.[24] In occupying, however, the De Spain mansion, which "would have to be the physical symbol of all them generations of respectability and aristocracy" (*Mansion*, 469), Flem moves beyond a tactically advantageous understanding *of* to long himself *for*—to attempt to *inhabit*—the signs of social position. He is a better seller than buyer, a better tactician than strategist. While the signs are available for purchase, their capacity for signification and occupancy proves less than desired. Flem is a crude iconographer, utterly inept at managing the symbols of plantation excess. Lacking the intervention of the French architect who tastefully curbs Sutpen's vision of "castlelike magnificence" (*Absalom*, 31), Flem tears down the portico and installs "extry big" columns (*Town*, 309) for his "Frenchman's Bend-dreamed palace" (*Mansion*, 651). As Ratliff explains, "even a feller that never seen colyums before wouldn't have no doubt a-tall what they was, like in the photographs" of "Confederit" sweethearts and beaux (*Town*, 309).[25] Flem imagines the De Spain mansion as a site of protection and security, but in his hands it proves no less susceptible to invasion than when under original management. Here, the invasion is performed not by Ab wearing excrement-smeared shoes, but by Mink bearing a rusty pistol. Although he contemplates the "white columned edifice with something like pride that someone named Snopes owned it" (*Mansion*, 699), Mink does not hesitate to enter it and bring Flem's design to an anticlimactic end. Long before that, however, the mansion is a dead space; as Polk elegantly puts it, "Flem fades into the walls of respectability, goes down not even swinging but just empty."[26] Like Flem's other monument to respectability—Eula's tombstone that declares a "virtuous Wife" to be "a Crown to her Husband" (*Town*, 312)—the mansion is also a monument to death: a "Snopes-colonial mausoleum," as Charles Mallison aptly describes it (*Mansion*, 645).

Although the mansion fails as a proper and a scene of propriety, the failure is not limited to Flem Snopes. His design to place himself in the culture has, as critics have long noted, been abetted throughout by "the town" whose spokesmen strive to narrate Snopesism as a story of "we" and "they." As Gavin Stevens (the foremost, self-appointed spokesman for "we") puts it, "when I say 'they' I mean Snopeses; when you say 'Snopeses' in Jefferson you mean Flem Snopes" (*Town*, 29). The ethnographic logic of what Stevens calls "our folklore, or Snopeslore, if you like" (Stevens likes) obtains a visual correlate (129). In the passage closest in all of Faulkner's fiction to the cartographic perspective occupied by its sole owner and proprietor, Stevens looks down on

> Jefferson, the center, radiating weakly its puny glow into space; beyond it, enclosing it, spreads the County, tied by the diverging roads to that center as is the rim to the hub by its spokes, yourself detached as God himself for this moment above the cradle of your nativity and of the men and women who made you, the record and annal of your native land . . . all bound, precarious and ramshackle held together, by the web, the iron-thin warp and woof of [man's] rapacity but withal yet dedicated to its dreams. (277)

But Stevens's "view of the whole" is hardly disinterested; his gaze falls last on Frenchman's Bend, "ant-heap for the north-east crawl of Snopes" (278). Invasion, in Faulkner, is always the spatial form of disavowal, the geographical cure for the symptoms from which "we," too, suffer. All of Faulkner's invaders threaten to reveal to the community what it does not wish to know about itself. As I have argued, the plantation serves as a recurrent trope and scene of disavowal, a place where rapacity and dream coexist intolerably. Stevens's vision momentarily integrates the two as being "bound" in the "fat black rich plantation earth still synonymous of the proud fading white plantation names whether we—I mean of course they—ever actually owned a plantation or not" (278). His correction is telling: it is *they*, not *we*, who owned the plantations and the proud (if fading) plantation names, among which Stevens names De Spain, Sutpen, and even Stevens, but not, of course, Snopes, the usurper. Is Stevens disavowing the rapacity or humbly refusing the pride of place the plantation (whether "ever actually owned" or not) confers? Therein lies the crux of the plantation's anxious position in Faulkner's geography. As guarantor of status and respectability within a social order, the plantation promises the smooth fit of synecdoche, the part representing the whole as, to borrow Faulkner's language, the "whole thing" falls into pattern "like a jigsaw puzzle when the magician's wand touched it." Such magic, however, is largely absent in Faulkner's fiction, where "actually owning" a plantation occurs on the peripheries of a center concerned mainly with the plantation's promise, its loss, its disavowal, its impropriety, and its profound resistance to habitation.

NOTES

1. The later map was produced by Random House based on a more detailed map Faulkner had designed for *The Portable Faulkner*. When describing the map that appears in that volume, I refer to features included on Cowley's copy of Faulkner's original map, available in Louis Daniel Brodsky and Robert W. Hamblin, eds., *Faulkner: A Comprehensive Guide to the Brodsky Collection*, vol. 1 (Jackson: University Press of Mississippi, 1982), n.p.

2. Quoted in William Faulkner, *The Sound and the Fury*, ed. David Minter (New York: Norton, 1987), 224. Recognizing the significance of Cowley's organization of his work Faulkner wrote to Cowley in December 1945 that the collection, which he suggested be advertised as a "chronological picture of Faulkner's apocryphal county," was "not a new work by Faulkner. It's a new work by Cowley all right though." See William Faulkner, *Selected Letters of William Faulkner*, ed. Joseph Blotner (New York: Vintage Books, 1978), 211. I share Thomas L. McHaney's view that Cowley's emphasis on Yoknapatawpha as an organizing principle of Faulkner's fiction "did affect the Mississippi writer's scale of reference to the county and may have affected what he came to write"; see McHaney, "First Is Jefferson: Faulkner Shapes His Domain," *Mississippi Quarterly* 47.4 (Fall 2004): 526. For a provocative survey of how Cowley's emphasis on Yoknapatawpha evolved among early Faulkner critics, see Lawrence H. Schwartz, *Creating Faulkner's Reputation: The Politics of Modern Literary Criticism* (Knoxville: University of Tennessee Press, 1988), 173–99.

3. David Harvey, *The Condition of Postmodernity* (Malden, Mass.: Blackwell Publishing, 1990), 253.

4. McHaney, especially 511–15.

5. William Faulkner, *The Hamlet*, in *William Faulkner: Novels 1936–1940* (New York: Library of America, 1990), 761. Text hereafter cited parenthetically.

6. William Faulkner, *The Mansion*, in *William Faulkner: Novels 1957–1962* (New York: Library of America, 1999), 620, 626. Text hereafter cited parenthetically.

7. Faulkner, *The Sound and the Fury*, 143.

8. Philip Weinstein, "The Land's Turn," in *Faulkner and the Ecology of the South: Faulkner and Yoknapatawpha, 2003*, ed. Joseph R. Urgo and Ann J. Abadie (Jackson: University Press of Mississippi, 2005), 20.

9. William Faulkner, *Go Down, Moses* (1942; New York: Vintage International, 1990), 284–85.

10. Tara McPherson, *Reconstructing Dixie: Race, Gender, and Nostalgia in the Imagined South* (Durham: Duke University Press, 2003), 26.

11. Edouard Glissant, *Faulkner, Mississippi*, trans. Barbara Lewis and Thomas Spear (New York: Farrar, Straus, and Giroux, 1999), 115–16.

12. James A. Snead, *Figures of Division: William Faulkner's Major Novels* (New York: Methuen, 1986), 145, 146.

13. Both Compson's Mile and Sutpen's Hundred are perfect squares, a shape that recurs throughout Faulkner's fiction to mark the anxieties associated with order, most famously, perhaps, in the concluding scene of *The Sound and the Fury*, where Benjy's experience of things "each in its ordered place" depends on the direction the square is

traveled (191). I note also that the straight lines of Yoknapatawpha's rectangular shape smooth out the irregularities of Lafayette, the Mississippi county on which it is based. The map's symmetries begin to look a bit suspicious.

14. William Faulkner, *Absalom, Absalom!*, in *William Faulkner: Novels 1936–1940*, 13. Text hereafter cited parenthetically.

15. Michel de Certeau, *The Practice of Everyday Life*, trans. Steven F. Rendall (Berkeley: University of California Press, 1984), xix–xx.

16. Fredric Jameson, *The Political Unconscious: Narrative as a Socially Symbolic Act* (Ithaca: Cornell University Press, 1981), 182.

17. John T. Matthews, *William Faulkner: Seeing through the South* (Malden, Mass.: Wiley-Blackwell, 2009), 194–95.

18. John T. Matthews, "Recalling the West Indies: From Yoknapatawpha to Haiti and Back," *American Literary History* 16.2 (Summer 2004): 256–57.

19. Glissant, 116.

20. William Faulkner, "Barn Burning," in *Collected Stories of William Faulkner* (New York: Random House, 1950), 8, 9. Text hereafter cited parenthetically.

21. William Faulkner, *The Town*, in *William Faulkner: Novels 1957–1962*, 26. Text hereafter cited parenthetically.

22. Brannon Costello, *Plantation Airs: Racial Paternalism and the Transformations of Class in Southern Fiction, 1945–1971* (Baton Rouge: Louisiana State University Press, 2007), 75.

23. Lucas Beauchamp in "The Fire and the Hearth" similarly misreads the status value of the plantation order as buried treasure.

24. Noel Polk, *Outside the Southern Myth* (Jackson: University Press of Mississippi, 1997), 46.

25. In *The Mansion* Charles Mallison observes that the Backus estate had been successfully "transmogrified" as "old Snopes had tried to do to the De Spain house with his Yoknapatawpha County gangster's money and failed"; the difference is that "the rich and lavish cash had been spent with taste" (651).

26. Polk, 46.

"My New Orleans Gang": Faulkner's French Quarter Circle

John Shelton Reed

"If I never much hankered after Paris during the expatriate years," Hamilton Basso wrote in the 1960s, "it was because, in the New Orleans of that era, I had Paris in my own back yard," and in the French Quarter of his youth a crowd of artists, writers, journalists, musicians, poseurs, and hangers-on had indeed worked with some success to create what Basso called "a sort of Creole version of the Left Bank." As the Vieux Carré evolved from the slum it had become at the turn of the last century into . . . whatever it is today, there was a moment when *les bons temps* rolled in a Bohemian sort of way.[1]

One participant in that scene, an artist and Tulane instructor named Bill Spratling, shared an apartment with someone he described later as "a strange young man who had yet to publish anything of great importance," a Mississippian named Bill Faulkner.[2] In 1926 the two Bills self-published some four hundred copies of a little book of Spratling's drawings of themselves and some of their friends, called *Sherwood Anderson and Other Famous Creoles*.[3] Anderson, who had recently settled in the Quarter, was one of the friends, and Faulkner wrote an introduction that was an unmistakable parody of the older writer's sometimes pompous prose.

Spratling said later that the book was meant to be "a sort of private joke," and certainly the title was.[4] Only two of the forty-three Famous Creoles (as I'll call them for short) were actually Creoles, as Creoles understand that word, and Anderson was the only one with any real fame other than local. The book was a strictly amateur production, it was full of allusions that were unintelligible to anyone not in the circle, some of the sketches were decidedly amateurish, and the authors even misspelled a half-dozen of their friends' names. Nevertheless, *Famous Creoles* (as I'll call the *book* for short) can serve as what Spratling called, looking back, "a sort of mirror of our scene in New Orleans."[5] The Famous Creoles included most of those whom Faulkner called "my New Orleans gang."[6]

Many of the Famous Creoles and their circle knew the Left Bank or Greenwich Village firsthand and did their best to follow those models, establishing artistic and literary institutions like the *Double Dealer* magazine, Le Petit Theatre du Vieux Carré, and the Arts and Crafts Club of New Orleans, as well as a good many coffee houses, bookshops, and galleries that supported the Dixie version of *la vie bohème*. But the life of the Quarter also reflected some characteristics of its habitués. The twenty-three Famous Creoles who actually lived in the French Quarter in 1926 included notable hosts (Anderson and his wife, Elizabeth Prall, and *Times-Picayune* columnist Lyle Saxon) and their most frequent guests and companions, as well as the most important of the journalists who covered the New Orleans cultural scene (Saxon, Natalie Scott, John McClure, Freddie Oechsner). Seventeen of the twenty-three were men, and only three of those were over thirty-five. Eliminate those three and throw in Basso (who spent so much time in the Quarter that he might as well have lived there) and you have most of the members of a group of newspapermen, freelance writers, artists, and Tulane faculty members who called themselves, for reasons now lost, the "Shasta Daisies society."[7] You also have a concentration of young men, nearly all unmarried—the makings of what Basso's biographer calls a "boyish and boisterous atmosphere" that often lent a sort of fraternity house flavor to the goings-on.[8]

Figure 1. Spratling and Faulkner, from *Famous Creoles*

The last drawing in *Famous Creoles* repays close study. It shows Faulkner and Spratling in their garret. Spratling, an art teacher who had written a pencil-drawing textbook, is holding his pencil at arm's length in the classic technique for determining proportions. The joke is that the proportions of the drawing are totally haywire. Faulkner holds a glass and under his chair are several liquor jugs. Next to the "Viva Art" motto on the wall hangs a pump-action BB gun, which (Spratling recalled) was used "on a rainy day, or when there were distinguished visitors to be entertained," to shoot out the windows of an empty house across the street. "From the street below no shot could be heard—only the slight tinkle of glass as it hit the pavement."[9]

The boys also shot passing pedestrians, and they had a scoring system posted on the wall. Bearded men were valuable, but "if you managed to pink a Negro nun, that rated ten points (for rarity value) and that was the highest you could go."[10] When Sherwood Anderson's teenaged son Bob visited New Orleans he became particularly fond of this sport, and made a nuisance of himself by coming around when Faulkner was writing. Bob didn't take hints, so one day Spratling and Faulkner "grabbed him, took his pants off, painted his peter green and pushed him out on the street, locking the door." After that, Spratling recalled, he "didn't bother us much."[11]

The walls of the apartment's bathroom featured nudes Spratling had painted, with shower faucets and parts of other fixtures incorporated as anatomical features.[12] Another attraction was what their friend Flo Field remembered years later as a "death-defying platform" built over the roof.[13] Reached through a window, it offered an escape from the stifling heat of a New Orleans attic, and at one party Faulkner unsuccessfully tried to persuade Mrs. Field to crawl outside—four floors above the street—with him.[14] The platform also offered access to adjoining roofs, across which, Ham Basso recalled, some daring partygoers once had "a fine game of tag."[15] (One of them was Faulkner: one slip would have profoundly altered American literary history.) Anthropologist Oliver La Farge, who shared a cook and dining expenses with Spratling and Faulkner, was very much a part of his messmates' larky scene. His tabletop mock-Indian "Eagle Dance" and his systematic destruction of some expensive drinking glasses became part of the circle's lore: he dropped them out the window, one by one, to hear the sound.[16]

For young Americans in the 1920s the French Quarter was an exotic and exciting place. La Farge described it in his memoirs as "a decaying monument and a slum as rich as jambalaya or gumbo":

There were sailors of all kinds, antique dealers, second-hand dealers, speakeasies galore, simple workmen, a fair variety of criminals, both white and
coloured nuns, the survivors of a few aristocratic Creole families clinging to
their ancestral homes, merchants of all sorts, and whole blocks of prostitutes.
Except for part of Royal Street and a section around the Cathedral which had
been brushed up and enjoyed the tourist trade, this was the real thing in slums.
. . . Anything could happen there, in the blocks of houses too beautiful to be
true, under balconies and in the shadows of the arches, and where the jangling,
jerry-built shacks have fought their way in among the ancient bricks. The hot
nights stirred you until you had a cat's longing to prowl, down streets turned
utterly silent, past speakeasies, by doors that gave out snatches of music, and
the blocks where the whispers and eyes of the whores behind the shutters
made a false promise of romance. Anything could happen in a town where the
signs on the trolleys along Canal Street showed that one line ran to Desire and
one to Elysian Fields.[17]

The Vieux Carré's version of Bohemia was tamer than the classic
nineteenth-century Parisian version, which floated on the surface of
an underworld of opiates and prostitution.[18] Some Bohemians patronized the relatively wide-open bordellos, but they didn't socialize with
the working girls, and for the most part the drug of choice was bootleg
alcohol.[19] Still, things were pretty spicy for 1920s America. The vice to
be found in the Quarter and nearby was a sort of tourist attraction, even
for tourists who weren't themselves in the market.[20] When New York
writer Carl Carmer and his wife, Betty, came to town, Carl was taken to
see Louise's, "a whorehouse of great distinction in the Quarter," while
Times-Picayune cartoonist Keith Temple took Betty to meet Aunt Rose
Arnold, a wealthy retired madam with a fondness for artists and writers.[21] Sherwood Anderson enjoyed Aunt Rose's company, introduced
Faulkner to her, and wrote the three of them into a short story.[22] John
McClure took the visiting H. L. Mencken to Tom Anderson's tavern on
Rampart Street, which had a brothel upstairs.[23] (The Cadillac Bar next
door was even dicier, allegedly with rooms for smoking opium.) Anderson's was a favorite eating and drinking place for McClure, Faulkner, and
Roark Bradford, while other members of the circle patronized Celeste's,
which Carmer described as "the lowest joint in New Orleans—filled with
lesbians, homosexuals, and the rest of us."[24] It was across from the police
station.

Flo Field stumbled on a link between the art scene and the demi-
monde of male prostitution when she met a young artist at an Arts and
Crafts Club exhibition.[25] When she went back to his apartment to see his
drawings, she found that he and his two roommates were "all starving."

The good-hearted Flo took them under her wing, bought them milk, and gave them money. But she was dismayed when one of them, "a boy like a beautiful 16 year old girl, but no front teeth" who worked as an artist's model, told her that the artist was "selling his body every night." (Flo wrote to her son, Sydney, that she regretted having been "a fairy godmother" to the three boys.)

A more respectable component of the Famous Creoles' circle was what Basso remembered as "a fairly dazzling collection of pretty girls [whose] part in this here twentieth century American literary renaissance will never be fully appreciated."[26] Half a dozen Famous Creoles met this description. Thirty years later William Odiorne particularly remembered cute Lucille Godchaux Antony, who often wore a painter's smock, and the elegant and vivacious pianist Genevieve Pitot.[27] Odiorne also recalled Odette Goldstein, a Brazilian reputed to be the most beautiful woman in New Orleans; and an Arkansas girl known as "Musetta," so chic she could have been a Parisienne, whom Spratling gallantly escorted to and from Tulane to pose au naturel for his art classes. But many of the pretty girls remain nameless, like the "New Orleans debutantes" Elizabeth Anderson remembered (not with pleasure), who "visited us regularly," one of whom "dropped her purse, knocked over her chair, and ran away in fright" when Sherwood rushed at her with his shirt completely open, to grab her for a dance.[28]

These girls and their boyfriends puzzled Sherwood. He wrote a friend that "one goes evening after evening among these women—at least these fellows do—and . . . one never goes to bed with one of them and gets clear. As far as that is concerned they will go further without going anywhere than any people I ever saw."[29] Adaline Katz agreed. A banker's daughter who took long walks with Anderson and appeared as a character in his novel *Many Marriages*, Katz recalled that though everyone probably believed in "free love" (certainly they talked about it a lot), there was less than one might have expected: the men, she told an interviewer (perhaps a bit scornfully), "drank a lot and talked a lot and then drank a lot."[30]

She was certainly right about that. Bootleg liquor was as much a part of the scene and emblematic of it as marijuana would be for a later generation of Bohemians. "The big thing that bound all those artistic people together was alcohol," Keith Temple claimed, and his neighbor and fellow Famous Creole Louis Andrews Fischer recalled that "*everybody* was a heavy drinker then."[31] Genevieve Pitot remembered "well lubricated" parties, where women might wear shawls in the summer heat to conceal bottles.[32] Liquor was a social necessity, Pitot said, and Spratling agreed. "We could do our friends proud," he said. "We always had plenty of liquor for all comers."[33] Elizabeth Anderson said, "We all seemed to feel that Prohibition was a personal affront and that we had a moral duty to undermine it."[34]

That wasn't difficult. James Feibleman acknowledged that Prohibition was in force, "but New Orleans did not seem to have heard of it."[35] When Faulkner's downstairs neighbors Marc and Lucille Antony had parties, they invited the neighborhood cops up for drinks.[36] The underworld organization run by Sylvestro "Silver Dollar Sam" Carollo, a "produce dealer" on St. Philip Street, insured that floods of liquor came from Cuba and the Bahamas to the Gulf and thence through any of several bayou routes to the Mississippi or Lake Pontchartrain.[37] (Faulkner spun fantastic yarns all his life about his involvement in this romantic business, complete with circumstantial details about hidden sandspits where Cuban schooners stashed barrels of alcohol.[38]) Once it reached the city, the thirsty could easily get a drink at one of the seventy-four French Quarter bars that Elizebeth Werlein once counted in a nine-block radius, or be served more discreetly in teacups at restaurants like Arnaud's.[39] Those who wanted a bottle could get one at an Italian grocery store like Joe Cascio's at St. Peter and Royal, or Manuel and Teresa across the street—although the "bourbon," "Scotch," and "gin" were most likely

Figure 2. Faulkner's bootlegger, "the bad priest," urinating against a wall (detail from the frontispiece to *Famous Creoles*)

Cuban grain alcohol flavored with iodine, creosote, and juniper-berry essence respectively.[40] (Faulkner's rum-running fantasy incorporated a little Italian lady who did the flavoring.) Alternatively, one could easily find a bootlegger. Spratling once bought ten large jugs from a woman whose bootlegger husband had died, and Faulkner's connection was a clergyman at the cathedral, "the bad priest" shown urinating against a wall in the frontispiece to *Famous Creoles*.[41]

Do-it-yourselfers could go "fishing," Keith Temple recalled, by paying a fisherman to rent a skiff and pick up a five-gallon can of alcohol stashed in the marshes.[42] Once you had your alcohol, you could make the popular "needle beer" by injecting (legal) near beer with it or your own mock gin with juniper essence from Solari's grocery at Royal and Iberville.[43] (Spratling rolled the cans across the floor for aeration; otherwise, he said, the taste was rather flat.[44]) As a well-connected local, musician Harold Levy got his alcohol and "essential oils" from a druggist friend.[45]

The favorite drink of all was what was called "absinthe"—probably the local product made without wormwood and sold legally after the end of Prohibition as Herbsaint—but whatever it was, as "the green fairy" it had a decadent Continental allure.[46] A Swiss man living in the Quarter made it himself and at six dollars a bottle (about seventy-two dollars in today's money) it wasn't cheap, but Spratling recalled making up "great pitchers for all our parties."[47] When it was poured over crushed ice with just a touch of water, to make an "absinthe frappé," Elizabeth Anderson attested, it had very little taste of alcohol, so "it was consumed in quantities."[48] "Was it good?" Temple asked of all this homemade hooch. "Indeed it was! It was cheap and tasted fine, and we certainly drank a very great deal of it."[49]

Above all, as Mrs. Anderson recalled, this was "a social and congenial time."[50] Even Faulkner was only occasionally antisocial, although by local standards he was an exceptional loner. Spratling wrote that he and his French Quarter friends "saw each other every day, almost every evening. If it wasn't at Lyle Saxon's house, it was at Sherwood and Elizabeth's or my own."[51] People just dropped in. According to Mrs. Anderson, "No one was ever invited, for that would make it seem as though they had to be invited before they would be welcome."[52] Almost every Saturday night the Andersons had a dinner party for a rotating group of friends and visitors to New Orleans.[53] Spratling remembered that the guests might include "John Dos Passos, or perhaps Carl Sandburg or Carl Van Doren or a great publisher from New York, Horace Liveright or Ben Huebs[c]h, all people we were proud to know."[54] If the Andersons weren't entertaining at home, they met friends for supper at one of the Quarter's inexpensive restaurants. Tujague's was a favorite, and so was

Tortorici's, a Sicilian place on Royal Street that people called "the Bucket of Blood."[55] After supper, the gang might move on to a newspapermen's hangout called Max in the Alley, where Elizabeth Anderson recalled "a large ceiling fan that languorously revolved, stirring flies into brief action [and] all the men dressed in rumpled, messy seersucker suits, patched with perspiration."[56]

Most days the *Double Dealer* crowd gathered at the Pelican Book Shop on Royal Street after business hours for "tea"—wine, salami sandwiches, and talk—just "a happy hour," Ham Basso recalled, not "an intellectual hour."[57] On Sundays Spratling and Faulkner often went for breakfast with Baron Hanno von Schucking, a Quarter character said to have a wealthy lady friend; drinks after breakfast extended into lunch, followed by more drinking, and the abandonment of whatever plans had been made for the day.[58] Most nights there were parties, often at Spratling's or Lyle Saxon's. At his apartment, "the Wigwam," Oliver La Farge recalled, "a bottle or so of absinthe, some sandwiches, some Saratoga chips were all we needed for a gathering which would last from nine o'clock to three the next morning."[59] Some Famous Creoles once famously took their socializing afloat when, on the eve of the Ides of March, 1925, they set sail for Mandeville, twenty-three miles across Lake Pontchartrain from New Orleans, a voyage immortalized, if that's the right word, in *Mosquitoes* (Faulkner's "one truly negligible book," in Hamilton Basso's opinion).[60]

The high point of the French Quarter's social calendar in the 1920s was a more or less annual costume ball modeled, the organizers said, on the Bal des Quat'z Arts, held in Montmartre each spring by students of the École Nationale des Beaux-Arts.[61] The first of these was held the night before New Year's Eve, 1922, as a fundraiser for the *Double Dealer.*[62] Ticket prices were steep—ten dollars for a single, fifteen for a couple—but tickets did entitle their holders to unlimited drink (illegal, of course, but the two hired policemen guarding the proceeds looked the other way) and more liquor had to be procured midway through the evening. There was also a band to pay and the organizers rented a parrot "which sort of lent color to the proceedings," so in the end the fundraiser netted only about two hundred dollars.

But the *States* called the party "one of the most sensational and interesting that has ever taken place in the social history of New Orleans"— which is saying something. At midnight a costumed crowd including artist Conrad Albrizio in a bear suit, someone in a police uniform that almost got him in trouble, and many others in what the newspaper described as "futuristic and original" garb arrived at the Quartier Club on Jackson Square to be greeted by "raucous ribald ragtime, jangling jazz, the moaning of saxophones, the blare of cornets, and the high, shrill notes of the clarinet."[63] The evening's entertainment began with a torchlight procession as "stalwart slaves" carried a "Moorish bride" on a palanquin from Ronald Hargrave's studio in the upper Pontalba building across Jackson Square to the club. (Hargrave had designed costumes for all of the wedding party, as well as "highly futuristic" murals to decorate the ballroom.) The nuptials that followed were the first of "several skits and stunts that added life and interest to the party"; others included "an up-to-date jazz dance by Miss Kingsley Black" and a "doll-dance" by a couple in costume. The highlight of the evening, however, was "the dance of Salome," which Genevieve Pitot performed in attire "that made the seven veils look like an arctic explorer's costume."[64] The *States* reporter found "words . . . entirely inadequate to describe this dance and costume" but tried anyway with "unique, bizarre, queer, original and startling." The dance, "greeted with much enthusiasm," was "one of the most Bohemian features of the evening's entertainment." (Pitot danced barefoot all evening and couldn't wear her shoes the next day.[65])

Lyle Saxon's *Times-Picayune* account of the evening led with sub-headlines including "Dowagers Dance Till 5 A.M.," "Riot of Color and Gaiety as Society Touches Fingers With Art," and "Old-Fashioned Girl in Low-Neck Nightie." A monumental figure of the "Great God Sile-nus" near the entrance "watched the whole rout with its pagan smile," as "bare-legged girls [in] fur-trimmed costumes of white . . . shrieked with delight"; "Turkish ladies reclined languidly on cushions upon the floor, smoke rising in long spirals from their cigarettes"; "pretty little talcum-powdered debutantes of this year's crop" were "'tasting life' with a vengeance, deliberately devilish"; and "more sophisticated girls of last year's vintage" wore "daring costumes of brilliant reds and greens." (Saxon himself was no doubt at least as interested in some dashing French naval officers from the ship *Jeanne D'Arc*, in their gold-braided uniforms.)

A couple of years later some students at the Arts and Crafts Club followed the *Double Dealer*'s example with the first of several Bals des Artistes. The announcement stated that the event would be "a cos-tume and mask affair and even those coming in evening clothes will be refused admission" and promised that the "stunts" would include many "features which are unmentionable—remember, it is the Bal des Artistes."[66] Spratling came to that one costumed "as a dashing Arab, bearded and turbaned and short-coated," and "won much applause." His girlfriend Esther DuPuy was one of the featured dancers; another hoofer had "studied under the personal direction of Ned Weyburn of the Ziegfeld Follies." (Faulkner—the only one not in costume—just sat

At the Arts and Crafts Ball

Figure 3. "This drawing by T. Kemp is one of the many which are being made to illustrate the spirit of the Arts and Crafts Club ball" (*Item-Tribune*, 1927)

on the floor and drank from a bottle in a paper bag. Later he wrote his mother, "More funny folks, all breaking their necks trying to have a good time."[67]) It's not clear which features were unmentionable—surely not the Russian puppet show. Nevertheless, the *Times-Picayune* announced triumphantly afterwards: "The Paris of America has its Montmartre."

The announcement had said that the ball was to be, "my dear, just another night of fun and frolic for members of the club," open to students and their guests at a dollar a head (Club members and their guests a bit more), but it also attracted a sizable contingent of slumming debutantes and their beaus—even a few dowagers.[68] Later, the ball was moved to a larger hall and opened to the public, and what had formerly been "a gorgeous hidden panorama for the artists themselves, a brilliant revel that most persons could only hope to read about in gay but ambiguous descriptions in the morning papers," now provided, as the *Times-Picayune* put it, "a spectacle that no other city in America can offer" for anyone with the price of a ticket, "something to make ordinary folk drop their jaws."[69] By 1927 newspaper society pages were listing the names of socially prominent partygoers, who by then outnumbered the more Bohemian element.[70] Admission charges had crept up, couples had become the basic unit, there were no longer cheap tickets for students, and proceeds went to upkeep of the Club's Royal Street quarters.[71]

These balls were not the only occasion for mixing between the Quarter's Bohemians and "Society." Spratling and Faulkner put a few club-women in *Famous Creoles* because the ladies knew and were known by the more obviously Bohemian element and shared their interests in art, drama, and literature. In fact, as William Odiorne recognized, looking back, uptown people founded, and funded, virtually all of the French Quarter's "Bohemian" institutions.[72] For a few years in the 1920s, Odiorne concluded, "society . . . with a capital S" was interested in "French Quarter Bohemianism" because "the revival of the old Quarter was a sort of civic project [and] we were useful."

Almost from the beginning, moreover, New Orleans's smart set was intrigued by what was going on in the Quarter. At the Green Shutter Tea Room on St. Peter Street, Lyle Saxon wrote, one could find both "artists in smocks discussing this business of life as they sip their coffee in the courtyard" and "a sprinkling of 'uptown' people who have come to see just what these artists are up to."[73] Apparently the uptown people liked what they saw of the artist's life, because as early as 1921 the *Item* was reporting that "the French Quarter . . . is now humming with the advent of Orleanians who have taken up the study of art."[74] After the Arts and Crafts Club's art school opened, the pace really picked up. "Someone always seems to be rushing off to a sculpture class or a life class or to a lesson in oil," a society columnist observed.[75] A reception at the Club for a student art exhibit attracted "a large gathering of society" ("Helene Stauffer was presiding at the tea-table in the reception room, all in green, with a large green hat[,] Betty Fenner was in pink, looking very pretty, and Dot Sharp wore a brighter pink").

Soon someone was grumbling that the Quarter was filling up with the kind of people "who rent an ordinary furnished room and call it 'my studio.'"[76] Lyle Saxon was less disapproving when he wrote a column about a shipping board engineer and his fashionable French wife, a childless couple in their early thirties who had moved from Uptown to a place across from the Green Shutter.[77] The wife wrote "poems in prose," Saxon reported, and her husband was "the perfect host," so "one always finds a group of artists and writers in her apartment." The couple's activities appeared frequently in the society pages. One "impromptu studio party" led a reporter to gush, "That's one of the advantages of being an artist . . . , you can give such wonderful parties!"[78] All in all, it appeared that the *New York Times* was right when it observed that "the French Quarter has suffered the fate of such quarters. It has become a fad. It has become, in a way, fashionable."[79]

Partly in consequence, the Bohemian moment turned out to be short-lived. As the 1930s began, the *New Orleanian* was complaining that the Quarter had become "a tourist camp," and that "as an artists' colony the spirit of the place grows more lethargic every year."[80] Most blocks not given over to tourists and seekers of nightlife had become too expensive

for most working artists and writers. A few Famous Creoles adapted
quite successfully—Marc Antony became a prominent society decorator,
for instance, and his wife, Lucille, went into real estate sales—but the
Andersons decamped for the mountains of Virginia and Spratling for the
mountains of Guerrero. Natalie Scott soon joined Spratling in Mexico;
Freddie Oechsner and Ham Basso moved north; William Odiorne was
in Paris and Ronald Hargrave somewhere in southern Europe. Eventually Roark Bradford and Oliver La Farge wound up in Santa Fe, and of
course Faulkner went back to Mississippi. By 1941 the WPA's guide to
Louisiana could refer to 1926 as "a time when the French Quarter was a
second Greenwich Village"—could refer to it, that is, as history.[81]

NOTES

This essay is adapted from portions of John Shelton Reed, *Dixie Bohemia: A French
Quarter Circle in the 1920s* (Baton Rouge: Louisiana State University Press, 2012).

1. Hamilton Basso, "William Faulkner, Man and Writer," *Saturday Review*, July 28,
1962, 11.

2. William Spratling, *File on Spratling: An Autobiography* (Boston: Little, Brown and
Company, 1967), 22.

3. William Spratling and William Faulkner, *Sherwood Anderson and Other Famous
Creoles: A Gallery of Contemporary New Orleans* (New Orleans: Pelican Bookshop Press,
1926).

4. Spratling, 28.

5. Ibid., 29.

6. W. Kenneth Holditch, "William Faulkner and Other Famous Creoles," in *Faulkner
and His Contemporaries: Faulkner and Yoknapatawpha, 2002*, ed. Joseph R. Urgo and
Ann J. Abadie (Jackson: University Press of Mississippi, 2004), 32.

7. James W. Thomas, *Lyle Saxon: A Critical Biography* (Birmingham, Ala.: Summa
Publications, 1991), 40.

8. Inez Hollander Lake, *The Road from Pompey's Head: The Life and Work of
Hamilton Basso* (Baton Rouge: Louisiana State University Press, 1999), 14.

9. Spratling, 28. The gun is a Daisy. Could this be where the Shasta Daisies got their
name?

10. Letter from William Wisdom to Carvel Collins, July 19, 1963, Flo Field folder,
6.8, Carvel Collins Collection of William Faulkner Research Materials, Harry Ransom
Humanities Research Center, University of Texas at Austin (hereinafter CCC); Spratling,
28.

11. Spratling, 28.

12. Interview with Caroline Durieux, Baton Rouge, March 26, 1963, CCC, 4.34.

13. Field to Spratling, October 1, 1962, Flora Field Papers, Newcomb Archives,
Newcomb College Center for Research on Women.

14. For Genevieve Pitot's recollection of the heat in the Spratling-Faulkner garret, see
W. Kenneth Holditch, "William Spratling, William Faulkner, and Other Famous Creoles,"
Mississippi Quarterly 51.3 (Summer 1998); on the attempt to persuade Mrs. Field, see
Joseph Blotner, *Faulkner: A Biography*, 2 vol. (New York: Random House, 1974), 1:495.

15. Basso, 12.

16. Alan Brown, *Literary Levees of New Orleans* (Montgomery, Ala.: Starrhill Press, 1998), 62.

17. Oliver La Farge, *Raw Material* (Boston: Houghton Mifflin, 1945), 117–18, 131.

18. Joanna Richardson, *The Bohemians: La Vie de Bohème in Paris, 1830–1914* (London: Macmillan, 1969).

19. On the bordellos, see, e.g., Edmund Wilson, *The Twenties: From Notebooks and Diaries of the Period* (London: Macmillan, 1975), 186.

20. Anthony Stanonis, "An Old House in the Quarter: Vice in the Vieux Carré of the 1930s," Department of History, Loyola University of New Orleans, 1996–97 (online at www.loyno.edu/~history/journal/1996-7/Stanonis.html).

21. Interview with Carl and Betty Carmer, August 23, 1965, 2479/008, Joseph Blotner Papers, Louis Daniel Brodsky Collection of William Faulkner Materials, Special Collections and Archives, Kent Library, Southeast Missouri State University, Cape Girardeau, Missouri (hereinafter JBP).

22. Holditch, "William Faulkner and Other Famous Creoles," 31; Sherwood Anderson, "A Meeting South," in *The World from Jackson Square*, ed. Etolia Basso (New York: Farrar, Straus and Company, 1948), 350.

23. Interviews with Joyce McClure, New Orleans, March 20 [1960?], CCC 9.14, and with Harold Dempsey, New Orleans, February 2, 1963, CCC 4.28.

24. Interview with Carl and Betty Carmer.

25. Letter to Sydney Field, April 4, 1931, in Flora Field Papers, Newcomb Archives, Newcomb College Center for Research on Women.

26. Quoted in Frances Jean Bowen, "*The New Orleans Double Dealer*: 1921–May 1926, A Critical History" (PhD diss., Vanderbilt University, 1954).

27. Interviews with W. C. Odiorne, Hollywood, February 15–16, 1963, CCC 11.1.

28. Elizabeth Anderson and Gerald R. Kelly, *Miss Elizabeth: A Memoir* (Boston: Little, Brown and Company, 1969), 89.

29. Letter to Jerome Blum, February 2, 1922, in *Sherwood Anderson: Selected Letters*, ed. Charles E. Modlin (Knoxville: University of Tennessee Press, 1984), 30–31.

30. Interview with Mrs. Ernest Samuel (Adaline Katz), Bay St. Louis, Mississippi, March 29, 1963, CCC 15.27.

31. Temple quoted in Stella Pitts, "The Quarter in the Twenties," *Dixie*, November 26, 1972, 44; Fischer quoted in Blotner, 1:496.

32. Kate Rose, "Unsung Composer Genevieve Pitot," *Figaro*, November 10, 1978. Clipping from Genevieve Pitot collection, M788, Louisiana Research Collection, Howard-Tilton Memorial Library, Tulane University.

33. Spratling, 27.

34. Anderson and Kelly, 90.

35. James K. Feibleman, *The Way of a Man: An Autobiography* (New York: Horizon Press, 1969), 217.

36. Interview with Marc and Lucille Antony, New Orleans, February 1 and 3, 1965, JBP, 2479/007.

37. Carl Sifakis, *The Mafia Encyclopedia*, 2nd ed. (New York: Facts on File, 1999); "occupation" and address from *Soards' 1921 New Orleans Directory*. On the bayou routes, see Calvert Stith, "New Orleans: Non-Guide-Book Style," *New Orleanian*, September 6, 1930, 37.

38. Blotner, 1:427.

39. Anthony Stanonis, "'A Woman of Boundless Energy': Elizabeth Werlein and Her Times," *Louisiana History* 46.1 (Winter 2005): 16. On liquor in teacups, see John W.

Scott, "William Spratling and the New Orleans Renaissance," *Louisiana History* 45.3 (Summer 2004): 317.

40. Blotner, 1:427.

41. Anderson and Kelly, 90; interview with Anita Loos, January 18, 1966, JBP, 2479/003.

42. Blotner, 1:427.

43. Thomas, 40; Holditch, "William Spratling, William Faulkner, and Other Famous Creoles."

44. Spratling, 28.

45. Interview with Harold Levy, New Orleans, Winter 1963, CCC 8.40.

46. Scott, 317.

47. Blotner, 1:524; Spratling, 28.

48. Anderson and Kelly, 90.

49. Quoted in Pitts, 44.

50. Anderson and Kelly, 83.

51. Spratling, 17.

52. Anderson and Kelly, 86.

53. Basso, 11.

54. Spratling, 17.

55. Interview with Louis Andrews Fischer, February 2, 1965, JBP, 2479/007.

56. Anderson and Kelly, 83.

57. Quoted in Inez Hollander Lake, "Paris in My Own Backyard: Hamilton Basso," in *Literary New Orleans in the Modern World*, ed. Richard S. Kennedy (Baton Rouge: Louisiana State University Press, 1998), 42.

58. Blotner, 1:523–24.

59. La Farge, 114.

60. On this famous voyage, see Walter B. Rideout, *Sherwood Anderson: A Writer in America* (Madison: University of Wisconsin Press, 2006), 1:572–73; Blotner, 1:417–19; and Anderson and Kelly, 118–21. For Basso's opinion, see Basso, 12.

61. On the Bal des Quat'z Arts, see, e.g., Felix Youssoupoff, *Lost Splendor*, trans. Ann Green and Nicholas Katkoff (London: Jonathan Cape, 1953), chapter 15, and Jacques Guiton, *A Life in Three Lands: Memoirs of an Architect* (Boston: Branden Books, 1991), 66.

62. This account of the Folies du Vieux Carré is taken (except as noted below) from an interview with Elise Friend and Albert Goldstein, M1151, Louisiana Research Collection, Howard-Tilton Memorial Library, Tulane University; "Scenes Attending Ball of Folies du Vieux Carre," *States*, January 7, 1923; clipping from MSS 247, Historic New Orleans Collection (hereinafter THNOC), and Lyle Saxon, "Moorish Wedding Starts First Annual Artists' Ball," *Times-Picayune*, January 1, 1923, 1–2.

63. See Bowen.

64. The "dance of Salome" reported in the *States* is almost certainly the one Pitot did, mentioned in Holditch, "William Faulkner and Other Famous Creoles," 35.

65. See Bowen.

66. "Bal des Artistes to Be Brilliant," unsourced and undated (but 1925) clipping in Dan Whitney folder, THNOC. The description of the ball that follows is taken from this story and from "Bohemia Skates Off Humdrum Air at Artists' Ball: Dancers' Costumes Vie with Decorations for Grotesque Honors," clipping from *Times-Picayune*, April 19, 1925, in Dan Whitney folder, THNOC.

67. Holditch, "William Faulkner and Other Famous Creoles," 35–36; Scott, 300–301.

68. Announcement of "Artist Ball," MSS 247, THNOC.

69. "Ball of Arts and Crafts Club Will Rival Any This Side of Paris, Say Leading Spirits of Quarter," *Times-Picayune*, November 20, 1927, 22.

70. E.g., "The Arts and Crafts Ball," unsourced clipping, MSS 247, THNOC.

71. Vertical Files, "Arts. Societies. Arts and Crafts Club. Undated and 1922–28," folder 1, Louisiana Research Collection, Howard-Tilton Memorial Library, Tulane University; "Spain is Theme of Artist Ball," undated (but 1927) clipping from *Item*, MSS 247, THNOC.

72. Interviews with W. C. Odiorne, Hollywood, February 15–16, 1963, CCC 11.1; letter to Carvel Collins, 15 March 1963, W. C. Odiorne folder (2 of 2), CCC 11.2.

73. Lyle Saxon, "What's Doing," *Times-Picayune*, October 25, 1925, 2.

74. Clipping from *Item*, February 6, 1921, in Ellsworth Woodward folder, THNOC.

75. Unsourced and undated (but 1927) clipping, MSS 247, THNOC.

76. Stith, 37.

77. Saxon, "What's Doing"; information on the couple from the 1920 census, on ancestry.com.

78. Unsourced clipping, November 7, 1924, in MSS 247, THNOC.

79. Silas Bent, "Greenwich Village on Royal Street," *New York Times Book Review and Magazine*, July 23, 1922, 4.

80. Josef Von Klinger, "Vieux Carre Soliloquy," *New Orleanian*, September 13, 1930, 30.

81. Louisiana Writers' Project, *Louisiana: A Guide to the State* (New York: Hastings House, 1941), 169.

"No Kind of Place": New York City, Southernness, and Migratory Modernism

Benjamin S. Child

The project of defining the South in Southern literature is obviously a matter of interest in a forum like the annual Faulkner and Yoknapatawpha Conference. As Scott Romine reminds us in his recent work, the "Real South of the late South" is, above all else, a product of cultural imagining and commercial branding. Of course, even before the arrival of the late South, we are forced to confront the presence of multiple Souths, microSouths as Romine calls them, all moving under the single sign "South"—and prominent among these various microSouths is a version that we might recognize as the "Faulknerian South." If we extend Romine's microSouth model beyond the scope of reproduction and representation bound up in postmodern capitalism, it becomes a helpful way to consider versions of the South that exist outside the purview of a Solid South, a site that is too easily imagined as a culturally and geographically bounded monolith.[1] Romine explains that to configure the meanings of the South involves "a way of mobilizing space in efforts of immense variety and scope," one variety being "localized efforts to generate more intimate and compelling microSouths."[2] Thus, an expansive approach to the microSouth might allow it to capture versions of the South that are carried within the individual consciousness, "Souths" that swell to the surface of mind because of a confrontation with some fragment of an individuated sense of one's own Southernness—or the ruptures that attend to that Southernness. This internal grappling with one's own heritage is, of course, a common feature of Faulkner's fiction, and thinking about it through a spatial prism allows us a different view of Faulkner's geographic imagination.

For this reason, and for the purpose of this essay, the common concept of a single Faulknerian South, with its suggestion of a total—or totalizing—vision, is too bold; better, perhaps, is a version of the Faulknerian microSouth that is more self-consciously grounded in perception and representation, more fluid and easily transportable. Contemporary critics are often willing to consider the South as a historical—and consistently historicized—conceit but, in this essay, I am interested in thinking about how this construct travels and in uncovering the variety and the diverse meanings of the Faulknerian South on the move.

In a memorable passage from *Intruder in the Dust*, Chick Mallison offers a perceptive theory of space: "not north but North, outland and circumscribing and not even a geographical place but an emotional idea."[3] Faulkner's visions of space are alive to the essential constructedness of place, to the possibilities of regions and spaces as "emotional ideas," and so it's worth trying to gather together the diffuse strands of "ideas" that swirl around the writer's representations of his region. In this way, the Faulknerian South is less strictly a set of geographic coordinates, signifying a "little postage stamp" of Southern soil, than a sociopsychological space representing a particular relationship with history. The South presented by Faulkner is thick with historical memory, and it operates as a site where racial and class-based tensions often propel individuals into generation-spanning conflicts. Richard Gray explains it this way: Faulkner's South is marked by a "habitual preoccupation with the past, [a] long romance with memory, and [a] rift" that highlights "the growing discontinuity it was experiencing between its notions of the past and the present."[4] Inherent to this configuration is an uneven relationship between modes of development, which includes the emergence of new technologies, participation in national trends of urbanization, and the normalization of more enlightened attitudes about race.[5] All this, of course, looks towards a discourse about modernization and its aesthetic counterpart, modernism. And it is easy to recognize this as a constellation of concerns that does not reside with Faulkner alone.

For this reason, I plan to examine these issues from two different angles: my first section will use movements represented in Rudolph Fisher's "City of Refuge" (1925) and in Flannery O'Connor's posthumously published "Judgement Day" (1965) to think about how the attitudes and power relationships of the South cling to the characters' respective rural-urban migrations. For the two main characters in these stories, certain traits and consequences of Southernness seem to be intensified through their experience in New York City. So much so, in fact, that the urban North itself may well come to act as the most Southern place on earth. The essay's second movement will take Faulkner's "Pennsylvania Station" as a lens through which to consider the ways in which tropes coded "Southern" in Faulkner's fiction respond to a geographic shift northward. By exploring three stories stretching from the 1920s to the 1960s, each of which uses New York City as a locus of modernity and charts migrations—specifically migrations catalyzed by rail travel—to and from the city, we can negotiate a range of responses to the arrivals and complications of modernity.

In addition to being set in New York City, each of these narratives is interested in the complications of migration and movement in the modern United States, particularly migration between the rural South and the urban North, and, correspondingly, each narrative works out a version of what we might tentatively call migratory modernism. In a recent essay, Leigh Anne Duck considers the "peripatetic modernism" of *Light in August*, focusing on movement that occurs within and between the rural provinces of Yoknapatawpha.[6] This essay is more specifically concerned with modern migrations from the rural districts of the South to the cities of the North; and in configuring the details of the modern in these narratives, Fredric Jameson's template becomes especially useful: Jameson makes the case that modernist art depends upon a tension between the "longing for . . . monadic closure" and the inability of the modern world to supply such closure.[7] As both a sociological subject and as a kind of embodied metaphor, then, the migrant is a productive figure since he or she is often seeking rootedness in an uprooted world, driven by the paradoxical impulse towards connection via disconnection.

Moving Up

When analyzing Faulkner's geographies in this way, we must first make peace with the possibility that what contemporary readers identify as the Faulknerian South doesn't necessarily originate with Faulkner. When Fisher's 1925 story "City of Refuge" ran in both the *Atlantic Monthly* and Alaine Locke's seminal anthology *The New Negro*, it appeared the year before the publication of Faulkner's first novel, *Soldiers' Pay*. And while Fisher is not typically identified as a Southerner—he was born and raised in that border space, Washington, DC—"City of Refuge" displays what hindsight marks as distinctly Faulknerian overtones. Throughout the story, for instance, as the characters struggle against the weight of their origins, there is a real sense in which, regardless of the location, Southern histories, or American pasts, to borrow a phrase of Temple Drake's, cannot be "fumigate[d]."[8]

The narrative shape of "City of Refuge" proceeds along familiar lines—an African American leaves the rural South for New York City, the cultural center of the industrial North. Yet unlike most participants in the Great Migrations of the early twentieth century, when the story's chief protagonist, King Solomon Gillis, makes it from Penn Station to Harlem, he is escaping the law in North Carolina, having killed an antagonistic white man. Unsurprisingly, then, he is amazed to find a black police officer directing traffic and marvels at the freedom of movement with which black bodies navigate the city. Here, at last, is the long-promised promised land, free from the oppressions of Jim Crow and the threatening specter of whiteness. And yet from the opening paragraph, the narration betrays a perceptible anxiety about the mechanized ethos of the urban landscape: "Confronted suddenly by daylight, King Solomon Gillis stood dazed and blinking. The railroad station, the long, white-walled corridor, the impassable slot-machine, the terrifying subway train—he felt as if he had been caught up in the jaws of a steam-shovel, jammed together with other helpless lumps of dirt, swept blindly along for a time, and at last abruptly dumped."[9] Dumped, like the materials from which machines craft the modern world. In the opening paragraphs, descriptions of hell, rifle fire, and Jonah struggling in the belly of the whale combine to usher Gillis violently into his new home. Of the Great Migration's transformative effects on the African American population at large, Lawrence Rodgers explains that "far more than simply a geographic relocation, the Great Migration transformed a rural farm folk to an industrial city folk."[10] This may be true, but "City of Refuge" suggests that the integration into a new space could be a deeply disruptive one. Thus, as Gillis moves through the streets of Harlem, his rural Southern blackness makes him an easy mark: early on, he sidles up to Mouse Uggam, a character who uses a shared Southernness to gain Gillis's trust and then cons him into unwittingly fulfilling the distribution end of a drug ring. When detectives break up the operation, Gillis ferociously resists arrest but is dumbfounded and stilled by the presence of a black police officer. The narrative's brief, parting glance at Gillis's interior is telling: "Harlem. Land of plenty. City of refuge—city of refuge. If you live long enough."[11] Although critics frequently recognize Fisher as a key participant in the Harlem Renaissance, this story severely complicates the spirit of that time and place, a phenomenon that is perhaps best summarized in a statement attributed to Ralph Ellison about Harlem acting as an "outpost of American optimism," particularly for African Americans.[12] According to "City of Refuge," Harlem and the Jim Crow South stand toe-to-toe as exemplary modes of a sadly familiar form of American cynicism. Exploitation may not operate along exclusively racial lines but, in Rudolph Fisher's Harlem, the disadvantages of Southern blackness migrate along with the migrants.

   This isn't a vision unique to "City of Refuge." In Fisher's "The South Lingers On" (1925), a story altered slightly and retitled for inclusion in *The New Negro*, we encounter a subtle variation on this same theme. The narrative explores the disorientation of a rural Southern preacher, Ezekiel Taylor, adrift in Harlem, where his charismatic religion becomes a metonym for the back-home South at large. When Lucky, a self-styled cynic who is himself the son of a Southern preacher, moves to disrupt

Taylor's revival, he is startled at his response to the proceedings: "Dam'
'f I know what it is—maybe because it makes me think of the old folks
or somethin' . . . it just sorter—gets me."[13] The South clearly does
linger on, if only in that most intimate of microSouths, the individual
consciousness.

In thinking about how Gillis's rural Southernness works to his disadvantage, we might look to Riché Richardson's recent investigations into
the relationship between black masculinity and the cultural meanings of
the country and the city. Richardson argues that throughout the twentieth century African American men from the rural South grapple with
a version of black manhood that so strongly privileges the urban that
to exhibit the signs of a rural identity is to be bracketed off as ignorant
and backwards at best, a docile and emasculated Uncle Tom at worst.
Uggam's description of Gillis underscores this dynamic: according to
Uggam, Gillis is simply "a baby jess in from the land o cotton and so
dumb he think antebellum's an old woman."[14] Although they walk the
ground of African American sovereignty, Uggam's comment infantilizes
Gillis in a manner that sounds suspiciously like the discourses of the Jim
Crow South.

In Walter White's essay "The Paradox of Color," which appears alongside "City of Refuge" in *The New Negro*, the author explains that even
though New York seems to be "as nearly an ideal place for colored people as exists in America," the city is still rife with "Southern whites who
brought North with them their hatreds" and, even more pervasively, with
oppressive attitudes about a "Negro who is either buffoon or a degen-
erate beast or a subservient lackey." In White's eyes, the result is the
"development of an intensive Negro culture and a definitely bounded
city within a city"—Harlem, in other words.[15] But, according to Fisher,
Harlem itself is not nearly impervious enough. As the narrator relates
in a subtle turn towards double-voiced discourse at the story's opening,
"In Harlem, black was white." Black may be white, but the experience
of King Solomon Gillis suggests that, in a system that mimics the hierar-
chical arrangement of the dominant culture, somebody still needs to be
black—a fact that the story's persistent interest in degrees of blackness
makes clear: Uggam is described as a "little yellow man" whose blackness fades as his authority seems to rise; the West Indian whom Gillis
replaces as a grocery worker is "nigger" and "monkey chaser." ("Anytime
y' can knife a monk, do it," Uggam tells Gillis.)[16]

Jolene Hubbs's recent account of Faulkner's rural modernism offers
a useful way to think about Gillis's difficulties adapting to his new urban
environment. Writing about *As I Lay Dying*, Hubbs describes a "peren-
nial obsolescence: a theory that poor whites are seen not in terms of

certain practices and objects that might be outmoded but rather as uniformly and perpetually archaic."[17] Although her analysis focuses exclusively on the experience of poor-white Southerners, it's a short step to apply it to rural blacks in the city as well. Mouse Uggam, for instance, is also a Southern migrant to New York, but his experience with Gillis suggests that the space itself grants a kind of provisional authority to the most thoroughly urbanized, the most fully assimilated to the attitudes and standards of modernity. Considering the dynamics of the "South in the City" in African American writing from the period, Farah Jasmine Griffin contrasts the "focus on [controlling] the body, which is so prevalent in the Southern sections of the migration" with an approach that "shifts to a focus on the migrant psyche . . . [since] the psyche is the realm where power is enforced."[18] From their first encounter outside the train station until the story's finale in a Harlem nightclub, Uggam corrals Gillis mentally, leading him along a course that can only end in a combination of both psychic *and* physical incapacitation.

O'Connor's "Judgement Day" shuffles the variables of Fisher's work and presents itself as a compelling counterpoint. The story tells of Tanner, a white native of rural Georgia, who leaves his home when the African American who owns the land he squats on insists that he work for him or move on. This inversion of the customary "Southern" power arrangement is further exaggerated when Tanner joins his daughter and her husband in their New York City apartment. Upon arriving in the city, he encounters an African American neighbor, with whom he tries to make a regional connection: "I ain't been up here long myself. It ain't much of a place if you ask me. I reckon you wish you were back in South Alabama. . . . I thought you might know somewhere around here we could find us a pond, Preacher."[19] "I'm not from South Alabama," the man says (544–45). "I'm from New York City. And I'm not no preacher! I'm an actor" (545). To which Tanner replies, "It's a little actor in most preachers, ain't it?" While this exchange offers a bit of obverse minstrel-style humor, we also recognize that it's a fundamental misreading of the cultural map that sets Tanner off as an outsider. Having fled a space where the power of his whiteness alone is no longer sufficient to keep him atop the cultural heap, Tanner's encounters with the neighbor operate as extensions of the very tensions that drove him out of the South in the first place. The region, along with the rest of the world, has shifted beneath his feet—and, if only for a moment, the narrator shows us how Tanner is forced to catch a glimpse of the black actor as a "negative image of himself" (538–39), but, as in rural Georgia, "the vision failed him before he could decipher it" (539). It may well be, as Tanner insists in his letters back home, that New York City is "no kind of place" (541), yet according to a series of qualifications that continually arrive with the onset of modernity in America, so too is rural Georgia. Could it be possible, to expand Gertrude Stein's famous phrase, that "there is no there there," anywhere you go?[20] O'Connor once infamously suggested that she would be willing to meet with James Baldwin in New York City but not at her home in Milledgeville. Yet there's a sense in which "Judgement Day" revises this statement by highlighting the final stages of the protracted evaporation of Jim Crow distinctiveness and its smothering sense of place.

In "The Geranium," an early version of "Judgement Day" and a selection from O'Connor's 1947 Iowa master's thesis, the Tanner character appears as Old Dudley, and although he is ill at ease in the City, he is inexplicably drawn to it by the power of the media images that emanate from the centers of culture: "He had . . . seen New York in a picture show. *Big Town Rhythm* it was. Big towns were important places. . . . It was an important place and it had room for him!"[21] And yet when he arrives at his daughter's working-class apartment building, he is shocked that she would share a building with an African American—this in spite of the fact that, like Tanner in "Judgement Day," Dudley's most intimate relationships in the South have been with African Americans, albeit African Americans who seem to indulge his outmoded visions of a racial hierarchy out of sympathy rather than submission. Of particular horror for Dudley are his experiences with the New York City train system: "People . . . rolled off the street and down steps and into trains—black and white and yellow all mixed up like vegetables in soup. Everything was boiling."[22] With its creation of a diverse public space, the modes of modernity facilitated by the transport train thus undermine an idea of order that precludes mixture; the train itself works to unravel the binarized racial thinking that buttresses the confidence of both Dudley and Tanner. As Florence Dore observes of O'Connor's work more generally, this anachronistic "desire for whiteness . . . is the object of biting satire."[23] In 1954's "An Exile in the East," a synoptic version of the story appearing between "The Geranium" and "Judgement Day," that turn toward satire is made all the more obvious: when the African American actor first encounters Tanner, he slips into a "mock southern accent" and provocatively whistles "Dixie," suggesting that for O'Connor, when the South encounters the City, the veils of deference are lowered and a clash is imminent.[24]

Consequently, the violence that is sublimated throughout "The Geranium" boils over in "Judgement Day," and Tanner's death at the hands of his new neighbor has a feeling of inevitability, as we see how northward, urban migrations might simply be the continuation—even the culmination—of confrontations that have rural southern roots. But even this conceit is troubled by the narrative: although roots have long served as an evocative image of stasis and stability, extending vertically to fix a subject in a given place, both "Judgement Day" and "City of Refuge" allow roots to spread out laterally, connecting the quarrels and interests of the rural South and the urban North in a dialogic embrace. To the extent that Gilles Deleuze and Félix Guattari's famous rhizome model emphasizes conditions "in the middle, between things, intermezzo, interbeing," it works as an optic for elucidating the urban-rural migrant's condition as it appears in these stories. Deleuze and Guattari further explain, "Making a clean slate, starting or beginning again from ground zero, seeking a beginning or foundation—all imply a false conception of voyage and movement."[25] Relocation is no kind of permanent escape; it's just the best way to keep trouble at bay. The terse philosophy of bluesman Robert Johnson, a modernist and traveler of the highest order, describes it this way: "I got to keep movin' / Blues fallin' down like hail."[26]

Still, for both Gillis and Tanner, the version of the South that appears in each of these stories is an accretion of cultural memory and experience that a change of venue cannot erase. It is a quality that also appears to bridge generations, as we're told that, after his death, Tanner's daughter lies awake at nights as long as her father's body lies buried in a New York cemetery. So she fulfills a version of Tanner's recurring dream by shipping his body back South, and now, the narrator tells us, she "rests well at night and her good looks have mostly returned."[27] The experience of these characters suggests, then, that even when the placeness of the South is troubled by modernization, and even when individuals look for freedom in the promise of modern mobilities, there's a residue of tradition that proves impossible to escape.

There and Back Again

Langston Hughes's 1932 poem "Pennsylvania Station" riffs along these same lines. The speaker notes the building's resemblance to a "vast basilica of old," recognizing it as an evocation of a "dream of God," and the trains pulling in and out of the station come to stand for the hope extended by increased mobility: movement is a mode of redemption.[28] Faulkner's take on "Pennsylvania Station" explores roughly the same ground, with a distinctly different note of emphasis. While "Pennsylvania Station" (1934) is certainly not the only place where New York City appears in Faulkner's fiction, it does present an opportunity to consider both the ways in which tropes coded "Southern" respond to a geographic shift northward and how Faulkner's version of New York corresponds to spaces represented in the migration narratives of Fisher and O'Connor.

One important point of contact: the very same station that serves as a portal to Gillis's new life in "City of Refuge" offers a temporary shelter to the unnamed narrator and his companion in "Pennsylvania Station." Yet the shape of migration that appears in "Pennsylvania Station" is an inversion of the familiar pattern, from the urban North down into Florida and then back again. And although the thrust of the narrative consists of little more than a shaggy dog story about a ne'er-do-well nephew named Danny who squanders the money his mother had set aside for a formal burial, the story's setting and its adoption of issues central to Faulkner's wider oeuvre bear noticing. For instance, in the story, Penn Station becomes a living index of past voices, coated and recoated with histories, much like Faulkner's South: the station is "filled . . . with a weary and ceaseless murmuring, like the voices of pilgrims upon the infinite plain, like the voices of all the travelers who had ever passed through it quiring and ceaseless as lost children."[29] This reading of Penn Station takes its place alongside the description of Frenchman's Bend that opens *The Hamlet* or the detailed picture of the jailhouse that appears in *Requiem for a Nun* (to list just two examples), each of which makes an extensive list of the forces that shape space, creating that familiar effect in Faulkner whereby the sedimentary layers of past events and their participants butt up against one other, overlapping and making a music of multiplicity. The proliferation and circulation of voices as a constitutive element of Faulkner's Penn Station, then, offers up a version of urban, northern space with distinctly "Southern" resonances.

Unlike "Mr. Acarius," the only other Faulkner story set in New York City, whose sole mention of the South comes with the appearance of a nurse from Alabama, or the word of Gavin Stevens, who describes New York City—Greenwich Village in particular—as "a place with a few unimportant boundaries but no limitations where young people of any age go to seek dreams," "Pennsylvania Station" goes farther toward making these regions speak to one another.[30] Although it occupies a minor place in the Faulkner canon, when critics have mentioned "Pennsylvania Station," they typically notice the story's unique narratalogical structure: an unnamed derelict provides the substance of the story, which is bookended by the observations of an omniscient narrator. Writing of the story's opening scene, Theresa Towner and James Carothers notice what is perhaps the narrator's unconscious nod to Southern culture by paying special attention to the text's description of shop windows that resemble "the eyes of people drugged with coffee, sitting up with a strange corpse."[31] Towner and Carothers go on to explain that "particularly in the

South, the dead body was watched over by family before burial," all of which implies that the voice guiding this "experiment in . . . urban realism" comes from the South.[32] Opening and closing the story, then, with an obliquely Southern sensibility, the text embodies a unique version of the South in the City, one that underscores the dialogic relationship between the two spaces.

If a mélange of fragmented voices and histories is key to the formation of Faulkner's version of modernism, it's not at all surprising to see that Faulkner's Penn Station is experienced as a compellingly modern site. As Marian Aguiar argues, "the train [holds] a central place as an overdetermined symbol of modernity. The railway's ability to reconstruct space and time through movement ma[kes] it a primary space for the constitution of new identities."[33] Certainly, the "constitution of new identities" seems to be on the docket for our train travelers but one thread that binds each of these stories is the fact that an old identity cannot be so easily elided. In all of the narratives, the promise of escape that the train represents folds back upon itself, and the originary conflict reemerges. Writing about what a "geography of modernism" might mean, Peter Brooker and Andrew Thacker explain that a "spatial history of modernisms would . . . ground the use of geographical tropes in the material practices and places of modernity, responsive to their discrete and palimpsestic local, regional, national and transnational provenances."[34] Geographies of modernism, then, are not about the wholecloth creation of new spaces but about remolding their polysemous, preexisting meanings. Or, as Dilip Gaonkar has it, "everywhere, at every national/cultural site, modernity is not one but many; modernity is not new but old and familiar; modernity is incomplete and necessarily so."[35] Ideas about these spaces—the South and New York City—paradoxically carry both the momentum and the inertia of history, and these contending forces work to shape and reshape collective imaginings about each region's meaning.

Houston Baker's evocative description of the railway offers some further insight: "The railway junction is marked by transience. Its inhabitants are always travelers—a multifarious assembly in transit."[36] Notice that Baker's statement encompasses not the moving train car but simply the junction itself, as if to say that in the modern world encapsulated by the railroad station, one can be in transit while sitting still. "Pennsylvania Station" thus becomes a variation on a familiar modernist theme about the impossibility of becoming a fixture in a contact zone that forever denies fixity.

Consequently, the figures populating "Pennsylvania Station" find themselves lodged in a liminal position—they belong in the places where they don't belong. This same principle extends to their racial identities. In some sense, the troubled nephew Danny in "Pennsylvania Station" functions as a less tragically inflected version of Samuel Beauchamp of "Go Down, Moses": he is entangled with the law but reached for, and possibly saved somehow, by the efforts of his family. Whatever the characters' racial makeup might be, their class positions mark them off from the dominant culture. They clean buildings, drift around the country, and can only grasp at prosperity through illegal activity. It's no coincidence, then, that in the *Collected Stories* volume, this piece is grouped in the "Middle Ground" series. But, as middle spaces often go, the position of the transients is unsteady, insecure: "they seemed to stand in the grip of a dreadful reluctance and inertia."[37] Working out a murky conflation of class and race, the characters in "Pennsylvania Station" stand as truly modern figures, marked by elliptically defined hybridity and motion. Jack Temple Kirby makes the case that "class . . . was the most important determinant of migrants' well-being and acculturation in new communities," but this story lets issues of race and class loose in the same orbit, declining to make any definitive comment but acknowledging the realities of the train depot as a contact zone where a whole panoply of people interact and react to one another and to their environment.[38] Like Joe Christmas, *Light in August*'s slippery, "parchmentcolored" protagonist, the figures in "Pennsylvania Station" are impossible to locate definitively, and they come to exhibit the ways in which constructions of whiteness and blackness respond to modernity's creation of a destabilized geographic center.

Spatial philosopher Doreen Massey recognizes a commonly made distinction between the fluid spaces of postmodern globalization and modernist conceptions of space, explaining that "in place of an imagination of a world of bounded places (modernism) we are now presented with a world of flows (postmodernism)."[39] But a world of flows is what we meet at every turn in all of these narratives, and, for the migrant of the modern period, these spaces operate in such a way that familiar narratives about regional difference begin to unwrite themselves. Massey further notes that these kinds of binary constructions create a glaring blind spot in critical analysis: "Both the romance of bounded place and the romance of free flow hinder serious address to the necessary negotiations of real politics."[40] In response to fears that the postmodern turn towards fluidity and openness might simply reinscribe a masculinist emphasis on individuality and frontier, Massey forwards Jacques Derrida's late concept of hospitality, defined by Derrida as our "manner of being there, the manner in which we relate to ourselves and to others, to others as our own or as foreigners," as a means of negotiating the potential problems of both bounded and open space.[41] While both "City of Refuge" and "Judgement Day" highlight instances wherein hospitality misfires, circumstances in which the host that Derrida conceived of as the necessary provider of hospitality is either absent or unwilling, "Pennsylvania Station" shows a community taking shape between the two transients, in defiance of the official power represented by the "man in the uniform of the railway company."[42] It's a community that includes its own ceremonies (the sharing of space and cigarettes, the telling of stories) and its own safe havens (the benches in Penn and Grand Central Stations) but remains under the direct jurisdiction of no single body.

These very qualities call up the question of the story's Southernness. At a time when the popular imagination often treated both a vibrant oral tradition and a sense of community as constitutive elements of a brand of Southernness under attack by industrial modernity, the text's decision to attach those characteristics to a pair of derelicts seeking refuge in Pennsylvania Station—one of industrial modernity's most prominent accomplishments—powerfully jostles both the meanings of Southernness and the shape of the standard migration narrative, as well as what we might call, with a nod to Homi Bhabha, the location of Southern culture. The Southern voice of the story's narrator thus presents a kind of microSouth that isn't South at all but stills bears some of the more abstract qualities of Faulkner's South more generally.

As characters in all three stories navigate a dislocated version of the Faulknerian South, they are consistently reminded of the historical scaffolding of their environment and of the effects that landscape can have on the creation, recreation, and decreation of identities. And each narrative can, in turn, be read as an examination of the portability—and durability—of Faulkner's microSouth. Commentators educated in the postmodern era have learned to set nearly every abstract idea or quality in scare quotes. Yet behind those marks lurk powerful forces that shape the texture and meaning of our lived experience. As all these stories work to prove, even, or perhaps especially, in the urban landscapes of the modern North, the South is not emptied of meaning in the course of the twentieth century but rerouted and reanimated in unexpected and provocative ways.

NOTES

1. In an essay now nearly three decades old, C. Hugh Holman argues that to approach the literature of the South strictly through the familiar models associated with the Agrarians and the Southern Renascence is "to shut too many doors to the fresh, the vital,

and the new." That we are still grappling with the legacies of a totalized South and the pull of its interpretive powers is a testament both to Holman's prescience and to the resilience of the monolith. The task of "dismantling the monolith," to borrow a phrase from Barbara Ladd, is the province of the new Southern Studies. See Holman, "No More Monoliths, Please: Continuities in the Multi-Souths," *Southern Literature in Transition: Heritage and Promise*, ed. Philip Castille and William Osborne (Memphis: Memphis State University Press, 1983), xxi, and Ladd, "Dismantling the Monolith: Southern Spaces—Past, Present, and Future," *South to a New Place: Region, Literature, Culture*, ed. Suzanne W. Jones and Sharon Monteith (Baton Rouge: Louisiana State University Press, 2002), 44–57.

2. Scott Romine, *The Real South: Southern Narrative in the Age of Cultural Reproduction* (Baton Rouge: Louisiana State University Press, 2008), 9.

3. William Faulkner, *Intruder in the Dust* (1948; New York: Vintage, 1991), 149–50.

4. Richard Gray, *Writing the South: Ideas of an American Region* (Baton Rouge: Louisiana State University Press, 1997), 216.

5. According to Jack Temple Kirby, while the 1920 census showed that the "American population had become statistically urban . . . not a single southern state's population met this modest definition" (49). The following decade, however, saw the first wave of the Great Migration, which sent many Southerners—primarily African Americans—to both the industrial centers of the North and Southern cities such as Memphis and Atlanta. Additionally, the arrival of industries such as textile production in the Piedmont region also pulled people away from the rural peripheries. Not surprisingly, the urbanization of the South, like that of the country at large, is a diachronic phenomenon with multiple movements. See Kirby, *Rural Worlds Lost: The American South, 1920–1960* (Baton Rouge: Louisiana State University Press, 1987), 49.

6. Leigh Anne Duck, "Peripatetic Modernism, or, Joe Christmas's Father," *Philological Quarterly* 90.2–3 (2011): 255–80.

7. Fredric Jameson, *The Geopolitical Aesthetic: Cinema and Space in the World System* (Bloomington: Indiana University Press, 1992), 163.

8. William Faulkner, *Requiem for a Nun* (1951; New York: Vintage Books, 1975), 133.

9. Rudolph Fisher, "City of Refuge" (1925), in *The City of Refuge: The Collected Stories of Rudolph Fisher*, ed. John McCluskey Jr. (Columbia: University of Missouri Press, 2008), 35.

10. Lawrence R. Rodgers, *Canaan Bound: The African-American Great Migration Novel* (Champaign: University of Illinois Press, 1997), 11.

11. Fisher, "City of Refuge," 47.

12. In *Considering Genius* Stanley Crouch contextualizes the quotation as a description of the golden age of "Ellingtonian Harlem"; he doesn't, however, offer a citation. This is unfortunate since the quote doesn't appear in Ellison's published oeuvre and it features prominently in Ken Burns's PBS documentary *Jazz*, a project on which both Crouch and his compatriot Wynton Marsalis worked extensively. See Crouch, *Considering Genius: Writings on Jazz* (New York: Basic Civitas Books, 2006), 145.

13. Fisher, "The South Lingers On" (1925), in *The City of Refuge: The Collected Stories of Rudolph Fisher*, 69.

14. Fisher, "City of Refuge," 35.

15. Walter White, "The Paradox of Color," in *The New Negro*, ed. Alain Locke (1925; New York: Touchstone, 1997), 364. Mark Hadden's description of the process whereby Locke assembled the anthology explains how the editor's vision for the anthology discouraged a strong Southern presence: "the focus on a lingering South was inappropriate if one was going to effectively and successfully market a *New Negro*." See M. A. Hadden,

"Harlem, the 'New Negro,' and the South: History and the Politics of Place," *Safundi: The Journal of South African and American Studies* 9.3 (2008): 258.

16. Fisher, "City of Refuge," 41.

17. Jolene Hubbs, "William Faulkner's Rural Modernism," *Mississippi Quarterly* 61 (2008): 464.

18. Farah Jasmine Griffin, *"Who Set You Flowin'?": The African-American Migration Narrative* (New York: Oxford University Press, 1995), 52.

19. Flannery O'Connor, "Judgement Day" (1965), in *The Complete Stories* (New York: Noonday, 1972), 544. Hereafter cited parenthetically in the text.

20. Romine reminds readers of the impossibility of ascribing a singular sense of place to the South when the region's "integrity" has something to do with "its peripheral relationship to a center." For our purposes, it's clear to see that even when "Southern literature" happens in the cultural center represented by New York City, the characters in these narratives—and the signs of the South that the narratives represent more generally—come to occupy the peripheries *within* the center. See Romine, "Where Is Southern Literature? The Practice of Place in a Postsouthern Age," in *South to a New Place: Region, Literature, Culture*, ed. Suzanne W. Jones and Sharon Monteith (Baton Rouge: Louisiana State University Press, 2002), 28.

21. Flannery O'Connor, "The Geranium" (1946), in *The Complete Stories*, 4.

22. Ibid., 7.

23. Florence Dore, "The Modernism of Southern Literature," in *A Concise Companion to American Fiction, 1900–1950*, ed. Peter Stoneley and Cindy Weinstein (Malden, Mass.: Blackwell, 2008), 241.

24. Flannery O'Connor, "An Exile in the East" (1954), in *Flannery O'Connor: The Growing Craft*, ed. Karl-Heinz Westarp (Birmingham, Ala.: Summa Publications, 1993), 152.

25. Gilles Deleuze and Félix Guattari, *A Thousand Plateaus: Capitalism and Schizophrenia*, trans. Brian Massumi (New York: Continuum, 1987), 28.

26. Robert Johnson, "Hellhound on My Trail," Vocalion, 1937.

27. O'Connor, "Judgement Day," 550.

28. Langston Hughes, *The Collected Poems of Langston Hughes* (New York: Vintage Books, 1995), 159. The poem appeared as "Terminal" in 1932 but was republished under the title "Pennsylvania Station" in 1962.

29. William Faulkner, "Pennsylvania Station" (1934), in *The Collected Stories of William Faulkner* (1950; New York: Vintage Books, 1995), 609.

30. William Faulkner, *The Town* (1957; New York: Vintage Books, 1999), 350.

31. Faulkner, "Pennsylvania Station," 609.

32. Theresa M. Towner and James B. Carothers, *Reading Faulkner: "Collected Stories"* (Jackson: University Press of Mississippi, 2006), 337, 334.

33. Marian Aguiar, "Inside the Technological Space of the Railway," *Cultural Critique* 68 (2008): 73.

34. Peter Brooker and Andrew Thacker, "Introduction," *Geographies of Modernism: Literatures, Cultures, Spaces*, ed. Brooker and Thacker (New York: Routledge, 2005), 4.

35. Dilip P. Gaonkar, "On Alternative Modernities," in *Alternative Modernities*, ed. Gaonkar (Durham: Duke University Press, 2001), 23; emphasis removed.

36. Houston A. Baker Jr., *Blues, Ideology, and Afro-American Literature: A Vernacular Theory* (Chicago: University of Chicago Press, 1984), 7.

37. Faulkner, "Pennsylvania Station," 624.

38. Kirby, 330.

39. Doreen Massey, *For Space* (Thousand Oaks: Sage, 2005), 81.

40. Ibid., 175.

41. Jacques Derrida, *On Cosmopolitanism and Forgiveness*, trans. Mark Dooley and Michael Hughes (London: Routledge, 2001), 17.

42. Faulkner, "Pennsylvania Station," 620.

Jamestown and Jimson Weed: Charting the Autochthonous Claim of William Faulkner's *The Sound and the Fury*

Kita Douglas

In the opening pages of Toni Morrison's *Beloved* (1987), Sethe washes chamomile sap from her legs as the unspeakable and repressed memories of her enslavement take sudden violent form in her consciousness:

> She might be hurrying across a field, running practically, to get to the pump quickly and rinse the chamomile sap from her legs. Nothing else would be in her mind. The picture of the men coming to nurse her was as lifeless as the nerves in her back where the skin buckled like a washboard. Nor was there the faintest scent of ink or the cherry gum and oak bark from which it was made. Nothing. . . . And then sopping the chamomile away with the pump water and rags, her mind fixed on getting every last bit of sap off. . . . Then something . . . and suddenly there was Sweet Home rolling, rolling, rolling out before her eyes, and although there was not a leaf on that farm that did not want to make her scream, it rolled itself out before her in shameless beauty.[1]

A traditional remedy for anxiety and sleeplessness, chamomile occludes the memories of Sweet Home that immediately resurface as Sethe washes away the herb. Equating the absence of chamomile with the return of Sethe's suppressed trauma constitutes more than an elegant and suggestive organic symbolism in the opening moments of *Beloved*. The plantation Sweet Home and its "shameless beauty" become embedded in a specifically sensual quality of memory for Sethe—she moves from "the picture of the men" to "the nerves in her back," from the remembered "scent of ink" to the present "breeze cooling her face"— that reaches across geographical space to claim her as surely as Schoolteacher's previous physical arrival at 124 Bluestone Road. The chamomile growing in the ground stains Sethe's legs and fragile consciousness as the metonymic bond between chamomile and memory reiterates both an articulation and repudiation of the symbolic premise of autochthony—to literally spring from the earth—an embedded claim to the human bodies of slaves necessarily imagined as inherent, prior, and embodied in this, the very territory of the New World. Thus the episode indicates how a vicious tautology of colonialism, slavery, and racism became naturalized in America's South by inscribing a violent cartography of race and territory on both bodies and land.

Morrison's evocative references to chamomile, likely *Anthemis cotula* or stinking chamomile, commonly known as dogfennel in Ohio where Sethe resides, summon a significant scene from William Faulkner's *The Sound and the Fury* (1929), a novel that I believe to be equally invested in probing slavery's imaginative conflation of the organic and the political. On the morning of April 7, 1928, Benjy Compson obliquely narrates a series of communications between himself and his caretaker, Luster Gibson, that includes a significant exchange of dogfennel for jimson weed, an indigenous flowering plant common to the South. In the initial scenes of his narrative Benjy shifts to the present while remembering a cold day at the gate waiting for Caddy. Caddy inquires in the past, "What is it. What are you trying to tell Caddy," as Luster interjects, *"What are you moaning about. . . . You can watch them again when we get to the branch. Here. Here's you a jimson weed."*[2] Luster again brings a moaning Benjy back to the present after he remembers an attack on a schoolgirl that resulted in his castration:

> "You fusses when you dont see them and you fusses when you does. Why cant you hush. Dont you reckon folks get tired of listening to you all the time. Here. You dropped your jimson weed." He picked it up and gave it back to me. "You needs a new one. You bout wore that one out. . . . Hush up. I the one got something to moan over, you aint. Here. Whyn't you hold on to that weed. You be bellering about it next." (54)

When Luster goes on to knock the jimson weed out of Benjy's hands, Dilsey intervenes, demanding to know whether Luster "been projecking with his graveyard" (55). Dilsey threatens, "Dont lie to me, boy," yet only the reader and perhaps Benjy may note that Luster indeed lies as he counters, "I aint been teasing him. . . . He was playing with that bottle full of dogfennel and all of a sudden he started up bellering" (56). Luster's substitution of dogfennel for jimson weed in his account to Dilsey marks a crucial distinction that has not yet registered within the significant body of criticism on this novel. Dogfennel's association with the chamomile family of plants, whose properties of easing anxiety, panic, and sleeplessness Morrison links with Sethe's memory to such powerful effect in *Beloved*, is exploited by Faulkner with equal skill as anxiety, panic, and sleeplessness are the very symptoms that seem to plague Benjy. In contrast, botanists, conjurers, and—we would assume since Luster lies to her—Dilsey would recognize jimson weed, or *Datura stramonium*, as an extremely powerful and dangerous hallucinogenic substance, and perhaps as a plant whose common name issues from a significant originary moment for the nation's trajectory: Bacon's Rebellion in the seventeenth-century colony of Jamestown, Virginia. While many readers might argue that the discrepancy between dogfennel and jimson weed constitutes no more than an insignificant lapse in Luster's diction, Luster's increasingly suspicious behaviors throughout April 7, 1928, suggest an oblique understory within the novel that demands closer attention if we want to probe the boundaries of Faulkner's geographical imagination in this early work.

I invoke Morrison and *Beloved* because I believe that Sethe's troubling encounter with the chamomile articulates how bodies might retain and speak living memories and histories. The insistent intrusion of the jimson weed on Benjy's fractured present disrupts the complex spatial and temporal structures of the narrative by evoking a significant historical moment from the nation's earliest colonial origins. In his widely read work *The History and Present State of Virginia* (1705), planter and local historian Robert Beverley writes of the etymological origin of jimson weed as "Jamestown weed," memorializing a notorious incident during Bacon's Rebellion in 1676.[3] Angry at governor William Berkeley's failure to condone his murderous attacks on the neighboring Pumunkey and Occoneechee peoples on the Virginia frontier, the planter Nathaniel Bacon initiated a rebellion against the colony of Jamestown. Bacon led an uneasy alliance of European and African indentured servants, frontiersmen, and recent freedmen into what may be America's earliest class and race war. Although Bacon's sudden death from dysentery undermined the rebellion, English soldiers were sent to the colony to suppress the uprising. Beverley describes the memorable incident of the soldiers' accidental ingestion of *datura*:

> The Jamestown weed . . . was gathered very young for a boiled salad, by some of the soldiers sent thither to quell the rebellion of Bacon; and some of them eat plentifully of it, the effect of which was a very pleasant comedy; for they turned natural fools upon it for several days: one would blow up a feather in the air; another would dart straws at it with much fury; and another stark naked was sitting in a corner, like a monkey, grinning and making mows at them; a fourth would fondly kiss and paw his companions, and [snear] in their faces, with a countenance more antic than any in a Dutch droll. In this fantastic condition they were confined, lest they should in their folly destroy themselves; though it was observed that all their actions were full of innocence and good nature. Indeed, they were not very cleanly, for they would have wallowed in their own

excrement if they had not been prevented. A thousand such simple tricks they played, and after eleven days returned to themselves again, not remembering anything that had passed. (139)

The possibility of a direct intertextual link between Faulkner's representation of Benjy's cognitive disturbances and the "pleasant comedy" of the British soldiers' "fantastic condition" remains tantalizing, and perhaps ultimately speculative. However, the indisputable importance of Jamestown and Bacon's Rebellion as a national—and, for the South, a regional—site and moment of reprehensible colonial origins offers a more concrete point of entry into examining Faulkner's thoughts on the interconnections between race and land.

Many historians have interpreted Bacon's Rebellion as a determining event in the evolution of American capitalism and racialized slavery, twin forces that hardened the plantation system. Theodore Allen's painstaking historical excavation of the ideological formation of race in the colonial period interprets Bacon's Rebellion as a crucial turning point in what he suggests was "the invention of the white race."[4] He documents the initial lack of race consciousness amongst the African and European American rebels even as they were motivated "by a desire to exclude the Indians from English-occupied territory" (204), and suggests that, in the wake of the rebellion, the Jamestown elite deliberately fostered a system of racial oppression to divert class struggle in the colony: "it was only because 'race' consciousness superseded class-consciousness that the continental plantation bourgeoisie was able to achieve and maintain the degree of social control necessary for proceeding with capital accumulation on the basis of chattel bond-labor" (240). Allen's thesis offers a compelling account of the class politics attendant to the historic legal construction of race in colonial America as an inheritable marker of exclusion and servitude that stems from Jamestown as the "pattern-setting" (241) model of plantation life, yet also defines the complex dynamics of the frontier as a zone of contested territorial possession and exclusion. Thus, the jimson weed references the interrelationship between black and white identities that converge on the central question of indigeneity, as Native Americans and their mandated displacement from the frontier seem to be a catalyst for reimagining laboring black bodies as visual markers of territorial expansion and agricultural settlement.

While I suggest that we refrain from too easily conflating Faulkner's and Allen's very different projects, I do believe there is some evidence that Bacon's Rebellion and the legal consolidation of race in colonial Virginia form a meaningful locale and moment for the cartography and genealogy of Yoknapatawpha. Kevin Railey convincingly reads *Absalom,*

Absalom! against the backdrop of Allen's thesis of class struggle in colonial Virginia. Railey suggests that Thomas Sutpen's origins on the Tidewater plantation in Virginia indoctrinate Sutpen into a social ideology of race and class struggle with a "direct connection to the historic ordeal of Virginia. . . . That the ordeal of Virginia became the ordeal of America is verified later in the novel and, one could argue, later in American history."[5] Jay Watson shrewdly infers from Railey's work that Sutpen's dramatic arrival and anxious reception in Jefferson "reads like a nineteenth-century version of the seventeenth-century social emergency known as Bacon's Rebellion" and that Sutpen effectively "export[s] that ideology to the frontier reaches of the developing nation."[6] Watson's identification of Mississippi and Yoknapatawpha as a frontier zone for the Virginian Sutpen resonates with Faulkner's own expression of what he thought Virginia might mean to the South and America. In a 1958 lecture at the University of Virginia, Faulkner posits Virginia as the historic site of an organic Southern identity that will set the tone for race relations in the future:

> And the place for this to begin is Virginia, the mother of all the rest of us [through] the South. Compared to you, my country—Mississippi, Alabama, Arkansas—is still frontier, still wilderness. Yet even in our wilderness we look back to that mother stock as though it were not really so distant and so far removed. Even in our wilderness the old Virginia blood still runs. . . . Virginia is a living place to that child long before he ever heard or cares about New York or, for that matter, America.[7]

Faulkner asserts that Virginia remains the symbolic site of origin for the white South and that the South itself, in the midst of the civil rights era, continues to be a frontier that looks to Virginia "as a child looks toward the parent for a sign."[8] Just as in *The Sound and the Fury* Quentin Compson's psyche begins to unravel one morning in Virginia as he stares at a man on a mule, realizing "a nigger is not a person so much as . . . a sort of obverse reflection of the white people he lives among" (86), Faulkner's own understanding of race hinges on Virginia as "a sort of obverse reflection" of an America still entrenched in the ideological struggles emerging from the dynamics of the colonial frontier. Railey's convincing argument for the ideological engagement of *Absalom, Absalom!* opens some new ways for thinking about *The Sound and the Fury* as an earlier iteration of colonial Virginia's discursive significance for Faulkner, a significance he returns to in *Absalom, Absalom!*'s interrogation of imperialist concerns. In my mind, it is *The Sound and the Fury*'s extended engagement with autochthony and indigeneity as imaginative modes of territorial organization that roots the text so deeply into the soil of the American psyche and establishes a crucial Yoknapatawpha mythos that links the trans-Atlantic foundations of coastal Virginia with the Mississippi frontier. The collision of British and European, African, and Native American peoples in the "pleasant comedy" of the British soldiers in Jamestown compels us to examine not only the content of the "sign" that the "parent" Virginia presents to its "child" the American South but also its particular form: the Jamestown weed.

The confusion between dogfennel and jimson weed in *The Sound and the Fury* forms a lapse in the text perhaps unconscious which indicates autochthony's fearful symbolic power in the regional imagination of a white South steeped in the traditions of colonial Virginia's mythic and legal legacies. What is Luster's intention in giving to a *"looney"* (19) a plant that Stephen Ross and Noel Polk helpfully define as "a large, rank-smelling, poisonous weed?"[9] In one of the few critical treatments of the jimson weed's textual significance for *The Sound and the Fury*, Charles Peavy notes that the plant is poisonous and carries "obscene sexual denotation. . . . Faulkner was doubtlessly aware of the phallic implications of the closed jimson flower clutched in the fist of a castrated Benjy."[10] Edmond Volpe claims jimson weed, also known as stink weed, may function as "an ironic symbol of the loss of Caddy who smelled like trees" and notes its use as a "contraceptive medicine" and "a symbol of the male sex organ," adding that "the two weeds in the bottle become a memorial to Benjy's sexuality."[11] According to ethnobotanist Donald Watts, *datura* carries a worldwide association with witchcraft, magic, conjuring, initiation rites, and the "development of second sight," producing hallucination, visions, and a loss of physical and mental agency. Watts notes the plant's association with hoodoo in the New World, citing a seventeenth-century medical tract: "seeds given to anyone will cause that victim to be at the complete mercy of the practitioner for 24 hours. . . . You can do what you like with him; he notices nothing, understands nothing."[12] In the final section of the novel, the description of Benjy's graveyard evokes this dangerous conjunction of sexuality, race, bondage, and toxicity: "Ben squatt[ed] before a small mound of earth. At either end of it an empty bottle of blue glass that once contained poison was fixed in the ground. In one was a withered stalk of jimson weed. Ben squatted before it, moaning, a slow, inarticulate sound" (315). In one sense, the connection between Benjy and the jimson weed might be read as an internal problem of kinship and patrimony for the Compsons. Quentin Compson links poison to his troubled ancestry and attendant class issues: "one of our forefathers was a governor and three were generals and Mother's weren't. . . . *Done in Mother's mind though. Finished. Finished. Then we were all poisoned*" (101–2). However, the strikingly performative relationship between Benjy and Luster, when read in the context of the jimson weed, also suggests racialized criminal intent and its miscegenous connotations for the nation, opening a window to the deep undercurrents of regional folklore and superstition embedded in the South's acute historic fear of slave insurrection. That poisoning exercised a "powerful hold over the imagination of white planters" is no surprise, as this fear indexes a deep anxiety for the planter that the enslaved may possess a deeper knowledge of the indigenous flora, a problem exacerbated by poison's apparent invisibility or tracelessness within the ocular oversight of the plantation system.[13] The sexualized undercurrents of Benjy and Luster's relationship evoke the monstrous freight of sexual bondage tied to miscegenation's disruptions of kinship and reproduction, as race, the faulty marker of difference and possession, threatens to break as a visible and thus logical marker of exclusion from colonial indigeneity and future citizenship.

Benjy and Luster's fraught relationship hinges on their careful performance of the bodily crossing implicit within autochthonous tales that blur categorical distinctions between self and other, master and slave, indigenous and colonizer. Benjy and Luster's doubling indicates the limits of a particular visual economy in the South; they demarcate the resistance of the enslaved towards the social substitution of laboring black bodies for white ownership within the plantation economy. While the reader occupies or possesses Benjy's consciousness in his own narrative, we only *see* Benjy in section 4: "a big man who appeared to have been shaped of some substance whose particles would not or did not cohere to one another or to the frame which supported it. His skin was dead looking and hairless; dropsical too, he moved with a shambling gait like a trained bear" (274). Dropsy is a colloquial term for the condition of edema, the swelling of tissues with fluid, and derives from the Greek word *oidema* (to swell) suggesting an allusion to the autochthon Oedipus's swollen foot manifested as lameness in Benjy's "shambling gait like a trained bear." Luster mirrors the autochthonous imagery of Benjy's "dead looking and hairless" body as he systematically reverts to and emerges from the space of the cellar throughout the day, "the obscurity odorous of dank earth and mold and rubber" (273), then lies (again) to Dilsey as he assumes Benjy's expression: "He met her gaze blandly, innocent and open" (273). Luster merges with Benjy as he brings wood into the kitchen: "he blundered again at the door a moment later, again invisible and blind within and beyond his wooden avatar" (273), reanimating Benjy's shambling, wooden movements in a mocking register that evokes the bodily play of minstrelsy as a strategic subversion of dominant racial codes. Reading Benjy as a Christ figure on Easter day remains a commonplace of criticism on *The Sound and the Fury*. However, Luster's affinity for the cellar's depths and Benjy's corpse-like pallor suggest chthonic origins crucially resurrected by Luster's ironic performance of labor. Cynthia Dobbs points out that black bodies are represented as necessarily static and naturalized throughout *The Sound and the Fury*: "Quentin's desire to see blacks as a sign of an immutable home pushes his description from the realm of cultural critique to a fantasy of naturalizing race: 'as if they had been built there with the fence and the road' becomes 'carved out of the hill itself.'"[14] Dobbs identifies an important conflation in the text between blackness, landscape, and historical memory, yet when we consider Benjy and Luster's autochthonous spectacle, I would argue that these figures also delineate a landscape cleansed of originary Native American presence as the mute and static Benjy is figuratively overlaid with Luster's laboring black body throughout the day. Luster's energetic parody undermines Quentin's fantasy of blackness as static or immutable, as Benjy and Luster's exchanges point to blackness as a type of active retention—of memory, knowledge, and material origins—that resists static naturalization.

I believe that Benjy and Luster's association with the Jamestown weed historicizes how tropes of autochthony and indigeneity within the colonial imaginary can subsume the central importance of Native and African Americans for the contiguous projects of naturalism and naturalization. To read *The Sound and the Fury* with and against Beverley's account of Bacon's Rebellion undermines the epistemological certainty of the colonial archive to which Beverley's text belongs: the constitutional assemblage of documents, desires, and classification strategies by which to order and claim the territory of the Americas. Beverley's history naturalizes settler origins by enacting an organizational authority that textually effaces and rewrites the indigenous ecologies and inhabitants of Virginia with settler historiography. Faulkner effectively re-presents the colonial archive by tracing an imaginative genealogy between colonial Virginia and his present Mississippi—Faulkner's parent and child—coeval with the development of race as the colonial management of bodies and their labor. Faulkner appears both to trouble and to be troubled by the central question of indigeneity and the frontier conquest of Native America relative to the visual and legal naturalization of race and plantation land tenure as the tenuous basis of citizenship. If Luster's retentive performance appears to unsettle colonial claims to a naturalized indigeneity that rests on the bodies of the possessed, the "pleasant comedy" of the Jamestown weed also marks the traces of the dispossessed. Beverley authorizes the substance of his project in the same terms with which he undermines its formal execution. He effectively plays Indian on the frontispiece, which states authorship "By *a* Native *and* Inhabitant *of the* PLACE," and in his preface, where he asks the reader "not to Criticize too unmercifully upon my [Stile]. I am an *Indian*, and don't pretend to be exact in my Language" (9). Beverley fails to overwrite completely the traces of earlier Native American presence as his claim to an authentic and indigenous knowledge production rests on the appropriation of a (newly) indigenous mode of inscription that could never hope "to be exact" according to colonial logic. Benjy plays Indian himself as his mother changes his name from Maury, a marker of his maternal ancestry, to Benjamin, which can be translated literally as "son of the South" in Hebrew.[15] Thus a disinherited Benjamin whose beloved pasture is sold becomes the autochthonous child of the South and its parent Virginia as he simultaneously elides and unearths what must be written over.

If colonial autochthony undermines itself as an organizational mode, I suggest we may productively read these substitutions, retentions, and erasures in terms of Joseph Roach's vision of how "culture reproduces and recreates itself by a process that can best be described by the word surrogation."[16] In his account of a modern circum-Atlantic culture Roach argues that the newness and invention of America "conceptually erases indigenous populations" and the "violent diasporic experience of African Americans" within the registry of official memory (4). However, Roach writes, "circum-Atlantic memory retains its consequences, one of which is that the unspeakable cannot be rendered forever inexpressible: the most persistent mode of forgetting is memory imperfectly deferred" (4). Roach works with the "three-sided relationship of memory, performance, and substitution" (2) to track the always imperfect effacement of the autochthonous, the indigenous, and the violently possessed within the circulation of substitution in circum-Atlantic modernity. Beverley's and Faulkner's works both fall within the realm of textual inscription that contests performance. However, Beverley's authorial performance of playing Indian, along with the multiple significations of the Jamestown weed within both the colonial archive and the resistant counter-history of the folklore and traditions of the enslaved and displaced, demonstrates how we might understand *The Sound and the Fury* as a work that colludes with *and* undermines any originary moment in Jamestown. I believe that Roach's focus on the *circulation* of bodies, performances, and memory in the Atlantic world can be extended by reading Faulkner, as Yoknapatawpha imaginatively *roots* itself within successive layerings of autochthonous myth as living palimpsest. This sedimentation of the movements of memories and peoples in the Americas and their always imperfect substitutions for preceding peoples, landscapes, and stories accretes in Faulkner's Yoknapatawpha as a bereaved yet continuously inventive modernity.

In one of the few treatments of autochthony in Faulkner's work, Richard Godden claims, "Faulkner tends to reach for an idiot when he has something precious to hide—witness Benjamin Compson"[17] While Godden posits that Benjy hides the secret of miscegenation in his longing for Caddy, exposing the sick logic of conceiving blood as sexual property to maintain abstract racial distinctions, Benjy's association with the jimson weed suggests that *The Sound and the Fury* also elides an originary moment of violent erasure, a concept that Godden intuits in the figure of the miscegenated idiot Jim Bond in *Absalom, Absalom!* as he points out how idiocy and autochthony hide problems of class and race for the planters: "They, like their subject, are caught in a class contradiction: their substance, whether as body, property, land, or language is haunted by black labor, a shade that must be repressed *and* embraced. Their solution is stylistic—a way of talking which buries the bound man alive in the language of those who own. Dead and buried, the bound man conceals the master's means to mastery" (17). Thus, Godden reads autochthony as "putting the black back into the ethnically cleansed ground" of the Jim Crow South (13). While I believe Godden correctly emphasizes the significance of effaced black labor, he misses the deeper dynamic of autochthony as a real condition for effaced *Native* American origins and continuity in Yoknapatawpha. In the important collection *American Indian Literary Nationalism* that he coauthors with Robert Warrior and Craig Womack, Cherokee scholar Jace Weaver delivers a "Red reading" of Faulkner and Yoknapatawpha central to their project of literary nationalism. Weaver argues that "[from] a Native standpoint, it is an ethnically cleansed landscape" stemming from Faulkner's refusal to acknowledge Chickasaw continuance in Mississippi after Removal in 1832.[18] If *The Sound and the Fury* elides the "master's means to mastery," it also necessarily unearths an earlier violence by means of a complex conjunction of the dispossession of Native Americans in colonial Virginia and the forced diaspora of indigenous Africans. Chickasaw critic Jodi Byrd clarifies how the experiences of diasporic Africans forced to labor in the Americas makes the colonization of the indigenous Americas possible: "that history of forced plantation slavery becomes precisely an original and autochthonous experience of violence in the conquest of the Americas."[19] Byrd's insight clarifies what I read within Faulkner's vision of an autochthonous Benjy—not the literal emergence from the land of bodies written with race or modern biologies but rather the eruption of a violent experience, an idea retained in the modern performances of intercultural memory.

If we accept that *The Sound and the Fury* continues to labor under the birth of a truly autochthonous experience of violence that dates back to Bacon's Rebellion, Faulkner's conception of the land and its memories offers a rich site for future critical and imaginative engagement. Weaver elaborates on how Faulkner's fraught representation of the land is rooted in the colonial struggle to claim indigeneity by possessing rather than emerging from a land. Acknowledging Faulkner's undeniable influence on Native American authors such as N. Scott Momaday and Louise Erdrich, Weaver contrasts the vastly different meaning that land holds for Native peoples to whom "land is an ordinate category": "When Natives are removed from their traditional lands, they are robbed of more than territory; they are deprived of numinous landscapes that are central to their faith and their identity, lands populated by their relations, ancestors, animals, and beings both physical and mythological. A kind of psychic homicide is committed" (64). In contrast, Weaver suggests, Faulkner represents the land as "a foreign and haunted landscape, populated by grinning demons, where the Amer-European is doomed to contest desperately with himself and the ghosts he has created in an effort to prove that he belongs, to establish his own indigeneity" (66). Weaver identifies Faulkner's fictional Yoknapatawpha County, "that place in which he sought rootedness" (66), as the source and end of Faulkner's struggle to contest these ghosts of both the dispossessed and the possessed:

> Yoknapatawpha is a kind of metaphor, indeed a powerful one, for Native existence in general and Native literature in particular. Not only have Natives been split from their lands . . . but since the arrival of Europeans, the land itself has been split, not only by the conqueror's plow, but by the conqueror's law. What was once home and family is now mere property, a commodity to be owned and possessed, bought and sold. The land that was once wholly Natives' has been split from them. A physical, but also a psychical, fissure has cleaved Native land from non-Native land. Call it what you will: "civilized" from "savage," "technological" from "natural," "possession" from "home." (67)

Weaver speaks of the incredible psychic damage inflicted on Native Americans dispossessed and removed from the lands and relations that shape their autochthonous identity, such as the Chickasaw and Choctaw peoples who textually, if not historically, vanish to make way for Yoknapatawpha.[20] Faulkner's representations of Native Americans throughout his work elegize indigenous absence as the tragic outcome of this split, particularly in *Go Down, Moses* but also in the Compson Appendix of *The Sound and the Fury*, which refers to Compson patriarch Jason

Lycurgus's purchase of the "solid square mile of virgin North Mississippi dirt" from the "Doom[ed]" Chickasaw chief Ikkemotubbe, "[a] dispossessed American King."[21] I suggest that the "split" also applies to African American slaves split from their own systems of kinship, homes, and indigenous communities. Weaver draws on Arthur Kinney's suggestion that Faulkner's Yoknapatawpha may not only be read in Chickasaw as "split earth" but may also stem from the Choctaw *yakni patafa*, meaning plowed or cultivated land, thus underscoring the agricultural labor that subtends this appropriation.[22] Given the centrality of land to ongoing indigenous struggles for tribal sovereignty and the long struggle for African American political and economic liberation, I suggest that we might productively read Faulkner's imagined and deeply influential Yoknapatawpha against these intellectual traditions to better understand the continuity of this "split" and the ways in which people have creatively sought to remediate this fissure.

One of the gravest outcomes of the "split" that Yoknapatawpha makes legible remains the breach between Native American and African American communities in and from the Southeast traumatized by the legacy of plantation colonialism in which one group's displacement was accomplished by the other's enslavement. Much critical work remains to be undertaken if this split is to be historically understood and given a different trajectory and future.[23] I believe that Faulkner's imaginative legacy of Yoknapatawpha offers a powerful site through which we can map the history of these triangulated relationships among Euro, African, and Native Americans. Faulkner's representation of the autochthonous American offers an important methodological strategy for aesthetic engagements by African and Native American thinkers and authors seeking to articulate what has been elided in the historical record but continues to be experienced. Weaver uses Faulkner's work as a paradigm of what is wrong with the legacy of colonialism in America for indigenous peoples and to point out how a "new human person" shaped in remediation of this damaging legacy may be reclaimed in the project of Native American nationalism and tribal sovereignty. His call for this "new human person" evokes Franz Fanon's earlier gesture towards a new humanism at the conclusion of *The Wretched of the Earth*, thus signaling a shared trajectory between indigenous and African diasporic intellectuals who critique the legacy of colonialism as fundamentally antihuman in principle and practice. Benjy materializes another type of new human born in the split between Jamestown and Yoknapatawpha, a moaning consciousness that conveys what Morrison's Sethe makes visible in a memory comprised of sensual pictures: the irrepressible violence of bodies and memories that erupt from the land itself. Thus, the stylized modernist expression of

Benjy's narrative captures something of the burden, the sheer strain on the imagination, posed by representing the fractured consciousness of a modern psyche shaped by the autochthonic myth of colonial America.

NOTES

This project was supported by the Social Sciences and Humanities Research Council of Canada.

1. Toni Morrison, *Beloved* (New York: Penguin, 1988), 6.

2. William Faulkner, *The Sound and the Fury: The Corrected Text* (New York: Vintage, 1990), 6. All subsequent references to this work refer to this edition unless noted.

3. Robert Beverley, *The History of Virginia, In Four Parts, Book II*, ed. Louis B. Wright (Chapel Hill: University of North Carolina Press, 1947), §18, 139. Hereafter cited parenthetically in the text.

4. Theodore Allen, *The Invention of the White Race, Vol. 2: The Origin of Racial Oppression in Anglo-America* (New York: Verso, 1997). Hereafter cited parenthetically in the text.

5. Kevin Railey, *Natural Aristocracy: History, Ideology, and the Production of William Faulkner* (Tuscaloosa: University of Alabama Press, 1999), 133.

6. Jay Watson, "Introduction: Situating Whiteness in Faulkner Studies, Situating Faulkner in Whiteness Studies," in *Faulkner and Whiteness*, ed. Watson (Jackson: University Press of Mississippi, 2011), xix–xx.

7. William Faulkner, "A Word to Virginians," February 20, 1958, transcript and Quicktime audio, *Faulkner at Virginia: An Audio Archive*, University of Virginia, http://faulkner.lib.virginia. edu/display/wfaudio20_read.

8. Ibid.

9. Stephen M. Ross and Noel Polk, *Reading Faulkner: "The Sound and the Fury"* (Jackson: University Press of Mississippi, 1996), 13.

10. Charles Peavey, "Faulkner's Use of Folklore in *The Sound and the Fury*," *Journal of American Folklore* 79.313 (1966): 438, http://www.jstor.org/stable/537508.

11. Edmond Loris Volpe, *A Reader's Guide to William Faulkner: The Novels* (Syracuse: Syracuse University Press, 1964), 103–4.

12. Donald Watts, *Dictionary of Plant Lore* (Oxford, UK: Academic, 2007), 380.

13. Junius P. Rodriguez, "Poisoning," *Encyclopedia of Slave Resistance and Rebellion, Vol. 2* (Westport: Greenwood, 2007), 382. See 381–84 for an indication of how poison features as an important discourse in African and African American Atlantic slave cultures outside of European cultural significations. See Nicholas Mirzoeff, *The Right to Look: A Counterhistory of Visuality* (Durham: Duke University Press, 2011), for a comprehensive account of the codevelopment of the plantation and ocular power in the Americas.

14. Cynthia Dobbs, "'Ruin or Landmark?': Black Bodies as Lieux de Memoire in *The Sound and the Fury*," *Faulkner Journal* 21 (2004–2005): 39.

15. I gratefully acknowledge Jay Watson for pointing out this important translation of Benjamin.

16. Joseph Roach, *Cities of the Dead: Circum-Atlantic Performance* (New York: Columbia University Press, 1996), 2. Hereafter cited parenthetically in the text.

17. Richard Godden, "A Phenomenological Reading of *The Hamlet* as a Rebuke to an American Century," in *Faulkner in America: Faulkner and Yoknapatawpha, 1998*, ed. Joseph R. Urgo and Ann J. Abadie (Jackson: University Press of Mississippi, 2001), 10.

18. Jace Weaver, "Splitting the Earth: First Utterances and Pluralist Separatism," in *American Indian Literary Nationalism*, by Weaver, Craig S. Womack, and Robert Warrior (Albuquerque: University of New Mexico Press, 2006), 58. Hereafter cited parenthetically in the text.

19. Jodi A. Byrd, *The Transit of Empire: Indigenous Critiques of Colonialism* (Minneapolis: University of Minnesota Press, 2011), 67.

20. Weaver points out that while the Choctaw were removed, many Chickasaw remained in Mississippi after Removal. See Patricia Galloway, "The Construction of Faulkner's Indians," *Faulkner Journal* 18.1–2 (2003): 9–31, for a comprehensive examination of Faulkner and the indigenous peoples of Mississippi. This journal volume, "Faulkner and Native America," includes a number of essays that examine Faulkner's representation of Native Americans in detail.

21. William Faulkner, "Appendix Compson 1699–1945," in *The Sound and the Fury: An Authoritative Text, Backgrounds and Contexts, Criticism*, ed. David Minter (New York: Norton, 1994), 203.

22. Weaver, 66. Weaver is drawing on Arthur E. Kinney, *"Go Down, Moses": The Miscegenation of Time* (New York: Twayne, 1996), 21–22. See Don H. Doyle, *Faulkner's County: The Historical Roots of Yoknapatawpha* (Chapel Hill: University of North Carolina Press, 2001), 24–25, for a thorough account of Yoknapatawpha's etymology and history.

23. For an indication of the complexity and controversy surrounding this issue, see Tiya Miles and Sharon P. Holland, eds., *Crossing Waters, Crossing Worlds: The African Diaspora in Indian Country* (Durham: Duke University Press, 2006). Tiya Miles, *Ties That Bind: The Story of an Afro-Cherokee Family in Slavery and Freedom* (Berkeley: University of California Press, 2005), and Claudio Saunt, *Black, White, and Indian: Race and the Unmaking of an American Family* (Oxford: Oxford University Press, 2005), both offer important historical accounts of Native and African American entanglements complicated by slavery in the Southeast where Faulkner writes.

South by Southwest: William Faulkner and Greater Mexico

JOSÉ E. LIMÓN

It is now well established that Faulkner's American geographies extend southeast of Mississippi across the Gulf of Mexico out to the Caribbean Sea but also directly southward to South America. His connection to the Caribbean is certainly well known, particularly to Francophone Haiti, in *Absalom, Absalom!*, Thomas Sutpen's immediate point of origin and formative moment before he shows up in Yoknapatawpha County, Mississippi. For Richard H. King, "it is the great proof text that links the (US) Southern Faulkner with the Latin American/Caribbean Faulkner."[1] However, Faulkner's extension southward toward most of Latin America proper is not based on his direct knowledge and/or incorporation of the Southern hemisphere into his work, for he does not do such to any degree that is in any way comparable to *Absalom, Absalom!* Rather, for the critics, this latter southward relationship is largely one of influence and/or comparability relative to that hemisphere's great writers and their social milieu, and that is the way he has been primarily connected to the Spanish-speaking world of South America and, to a lesser extent, to Brazil.[2]

However, we should recall that while most of Latin America does lie on a direct line south from Mississippi, not all of it does. There is another kind of Latin America, not toward the southeast or directly south, but rather toward the southwest by west. This other line takes us from Mississippi across Louisiana into first, Texas, then across the US-Mexico border but also directly westward toward California and therefore into the territories and peoples that the late Américo Paredes called Greater Mexico: "all of the area inhabited by people of Mexican culture—not only within the present limits of the Republic of Mexico but in the United States as well—in a cultural rather than a political sense."[3] Even after his death in 1999, Paredes remains the leading literary intellectual of Mexican ancestry who was born and worked primarily in the United States, a Mexican American who devoted most of his career to the critical exploration of the verbally expressive world of Greater Mexico, its folklore and its literature.[4] We shall return to him later.

This essay explores Faulkner's relationship to Greater Mexico, one previously addressed in part, but of which much more may be said. I offer an argument that proceeds in two broad parts. First, I propose that Greater Mexico's relationship to the US South makes possible the construction of Faulkner's fictional world keyed as it is on the US Civil War and its aftermath for the South. The second part of my argument proposes that, if Greater Mexico had this enabling relationship to Faulkner's fiction, then conversely, certain writers but also filmmakers from Greater Mexico have drawn on that same Faulkner for their own representations of Greater Mexico. But my argument then also loops back to another aspect of my first proposition, namely that the Greater Mexican world such artists represent is one that was engendered by the US South.

In the totality of his work, Faulkner himself rarely referred to this relationship between Greater Mexico, the South, and his work, although he surely knew of it, for he does do so at length in at least one important place. Let us remember the beginnings of *Light in August*. I am not talking about its literal beginning with Lena Grove making her way from Alabama to Jefferson in search of her Lucas Burch. Rather, I wish to note the way that the novel reminds us of the historical beginnings that set in motion the narrative substance of this particular text but also much of Faulkner's other work. *Light in August* offers us such a historical entry point although it comes later in the novel, as Faulkner takes his usual modernist liberties with conventional time and narration. In chapter 11 Joanna Burden tells us of her grandfather, Calvin, and her father, Nathaniel, both of whom ran away from their respective homes to spend time in the Southwest in different periods.

In her own previous exploration of this topic, Leigh Anne Duck has taken note of these travels but does not precisely specify the time periods for these two journeys nor what happens in the Southwest in between.[5] They span the first two-thirds of the nineteenth century: Calvin in California when it was still a Mexican possession; Nathaniel in Colorado, New Mexico, and Texas after 1848 but also in "old Mexico." Indeed, when Nathaniel returns home to his father, Calvin, and his sisters, he brings with him Juana, a Mexican woman, but also their baby son, also named Calvin after his grandfather. More on them later. For the moment, let us focus on what Faulkner implies but does not really say either here or elsewhere. The elder Calvin visits Spanish-Mexican California, it would seem, sometime before 1848, and his son, Nathaniel, enters Greater Mexico precisely in 1850. What Faulkner does not foreground is the temporal space in between these two Burden excursions, as if he is repressing an event that then leads irrevocably to Faulkner's world.

That event is the US-Mexico War, itself tied to the movement of

Americans into Mexican Texas in the 1820s and '30s, leading to Texas's independence from Mexico in 1836 and the US-Mexico War of 1846–47 in support of the Texas desire for annexation to the United States. As I have noted elsewhere, historians have pointed to a variety of interests—chief among them the idealistic "Manifest Destiny"—that led to this chain of events and the eventual US imperialistic acquisition of the northern provinces of then national Mexico.[6] But among these American interests, the demands of the Southern political economy at the time were central. According to the still authoritative Clement Eaton, "the South was eager for the annexation of this region because it offered a field for the expansion of the cotton kingdom and slavery," an expansion also "motivated by the high birth rate in the South, for the large families of strapping boys had to make elbow room for themselves." Moreover, "the opening of new cotton lands would give vitality to Southern slavery by increasing the demand for additional slaves, thus enhancing the value of slave property in the South."[7] And from this new "elbow room," this new "imperial domain," as many as "five slave states could be carved out" to create "a reserve of future slave states to keep the balance of power in the Senate."[8] (The expansion of slavery was not entirely confined to future cotton production. After the Mexican War and the California Gold Rush of 1849–50, no less a figure than Jefferson Davis imagined great profits to be derived from using slaves to mine California's gold).[9]

The South had political and military power to fulfill its needs and demands. As the process for annexing unfolded, the president of the United States, James K. Polk, a Southerner, ordered a fellow Southerner, commanding General Zachary Taylor, to march into Texas and then into internal Mexico. The war commenced with a series of battles in southern Texas and northern Mexico in which the Mexican armies were defeated and fell back, losing even Mexico City to the invading American troops.[10] Among those troops we find a Mississippian, the afore-mentioned Colonel Jefferson Davis, Taylor's son-in-law, in command of a volunteer unit he had raised called the Mississippi Rifles. The unit fought at the Battle of Buena Vista, for which current day Buena Vista, Georgia, was named when it incorporated in 1850. For indeed, the clear majority of the US troops were from the Old South, a telling number given the greater population base of the North and Midwest at that time. As Eaton summarizes the matter: "the Mexican War was an adventure in imperialism of the South in partnership with the restless inhabitants of the West. It was provoked by a Southern president and fought largely by Southern generals and Southern volunteers."[11]

Among these Southern volunteers we find Faulkner's great-grandfather, W. C. Falkner, who fought in the Mexican War as a lieutenant from 1845 to October 1847, probably with Davis's Mississippi Rifles, and later served as a colonel in the coming Civil War. Out of the Mexican experience the Colonel became something of a writer himself, penning a poem on the siege of Monterrey and a novel, *The Spanish Heroine*.[12] According to Joseph Blotner, but also Robert Cantwell, through family stories W. C. Falkner figured prominently in Faulkner's imaginative life, particularly for his experiences in the Civil War.[13] It seems likely that Faulkner also had some awareness of the Colonel's previous military experience in the Mexican campaign and possibly might have read the Colonel's two literary works based on that experience. Yet, as Blotner says, "it is hard to know with any certainty the total picture Faulkner had in his early years of this ancestor who loomed so over the whole family."[14]

As is now common knowledge, W. C. Falkner and the Falkner family lore he inspired would later be transformed into the figure of Colonel John Sartoris in Faulkner's 1929 *Sartoris*, an abridgement of the 1927 manuscript *Flags in the Dust*. Even as an abridgement, *Sartoris*, the first of the novels set in Yoknapatawpha County, explores the decay and moral convolutions of the Old South and its white aristocracy after the Southern defeat in the Civil War. But W. C. Falkner, this bridging figure in Faulkner's own family, and his representation in Faulkner's fiction serve to remind us that the white South reaped the consequences of the violent imperialism it had principally led against Greater Mexico in pursuit of expanding that slavery and cotton-based Southern aristocracy. Again Clement Eaton puts the matter succinctly: "One of the most important consequences of the Mexican War was that it precipitated a great sectional struggle between the North and the South over the status of slavery in this territory, a controversy that led eventually to the Civil War."[15] Thus the Southern-led conquest and racial destabilization of Greater Mexico led to the demise of the South over the question of slavery and therefore to the narrative substance of Faulkner's world. This world, of course, is about nothing else but the traumatic and racialized consequences of the Civil War and whether the people of the South could, in Faulkner's own words, endure and prevail through this trauma and emerge as a better humanity.

However, in its own forms, such racialized trauma also characterized Greater Mexico after its experience of the Southern-led US-Mexico War. How did this happen? Again, we can turn to *Light in August* to gain entry into this question for Greater Mexico. Nathaniel, we shall recall, is the elder Calvin's son conceived with his French Huguenot wife, Evangeline, whose phenotype gives Nathaniel a particular racial cast such that we see Calvin and his child Nathaniel comparatively as "the tall, gaunt, Nordic man, and the small, dark, vivid child who had inherited his mother's build and coloring, like people of two different races."[16] As noted earlier, like his father before him, Nathaniel runs away in 1850, at the age of fourteen, to Colorado, Mexico, and Texas, finally returning sixteen years later to his father's house in the company of a Mexican woman, Juana, and their child. They have come home to marry.[17] When the elder Calvin sees Nathaniel and Juana's baby, his namesake, he is outraged: "'Another damn black Burden,' he said. . . . 'Damn, lowbuilt black folks: lowbuilt because of the weight of the wrath of God, black because of the sin of human bondage staining their blood and flesh.'"[18] Though the Burdens have clear ties to the North, Faulkner uses them, in André Bleikasten's words, "to explore the hidden recesses of the Southern mind," presumably the white Southern mind.[19] For though the elder Calvin is an abolitionist, that does not keep him from also being a racist, whose "theological fanaticism" makes him, according to Bleikasten, "a worthy match for Doc Hines," as both men "regard the black man as the accursed of God" in taking up "antithetical rationalizations of the same racist delirium." In her own searching analysis of this racial moment, Duck observes that while "equating different regional associations with different bloods . . . the Burden family narrative provides no consistent meaning for race, [but] it does suggest a prominent and consistent association: repeatedly, the language of race is mobilized when groups or individuals are responding to perceived threats against cherished aspects of identity."[20]

Calvin Burden's racist equation between blackness and in this case a half-Mexican child was indeed carried by Southerners into Greater Mexico not only during the US-Mexico War but even before and certainly afterward as more Southerners moved into Greater Mexico after the Civil War. Their encounter with full-blooded Mexicans generally produced a racial hierarchy and system of segregation, a system that prevailed well into my own lifetime in Texas. As if such racism needed exacerbation, we should also recall that these Southerners were also prejudiced against Indians, having fought them throughout Southern history. That Mexicans were also half-Indians did not escape their notice and contributed to the disparagement of Greater Mexico as a nation of "half-breeds." Moreover such Southerners were also for the most part fundamentalist Protestants encountering a Catholic culture exactly at the time of anti-Catholic hysteria in the United States directed principally against the Irish. As with African Americans in the South, this racial hierarchy came to be highly correlated with labor exploitation of Mexicans, both those who were resident in what was to become the United States and those entering the United States, especially after the Mexican Revolution of 1910. Most of this latter group entered into the very territories acquired in the Mexican War—most, but not all, as we shall see later.

With Mexican immigration after 1910, we come to another dimension of the plight of Greater Mexico. For it can be argued with some conviction that the Southern-led invasion of national Mexico in 1846–47 not only severed Mexico from its northern territories, depriving that country of all manner of natural resources, but also destabilized internal Mexico as wars can do. In the nineteenth century the Mexican political and economic system never achieved a stable coherence even after the US troops withdrew. Internal factionalism and foreign debt led to the French occupation and the imposition of an Emperor and Empress of Mexico, Maximilian and his wife, Carlota. Coming in the middle of the US Civil War, the occupation proved to be to the benefit of the Confederate South. French sympathy for the Confederate cause provided an overland outlet through Texas for Southern cotton, evading the Union blockade and materially lengthening the war and therefore slavery. Maximilian's support for the Confederacy continued even after the Civil War with his invitation to ex-Confederates to move to Mexico and establish settlements to be called "Carlota's Colony."[21] In 1867 the invitation was presumably withdrawn when, with the support of the now triumphant and (re)United States, the French were expelled by Mexican rebels and Maximilian was executed while the Empress Carlota was in Europe seeking support for her husband and his regime. It was a moment in Mexico's history known to Faulkner, as witness the reference to Maximilian and (especially) Carlota in *Requiem for a Nun*, in the conversation between the "host" native to Yoknapatawpha County and the educated "stranger" passing through town. Carlota's image and that part of Mexico's tragic history are conflated with the tragedy of the South expressed through the figure of Cecelia Farmer and her lingering signature on the glass.[22]

After the expulsion of the French, political and economic stability proved elusive for Mexico, and the result was the oppressive dictatorship of Porfirio Diaz beginning in 1876 and lasting until the Mexican Revolution of 1910, with its own violent and further destabilization of Mexico and the beginning of massive immigration into the United States and its Southern-created segregated society for most Mexicans whether immigrant or native-born. But as we broach the question of a racialized Mexican immigration into the United States through the 1930s, we can return to *Light in August* to remind ourselves of what I call the second reappearance of Greater Mexico in that text. The first, as we have seen, had to do with the Burdens going out into the nineteenth-century West and with Nathaniel's Mexican Juana, whose son, Calvin, complicates the

racial thematics of the novel. But there is also some considerable suggestion that Joe Christmas himself may be at least part Mexican through his
father, an employee with a traveling circus who impregnates his mother,
Milly.[23] Ramón Saldívar reminds us of the way in which the racial contradictions surrounding Joe Christmas take up Mexican raciality as a
mediator between black and white, and John T. Matthews speaks of Joe's
"ambiguous paternity."[24] Milly's father, Doc Hines, will have none of this,
choosing to see Joe and his circus father as "niggers."

My point is not to settle this rich racial ambivalency but simply to
underscore the familiarity of Faulkner's characters with Mexicans in the
1920s and '30s. Since these characters, like Doc Hines, are largely not
people who could be tourists in Mexico, the only other likely possibility
for this time period is that Mexicans are starting to appear in Faulkner's
South in significant numbers, although not without interesting prec-
edents that foreshadow the discussion around Joe Christmas. Historian
Neil Foley tells us of one Santiago Tafolla from New Mexico who, in
1848, ran away from home and made his way to the Old South, where
he found work as an overseer on a plantation near Talbaton, Georgia.
Within the Southern binary of black and white, Tafolla and others soon
came to identify him as the latter even as he was also referred to as
Mexican Jim, "perhaps history's only Mexican overseer on a slave plantation in the antebellum South."[25] As historian Jerry Don Thompson has
shown us, in 1861 the Civil War brought Mexicans from Texas to the
South, Mexicans who ironically decided to throw in their lot with the
Confederacy as soldiers in the Sixth Texas Infantry, which saw action at
Chattanooga and Chickamauga. One can only wonder how they were
received within the black-white binary.[26]

Faulkner himself probably knew nothing of this nineteenth-century
contact, but it is likely that, like many Americans, he was at least somewhat familiar with the dramatic events in Mexico concerning the Mexican Revolution and the subsequent immigration of Mexicans into the
United States primarily as agricultural labor, a demographic shift that
occasioned much public hysteria and the partial deportation of Mexicans.[27] Mexican immigration was quite evident in nearby Texas, and, citing Blotner, Duck suggests that "Faulkner would have had ready access
to information regarding this history from his in-laws, who moved to
Mississippi from the Blackland Prairie—the hub of Texas cotton farming—in the late nineteenth century."[28] However, even if Faulkner had
such conversations with his in-laws—and we do not know that he actually did—this would have been information about such labor activities in
Texas, not Mississippi, and in the nineteenth century, not the twentieth.
Duck makes a further inferential and conditional argument: "But these

tensions among agricultural workers continued to develop during the course of Faulkner's lifetime taking forms almost certain to draw the attention of a Mississippian interested in relations created by plantation agriculture and the social changes initiated by an increasingly mobile labor force."[29]

Faulkner had other more direct possible sources for knowledge about early twentieth-century Mexico and Mexican labor migration. William Spratling, Faulkner's close friend, roommate, and coauthor from his New Orleans days, had visited Mexico in the mid-twenties and moved there permanently in 1929 to launch his famous career as a silversmith.[30] But he continued to visit Faulkner in the United States into the 1930s, including during one of Faulkner's sojourns in California.[31] It seems quite unlikely that Mexico would not have come up as a subject of conversation between the two friends.

Julie M. Weise, however, provides direct and substantial evidence that lends fulsome support to the likelihood that the presence and racial ambiguity of Mexicans in the Mississippi world of the 1920s and 1930s inform *Light in August*. By Weise's accounting it is quite clear that there were substantial numbers of Mexican sharecroppers in Mississippi from 1908 up to World War II and that, in the face of racism, they often claimed the racial status of "whiteness" even as some of them married black women. In pursuing this whitening strategy, they were perhaps remembering similar governmental policies in pre-Revolutionary Mexico under Porfirio Diaz, in which Mexican indigenous society served as the racial Other. However, they could play such a white card in large part because Southerners were largely unaccustomed to and ambivalent about this relatively new racial category.[32] Nowhere does Faulkner speak explicitly of this Mexican sharecropper presence in his Mississippi backyard, but the imagined identification of the figure of Joe Christmas in these ethnic terms may be evidence enough that he knew of it. (It is highly probable that this Mexican presence helps account for the popularity of *tamales* in the Mississippi Delta, a food now taken up largely by African Americans.)[33]

Thus a kind of Faulknerian world of race, historical memory, social conflict, displacement, and historical tragedy also came into existence for Greater Mexico, but I say again a Greater Mexico for which the US South bears some large responsibility. Greater Mexico has not lacked for its own writers and filmmakers to record and explore the material and moral vicissitudes of this world rent with racialized contradiction and conflict. Paradoxically enough, some of these artists have turned to or are seen in relation to William Faulkner as a model. We begin with four major writers who will serve as examples in ascending order of reputation, significance, and thematic and stylistic proximity to Faulkner. In this order, these are Américo Paredes, Rolando Hinojosa, Carlos Fuentes, and Cormac McCarthy.

I began my definition of Greater Mexico by referencing the term's coinage by Américo Paredes, whom I also identified as the leading Mexican American literary intellectual of our time. In the 1930s Paredes wrote a novel called *George Washington Gómez* set in predominantly Mexican American southern Texas, specifically in Paredes's hometown of Brownsville, where the Rio Grande meets the Gulf of Mexico to form its own Delta country.[34] The novel fictively calls the town "Jonesville," its English-language name already suggesting that, even though the area was predominantly Mexican American, in the 1930s it was politically and economically dominated by white Anglos, many from a Southern lineage. The novel is in the form of a bildungsroman—a coming of age story—which begins with the birth of the central protagonist named George Washington Gómez in 1915, charts his life story through his education in the local schools and at the University of Texas at Austin, and closes as he is starting a career as a lawyer and a national security agent at the beginning of the Second World War. However, this life story is fraught with internal conflict as the protagonist struggles with his ethnic identity. Given the history of ethnic conflict in southern Texas, reflected in the tortured name that his parents have given him, should he be loyal to his Mexican origins, or should he become a full-fledged assimilated American?

There is no evidence that Paredes ever turned consciously to Faulkner as a model for his own work. However, Ramón Saldívar has astutely compared this novel to Faulkner's *Absalom, Absalom!*, not in terms of their formal features or general narrative structure, which are very different, but rather with a focus on the respective central protagonists, Thomas Sutpen and George Washington Gómez. Sandívar argues that in both characters absolute notions of racial or ethnic identity are being negotiated but ultimately that each man gives way to an identification with the subject position that historically has dominated him. In Sutpen's case, his initial definition as a member of the white Southern peasantry is then overlaid and made potentially socially productive by his immersion in the racially fluid world of Haiti. However, these amplifications are then constricted when he comes back to the South—to Mississippi—where, with his "design," he will emulate the racist and economic dominance of the white planter class and suffer the consequences as his past, by way of Wash Jones, returns to haunt and eventually destroy him. In somewhat similar fashion, in his own racialized and class-stratified world, George Washington Gómez will also try to emulate white society but not without contradiction. Though he does not die as does Sutpen, his new identity will be psychologically fraught and alienated as evidenced in a recurring dream about his past.[35]

The racially and economically conflicted world of Mexican American south Texas has also yielded another writer who addresses these issues, but in this instance the indebtedness to Faulkner is quite clear, as critic Mark Busby has shown us.[36] Rolando Hinojosa, who currently teaches at the University of Texas at Austin, has explicitly acknowledged Faulkner not only as his favorite writer but as a model for his construction of his "own little postage stamp of native soil," specifically a fictive county in south Texas that he calls Belken County, in which he has set a series of short novels. For the most part, and in a manner that recalls Paredes, these novels trace the lives of two protagonists—Rafe Buenrostro and Jehu Malacara—whose ancestral origins go back to pre-1848 Texas before the coming of the Anglos to south Texas. We follow them from their childhood beginnings as poor Mexican American kids growing up in the 1920s in Belken County, through their education, especially at the University of Texas at Austin, and their service in the Korean War, to their eventual return to Belken County as professionals. The more significant of the two—Rafe Buenrostro—is especially aware of the racial and economic contradictions of his existence, but unlike George Washingon Gómez or Thomas Sutpen, he does not give himself over to an assimilated existence among those who dominate. Rather, with a vivid Faulknerian memory of his ancestral past and with all of its contradictions but also its strengths, he successfully fashions a bilingual and bicultural existence even as he puts himself at the service of his community as a mature adult in the 1970s. Also trained as a lawyer at the University of Texas at Austin, he foregoes a lucrative career defending the drug lords in the area that are so much in the news today and instead becomes a police detective hunting these people down.[37]

Even though they have these affinities with Faulkner's work, neither Paredes nor Hinojosa shares his complexity of form and depth of consciousness, but that does not mean that they have not written compelling work. Closer to Faulkner by way of complexity and depth are my final two authors from Greater Mexico, Carlos Fuentes and Cormac McCarthy.

The late Carlos Fuentes continues to be the Republic of Mexico's leading literary intellectual and was well known in the United States as a visiting professor and lecturer at our leading universities. Most, if not all, of his work has been translated into English, although he had great facility with the language, having spent considerable time in the United States and its schools as a child. Thus, although not a US citizen, he was in his own way a citizen of Greater Mexico as we have defined it here. Gabriel García Márquez, the great Latin American writer from Colombia, has written about a wonderful encounter at a 1995 dinner party with President Bill Clinton, a party "given by William Styron in his summer house on Martha's Vineyard in August 1995," with Carlos Fuentes also present. The gathered company got around to naming their favorite book, their bed-time reading, and "Clinton said his was the 'Meditations of Marcus Aurelius,'" but, according to García-Márquez,

> Carlos Fuentes stuck loyally to "Absalom, Absalom" [sic], Faulkner's stellar novel, no question, although others would choose "Light in August" [sic] for purely personal reasons. Clinton, in homage to Faulkner, then got to his feet and, pacing around the table, recited from memory Benj[y]'s monologue, the most thrilling passage, and perhaps the most hermetic, from "The Sound and the Fury."[38]

García-Márquez continues, "Faulkner got us to talking about the affinities between Caribbean writers and the cluster of great Southern novelists in the United States."[39]

Fuentes's selection of *Absalom, Absalom!* does not at all surprise, and several critics have written on Faulkner's influence on Fuentes, among them most recently Wendy Faris.[40] Her perceptive essay focuses on *As I Lay Dying* in relation to Fuentes's novel *The Death of Artemio Cruz*, arguably his most important work. She is interested in both Fuentes's and Faulkner's use of what she calls "narrative excess," or "the expenditure of more narrative time and descriptive detail than is strictly necessary for the recording of an event or a scene," and for this purpose, *As I Lay Dying* seems to her a better partner for *Artemio Cruz*.[41] However, as she also notes, "these two texts do not compare smoothly," for "history in *As I Lay Dying* is private history, the burden of the past is generalized and focused through the Bundren family, so that for the most part it eludes the specifically racial and historical questions that pervade much of the rest of Faulkner's fiction." Indeed, she continues, "because of its present time orientation, *As I Lay Dying* represents a respite from the relentless historicity of the other texts, which are in that respect closer to *The Death of Artemio Cruz*," in which the central protagonist, a failed leader in the also-failed Mexican Revolution of 1910, bears a close resemblance to Thomas Sutpen but also to a composite of Calvin Burden, the Reverend Hightower, and Joe Christmas.[42]

For myself, I prefer the relentless historicity, but I also follow Fuentes's own preference for *Absalom, Absalom!* and *Light in August*, as these texts share with *Artemio Cruz* what Louis D. Rubin called "the impossible load of the past," a past that seems to offer a heroic beginning but then ends in failure. For the US South, the heroism of the Confederacy is premised on slavery and leads to defeat; for Greater Mexico, the ideals of the independence movement of 1810 and the revolution of 1910 are premised on a racialized and exploited peasantry and also end in failure. I have noted the way in which these two seemingly disparate histories are in fact causally intertwined. So it seems only just that Fuentes's *Artemio Cruz* is intertwined with Faulkner. As Faris notes, Fuentes actually wrote a critical essay on Faulkner, "The Novel as Tragedy," shortly after he published *The Death of Artemio Cruz*.[43]

Finally, I close my readings of these authors of Greater Mexico influenced by Faulkner with the endlessly fascinating Cormac McCarthy. Of all our writers, including Fuentes, it is surely McCarthy who is closest to Faulkner. He certainly shares Faulkner's primary geography, as he was raised in nearby Tennessee and spent his early adult life in the South. His early novels set in the South certainly attest to the Faulkner influence, sometimes greatly. The first of these, *The Orchard Keeper*, was published in 1965, three years after Faulkner's death, with Faulkner's publisher and indeed his editor as well. An exploration of the passing life in rural Tennessee right before World War II, the novel, according to one critic, "has a Southern Gothic atmosphere and descriptive energy clearly reminiscent of William Faulkner. One can sense Faulkner's influence in the supernatural light McCarthy casts on rural life, in the shifting narrative perspectives, and in the heightened language that infuses seemingly discrete actions with universally mythic resonance."[44] Indeed, the novel won a William Faulkner Foundation Award for the best first novel by an American writer. Later Southern-based novels such as *Outer Dark* continued in this tradition. Yet although his third novel, *Child of God*, is based on an actual historical account of serial murder and necrophilia, McCarthy's early work does not seem Faulknerian in a large and profound historical sense. That is, in his early fiction, he does not draw on or interrogate the large historical Southern themes concerning slavery, race, the Civil War, the Cavalier tradition and its failure, social violence, and the Southern mind. That remained a project for McCarthy's novels of the 1980s and beyond, in which we can see the younger writer forging a distinctive body of later work while remaining indebted to his literary master, in ways that recall Harold Bloom's ideas about the anxiety of influence.[45]

In 1976, as if by some providential design for the purpose of the present essay, McCarthy shifted his geography and moved into Greater Mexico, specifically to El Paso. In preparation for new writing, he undertook rigorous research, including scouting trips throughout the

Southwest and into Mexico, and mastered Spanish. In four subsequent novels set in this new country, McCarthy becomes not only a writer of Greater Mexico but the best one in my estimation. In this new work we do find the large historical inquiry absent in the early work. Especially in the first of these novels, *Blood Meridian*, it is as if McCarthy, more so than anyone else, is now rendering in a gripping, poetically apocalyptic fiction the theme with which I began this essay: the violent engendering of Greater Mexico by the US South.

The action of the novel begins immediately after the Treaty of Guadalupe Hidalgo ending the US-Mexico War and features two central protagonists. The first, known simply as the "kid," appears to be a runaway teenager who has made his way from Tennessee into eastern Texas, now American territory as is the rest of the Southwest. He joins up with another memorable character named Judge Holden, a combined Colonel Sartoris and Thomas Sutpen raised to the Nth power, who leads the "kid" and other grotesque characters in an orgy of violence throughout the Southwest but also down into national Mexico. Their goal is to get profitable scalps from Indians to be paid for by the Mexican government, but the violence escalates against Mexican nationals as well, for who can really tell the difference between Indians and peasant Mexicans who are half-Indian anyway?

Such situated and racialized violence has been read as "sacred" or redemptive violence in this and other McCarthy novels, recasting his work as a product of religious humanism.[46] In similar fashion the "Western" novels, including *Blood Meridian* and the Border Trilogy, have come to be critically "characterized by deep philosophical musings on history, God, and the very nature of being."[47] We may, then, be witnessing McCarthy's critical refashioning as an exemplar of the universalist and modernist artist emulating Faulkner's own universalization.[48] But such a universalist reading need not displace the historical and cultural drama that is also unfolding in *Blood Meridian* as McCarthy charts a Southern and racial violence that was forcibly introduced into Greater Mexico, shaping that society in distorting ways that have endured. While the subsequent Border Trilogy continues this interrogation in a lower key, it also addresses broad historical themes such as the ending of the frontier in mid-twentieth-century Texas and New Mexico and the development of an elitist ruling class and state corruption in Mexico.[49] The later *No Country for Old Men* then moves us into the present-day Texas with an exploration of the culture of drug-induced violence that is now afflicting the Texas border with Mexico. As such, all of McCarthy's works parallel Faulkner's explorations of the South and do so in the same idioms.

Like Faulkner, McCarthy's work has been transformed into film, most notably and successfully, for our purposes, in *No Country for Old Men*, directed and produced by the Coen brothers. I close this section by noting Faulkner's influence on other films concerned with the vicissitudes of Greater Mexico. In a provocative and ingenious analysis, film critic Jerry W. Carlson argues for the influential presence of Faulkner in two major films that take up this theme: *El Gallo de Oro* (1964) and *The Three Burials of Melquiades Estrada* (2005). The first is set in post-Revolutionary Mexico in the 1930s; the second, in Mexican American south Texas in our own time. Both have fascinating linkages to Faulkner. *El Gallo* was "based upon an extended treatment developed and written by the Mexican novelist, Juan Rulfo," who is closely associated with Faulkner. The script was written by the director Roberto Galvandón, with none other than Gabriel García Márquez and Carlos Fuentes.[50] Guillermo Arriaga, the screenwriter for *The Three Burials*, "consistently cites William Faulkner as the inspiration for his work," while this film's director and lead actor was Tommy Lee Jones, who "tried to develop an adaptation of Faulkner as his first directorial project."[51]

Intriguing though they are, Carlson eschews such biographical linkages. Instead, drawing on Wayne Booth's concept of an "implied author," he asks how these films "produce a Faulknerian world that lets us construct an implied Faulknerian author?" Based on the commonalities of Greater Mexico and the South noted in this essay, Carlson reads *El Gallo* in terms of its plot and style as it renders an early twentieth-century rural Mexican society struggling between feudalism and modernity much as Faulkner's South was. As such, the film's *"implied Faulkner"* is "most closely related to that of the Snopes stories and novels."[52] *The Three Burials* deals with the accidental killing in Texas of an illegal Mexican worker, Melquiades, and with the effort of a Texas cowboy to take him back to Mexico for burial. Carlson sees an explicit connection between Melquiades and Joe Christmas. If Joe is "an ambiguous figure looking for his place within Mississippi of the 1930s . . . Melquiades is a man trying to find a life in the isolated ranching world of south Texas," a man "whose past," like Joe's, "becomes less clear as it is incrementally revealed." Moreover, "the characters and events are further rendered Faulknerian by the film's principles of plot. The structures of both *Absalom, Absalom!* and *As I Lay Dying* inform the plotting of *The Three Burials*."[53] The continuity of the historical crisis between the US South and Greater Mexico thus "calls forth the Faulkner who struggled with the narrative forms for the chaos of Southern history and its legacy of massive displacement of peoples," problems that, I may add, also characterized Greater Mexico's engendering by this same South. Fittingly, then, the region's artists now enlist Faulkner's assistance in making sense of their own crisis.[54]

In the foregoing I have attempted to connect Faulkner's project and its geography to what I have called Greater Mexico by two routes: first, by showing how Greater Mexico was created by the Southern-led incursion into Texas and then the rest of the Southwest, an incursion that led irrevocably to the Civil War and its consequences for the South, which became the stuff of Faulkner's fiction; and second, by proposing that this fiction has been of great service as a model for certain writers and filmmakers of Greater Mexico as they record and interpret the vicissitudes of the region's encounter with the United States by way of the South. I now present one final closing comment. If the US South indeed bears some historical responsibility for Mexico's nineteenth- and early twentieth-century social crisis, I would further argue that the crisis continues into the present day, as witness the large numbers of Mexican immigrants coming into the United States. But those residing in the South are now living out a fascinating historical irony. The continuing crisis in Mexico, in conjunction with changes in US regional economies outside the South, is now producing unprecedented levels of Mexican immigration into the states of the Old South. At some historical distance the Old South is now reaping what it once sowed, inasmuch as there is a relatively straight line from the instability and disorder that the South helped to create in Greater Mexico in 1846–47 to the current instability and disorder in national Mexico today that have produced such emigration from that beleaguered country. The reaction of the South—white and black—to immigration from Mexico is now producing a complex and fascinating conundrum of history, race, economics, politics, and culture perhaps on a par with that which Faulkner inherited and made narratively memorable for us in his time.

Who will speak to us imaginatively of this new world in today's South? In one of my critical fantasies, I sometimes wonder if out there somewhere, in Tuscaloosa, Raleigh, Macon, or better yet, Oxford, Mississippi, there might be a Mexican youngster, born of immigrant parents and raised in the South in our time. Such a young person may already be trying to imagine such a US Southern–Greater Mexican world in fiction; perhaps after reading *Light in August* in an English class at Ole Miss; perhaps first mouthing the words to such a story in a Southern-inflected English but also with a slight Spanish accent, before committing them to writing; perhaps, while still a novice writer, initially imagining a pregnant Lena (for it is also a Spanish name) García coming up Highway 278 from Mexico into Mississippi looking for her meandering immigrant husband,

Lucas (a Spanish name as well). "I have come from Zacatecas: *muy lejos*. All the way from Zacatecas *a pied*." Or, like Faulkner, perhaps this maturing writer will later creatively shape materials from real life such as the ethnographic report from anthropologist David Sandell that tells us about a Mexican immigrant who lost his life in the deserts of Arizona and about his family's mourning in Mexico. Looking for a new beginning, his distraught widow in Mexico decided to emigrate to Georgia.[55] Given the vexed history between the US South and Greater Mexico, such a writer and such writing would be the most poetic justice. I hope she is out there.

NOTES

My great appreciation goes to Ms. Mary Buechler at the University of Notre Dame for her invaluable research assistance for this essay.

1. Richard H. King, "Allegories of Imperialism: Globalizing Southern Studies," *American Literary History* 23 (2011): 153. King also comments, however, that "Jeff Karem shrewdly corrects the critical emphasis upon Haiti when he notes that Faulkner's treatment of the events there is 'overdetermined and underrepresented' (162). It is, to be sure, a 'capacious symbolic reserve' (163), but the lack of specificity and murkiness of the passage means that it can hardly bear the historical or political importance claimed by Faulkner critics" (153). Quotations and page numbers from Jeff Karem refer to his "Fear of a Black Atlantic? African Passages in *Absalom, Absalom!* and *The Last Slaver*," in *Global Faulkner: Faulkner and Yoknapatawpha, 2006*, ed. Annette Trefzer and Ann J. Abadie (Jackson: University Press of Mississippi, 2009), 162–73.

2. See Part 3, "William Faulkner and Latin America," in *Look Away! The U.S. South in New World Studies*, ed. Jon Smith and Deborah Cohn (Durham: Duke University Press, 2004), 311–449; Deborah Cohn, "The Case of the Fabricated Past: Invented Information and the Problems of Reconstructing the Past in *Absalom, Absalom!* and *The Real Life of Alejandro Mayta*," in *History and Memory in the Two Souths: Recent Southern and Spanish American Fiction* (Nashville: Vanderbilt University Press, 1999), 45–93; and Cohn, "'He Was One of Us': The Reception of William Faulkner and the U.S. South by Latin American Authors," *Comparative Literature Studies* 34 (1997): 149–69.

3. Américo Paredes, *A Texas-Mexican Cancionero: Folksongs of the Lower Border* (Urbana-Champaign: University of Illinois Press, 1976), xiv.

4. José R. López-Morín, *The Legacy of Américo Paredes* (College Station: Texas A&M University Press, 2006); Ramón Saldívar, *The Borderlands of Culture: Américo Paredes and the Transnational Imaginary* (Durham: Duke University Press, 2006); Manuel F. Medrano, *Américo Paredes: In His Own Words, an Authorized Biography* (Denton: University of North Texas Press, 2010); and José E. Limón, *Américo Paredes: Culture and Critique* (Austin: University of Texas Press, 2012).

5. Leigh Anne Duck, "Race, Labor, and Hispanic Migration in *Light in August*," in *William Faulkner y el Mundo Hispanico: Dialogos Desde el Otro Sur*, ed. Beatriz Vegh and Eleonora Basso (Montevideo: Libreria Linarde y Risso, 2008), 61.

6. José E. Limón, *American Encounters: Greater Mexico, the United States, and the Erotics of Culture* (Boston: Beacon Press, 1998), 7–14.

7. Clement Eaton, *A History of the Old South* (New York: Macmillan, 1949), 367.

8. Ibid., 346.

9. Gene Dattel, *Cotton and Race in the Making of America: The Human Costs of Economic Power* (Chicago: Ivan R. Dee Publishers, 2009), 83.

10. K. Jack Bauer, *The Mexican War, 1846–1848* (Lincoln: University of Nebraska Press, 1992).

11. Eaton, 365–66.

12. Joseph Blotner, *William Faulkner: A Biography*, 2 vol. (New York: Random House, 1974), 1:23–28.

13. Robert Cantwell, "The Faulkners: Recollections of a Gifted Family," in *Conversations with William Faulkner*, ed. M. Thomas Inge (Jackson: University Press of Mississippi, 1999), 30–41.

14. Blotner, 24.

15. Eaton, 365–66.

16. William Faulkner, *Light in August:* The Corrected Text (New York: Random House, 1990), 242.

17. Ibid., 243–47

18. Ibid., 247.

19. André Bleikasten, *"Light in August:* The Closed Society and Its Subjects," in *New Essays on "Light in August,"* ed. Michael Millgate (New York: Cambridge University Press, 1987), 85.

20. Duck, 62.

21. Andrew F. Rolle, *The Lost Cause: The Confederate Exodus to Mexico* (Norman: University of Oklahoma Press, 1992), 92–99.

22. Noel Polk, *Faulkner's "Requiem for a Nun": A Critical Study* (Bloomington: Indiana University Press, 1981), 186.

23. Faulkner, 373–76.

24. Ramón Saldívar, "Looking for a Master Plan: Faulkner, Paredes, and the Colonial and Postcolonial Subject," in *The Cambridge Companion to William Faulkner*, ed. Philip M. Weinstein (New York: Cambridge University Press, 1995), 117; John T. Matthews, "This Race Which Is Not One: The 'More Inextricable Compositeness' of William Faulkner's South," in *Look Away! The U.S. South in New World Studies*, 201–26.

25. Neil Foley, *The White Scourge: Mexicans, Blacks, and Poor Whites in Texas Cotton Culture* (Berkeley: University of California Press, 1997), 23.

26. Jerry Don Thompson, *Vaqueros in Blue and Gray* (Austin: Presidio Press, 1976), 26. Thompson adds that Mexicans from Texas also fought in Texas itself, both for the Confederacy and for the Union, reminding us in turn of another irony: the last battle of the Civil War—whose ending brought us Faulkner's world—was fought in Mexican South Texas near Palmito Ranch, one of the places that Zachary Taylor's troops had crossed as they invaded internal Mexico in 1846.

27. Mark Reisler, *By the Sweat of Their Brow: Mexican Immigrant Labor in the United States, 1900–1940* (Westport: Greenwood Press, 1976), 151–69.

28. Duck, 65.

29. Ibid.

30. William Spratling and William Faulkner, *Sherwood Anderson and Other Famous Creoles* (New Orleans: Pelican Press, 1926).

31. Blotner, 379.

32. Julie M. Weise, "Mexican Nationalisms, Southern Racisms: Mexicans and Mexican Americans in the U.S. South, 1908–1939," *American Quarterly* 60 (2008): 753, 759–60.

33. http://www.tamaletrail.com/introduction.shtml. In *The Awakening*, however, Kate Chopin records the presence of Mexicans and tamales in New Orleans in the late nineteenth century through her character Adele Ratignolle. See Chopin, *The Awakening and Other Writings*, ed. Suzanne L. Disheroon, Barbara C. Ewell, Pamela Glenn Menke, and Susie Seifres (Buffalo: Broadview Press, 2011), 85.

34. Américo Paredes, *George Washington Gómez: A Mexico-Texan Novel* (Houston: Arte Público Press, 1990).

35. Saldívar, "Looking for a Master Plan," 96–120.

36. Mark Busby, "Faulknerian Elements in Rolando Hinojosa's *The Valley*," *Melus* 11 (1984): 103–9.

37. The entire series of Hinojosa's novels is called *The Klail City Death Trip Series*. See *Rites and Witnesses* (Houston: Arte Público Press, 1982); *The Valley* (Tempe: Bilingual Press, 1983); *Dear Rafe* (Houston: Arte Público Press, 1985); *Partners in Crime* (Houston: Arte Público Press, 1985); *The Useless Servants* (Houston: Arte Público Press, 1993); and *Ask a Policeman* (Houston: Arte Público Press, 1998).

38. Gabriel García Márquez, "The Mysteries of Bill Clinton," http://www.salon.com/news/1999/02/cov_02news.html.

39. Ibid.

40. Wendy Faris, "Southern Economies of Excess: Narrative Expenditure in William Faulkner and Carlos Fuentes," in *Look Away! The U.S. South in New World Studies*, 311–32.

41. Ibid., 334.

42. Ibid., 335.

43. Ibid., 336.

44. Erik Hage, *Cormac McCarthy: A Literary Companion* (Jefferson, N.C.: McFarland & Company, 2010), 124.

45. Harold Bloom, *The Anxiety of Influence* (New Haven: Yale University Press, 1973).

46. Wade Hall and Rick Wallach, eds., *Sacred Violence: A Reader's Companion to Cormac McCarthy* (El Paso: Texas Western Press, 1995).

47. Hage, 11.

48. David Holloway, *The Late Modernism of Cormac McCarthy* (Westport, Conn.: Greenwood Press, 2002); Lawrence A. Schwartz, *Creating Faulkner's Reputation: The Politics of Modern Literary Criticism* (Knoxville: University of Tennessee Press, 1988).

49. McCarthy's *Border Trilogy* includes *All the Pretty Horses* (New York: Random House, 1992), *The Crossing* (New York: Vintage Books, 1995), and *Cities of the Plain* (New York: Vintage Books, 1999)

50. Jerry W. Carlson, "William Faulkner in the Light of Mexican Film," in *William Faulkner y el Mundo Hispanico: Dialogos Desde el Otro Sur*, ed. Beatriz Vegh and Eleonora Basso (Montevideo: Libreria Linarde y Risso, 2008), 23.

51. Ibid., 24.

52. Ibid., 27.

53. Ibid., 28–29.

54. Ibid., 31.

55. David P. Sandell, "Where Mourning Takes Them: Migrants, Borders, and an Alternative Reality," *Ethos: Journal of the Society for Psychological Anthropology* 38 (2010): 179–204.

Thomas Sutpen's Geography Lesson: Environmental Obscurities and Racial Remapping in Faulkner's *Absalom, Absalom!*

RYAN HERYFORD

The design that will later entail Sutpen's Hundred begins with a geography lesson, or lack thereof. In a "one-room country school in a nest of Tidewater plantations"[1] Thomas Sutpen's teacher reads to the class from a book on Haiti and other Caribbean nations: "That was how I learned of the West Indies. Not where they were, though if I had known at the time that that knowledge would someday serve me, I would have learned that too. What I learned was that there was a place called the West Indies to which poor men went in ships and became rich, it didn't matter how, so long as that man was clever and courageous."[2] Geography, or the "where they were" of points within and outside one's own frame of reference, is obscured within the semiotic systems by which the Caribbean islands were represented to those inhabiting the industrialized metropolises and tidewater plantations of the United States. Haiti, as translated through the geographically impoverished narratives of Thomas Sutpen, becomes located not by latitudinal coordinates but by a colonialist cartography, symbolically mapped as a "spot of earth which might have been created and set aside by Heaven itself . . . as a theatre for violence and injustice and bloodshed and all the satanic lusts of human greed and cruelty, for the last despairing fury of all the pariah-interdict and all the doomed."[3]

Ironically, the apocalyptic rhetoric used to define and locate Sutpen's Haiti is not too dissimilar from popular ecological depictions of the US South throughout the nineteenth and twentieth centuries. By 1867 a malaria-ridden John Muir had already begun to cast "the border which sweeps from Maryland to Texas" within a diseased topography of fevers and plagues: "The world, we are told, was made especially for man—a presumption not supported by all the facts. . . . But when man betakes himself to sickly parts of the tropics and perishes, he cannot see that he was never intended for such deadly climates. No, he will rather accuse the first mother of the cause of the difficulty, though she may never have seen a fever district; or will consider it a providential chastisement for some self-invented form of sin."[4] If climates, ecologies, and theological renderings alone could usurp and reenvision the boundaries of the nation-state—and the Southern United States does share just as many ecogeographic traits with the Caribbean islands as with its Northern neighbors—both Haiti and Yoknapatawpha County might potentially be remapped together on one side of what Amy Kaplan refers to as the geopolitical "distinction between images of the 'jungle' and 'wilderness,'" their ecologies and climates contained within a more expansive Global South.[5]

The jungle, as an incorporative concept of place, would speak not only to the shared ecological and geographic attributes of the Global South but to the common histories of exploitation, slavery, reconstruction, and military occupation that worked in part to define Haiti and Mississippi throughout the nineteenth and twentieth centuries. Both the historical narrative within *Absalom, Absalom!* and the events contemporary with its publication were embedded in myriad historical specificities particular to and incorporative of each locale. The story of Sutpen's Hundred, built and sustained by the labor acquired through a transatlantic voyage, and collapsing not long after the official conclusion to the Reconstruction of the southern United States, was simultaneously interpreted by an American readership immersed in news surrounding the 1915–1934 US occupation of Haiti, where certain technologies of antebellum plantation violence and military paternalism were exported from the US South and into presumably independent nations throughout the Caribbean.[6] The Global South thus figures into Faulkner's novel as a multilayered palimpsest where prerevolutionary Haitian sugarcane plantations, the antebellum South, military-based Reconstruction, and the twentieth-century occupation of Haiti are all condensed and conflated into a Judeo-Christian fable of the hemispheric jungle, its providential chastising, its exploitation, and its eventual collapse.

Yet to situate Yoknapatawpha County and Haiti within this homogenizing geography ignores the racially coded divides separating the wilderness from the jungle. Indeed, if such distinctions are to exist, they are determined by ideology and not ecology. The wilderness, as a signifying frontier of white masculinity, is often premised upon its contrasting binary, what Kaplan more specifically calls "the enervated 'barbaric tropic' marked by its unspoken connotations of blackness."[7] Race and its ideological constructs, as Thomas Sutpen learns on his voyages throughout both the Caribbean and the Southern United States, are far more determinative of Western cartography than any shared ecologies, histories, or geographic proximities.

Racial mapping, as a practice that supplants other modes of geographic organization, not only pertains to divides at the hemispheric level, but codes and contextualizes the more intimate geographies of nations, states, cities, towns, and even families. From genealogical geographies of racial miscegenation and antebellum lineage, to the de jure segregation of post-Reconstruction Jim Crow cities, to what Mary Renda refers to as "Woodrow Wilson's wholly racialized vision of liberal internationalism"[8] wherein diplomatic racism structured a nation's, and an individual's, potential for self-determination, race becomes the imperial mapmakers' primary tool in exercising sovereignty. It is likewise an ontological exercise, as concerned with various peoples' mappings of their place in space as it is with the cartographic construction of the subjects themselves.

Thomas Sutpen's geography lesson then comes not from the abstract and obscured passages read in his one-room Tidewater schoolhouse, but through our own narrative recapitulations of the conflated routes by which he traveled. Geographic knowledge—to the slaveholder, the occupying marine, the imperial entrepreneur—is an active process of constant disassembly and remapping, wherein the Global South, its jungles, and its wildernesses are determined not by latitudinal degrees but through racist technologies of violence and the production of both sovereign subjects and life stripped bare, made base and expendable: what Giorgio Agamben refers to as *homo sacer*, and perhaps more appropriately, what Achille Mbembe calls the necropolitical subject, whose agency and voice, born as they are within the banality of everyday violent acts, must find alternate means and modalities for expression, outside and apart from the confines of social and civil death.[9] It is this ontological path that I hope to chart as I, in my own right as a reader of *Absalom, Absalom!*, attempt to reconstruct and narrate the map of Faulkner's Caribbean.

The story of Thomas Sutpen's journey to acquire the slave labor necessary for his design is premised on the disavowal and abstraction of temporal movement through and between actual geographic coordinates within the Global South. As General Compson remembers, there was "no more detail and information about that than about how he got from the field, his overseeing, into the besieged house when the niggers rushed at him with their machetes, than how he got from the rotting cabin in Virginia to the fields he oversaw."[10] This strategic refusal to contextualize these distinct and specific places within a sequential travel narrative allows Sutpen's listeners to imagine the "rotting cabin in Virginia" and the Caribbean "fields he oversaw" as both one and the same, providing the necessary overlaps that could arguably explain many of the tale's inconsistencies and seeming impossibilities. Indeed, this conflation of both space and time opens the possibilities for not only a cartographic but a chronological recomposition of the Caribbean voyage. The absence overlaying the geographic particularities in Sutpen's journey is matched, for instance, by a historical ambiguity that exposes certain contradicting discrepancies between Sutpen's conveyed dates and the actual history of Haiti as an independent nation.

According to the timeline of the novel, Sutpen's single-handed suppression of the plantation revolt occurred in or around 1824. This event, however, would have happened twenty years after the Revolution and subsequent declaration of Haiti as an independent nation. By 1824, the year of Sutpen's profiteering in the West Indies, Haiti was under the leadership of President Jean Pierre Boyer, who had unified and asserted complete authority over the previously divided island. It was during this time that Boyer freed all remaining slaves in Santo Domingo. It was also in September of this same year that the American Colonization Society attempted to arrange for the transportation of 6,000 free African Americans from the United States to Haiti. By the early 1820s white ownership of any land in Haiti was both legally disallowed and culturally stigmatized.[11] While Boyer's presidency did institute the Code Rural, a law designed to tie formerly enslaved peasant laborers to plantation land by denying them certain rights of mobility, Sutpen's account, which explicitly implies slave revolts and the transnational dealing of peoples as commodities, is, if not entirely inaccurate, at least suggestive of the possibility that these particular historical discrepancies might beg for a reading of Sutpen's time in Haiti as an *impossible journey*.[12]

The obscurations and misrepresentations of geographic place and historical dates have often been interpreted via Faulkner's interest in cyclical versus linear models of time, narrative, and history. The possibilities that cyclical history might disassemble and replace dominant Western teleology are embraced by many of Faulkner's narrators who employ tactics of repetition as a means for unearthing deeper historical truths. As illustrated most vividly in a passage spoken by Quentin Compson, it becomes clear that the history of *Absalom, Absalom!* cannot be contained within a chronological trajectory of specific dates and locales but is transient and repetitive, a specter that continues to haunt contradictions left unresolved: "Maybe nothing ever happens once and is finished. Maybe happen is never once but like ripples maybe on water after the pebble sinks, the ripples moving on, spreading, the pool attached by a narrow umbilical water-cord to the next pool which the first pool feeds, has fed, did feed, let this second pool contain a different temperature of water, a different molecularity of having seen, felt, remembered, reflect in a different tone the infinite unchanging sky, it doesn't matter."[13] Quentin's tone, which shifts from an intricate allegorical articulation of historical understanding to near-abstract nihilism, opens up theoretical conversations concerning narrative time at the same moment that it forecloses possibilities for historical distinction and revolutionary agency. Indeed, repetition, like geographic abstraction, when treated as uninterruptible and unchanging, neglects the power of particularities to reveal historical injustice and alternative means for resistance and sociopolitical reimagining. Quentin's unchanging sky, while aiding in a cross-historic, hemispheric critique of national narratives, ignores the fracturing power of events like the Haitian Revolution, as well as the very real diasporic movements of imperial investments and forced passages wherein both "poor men went in ships and became rich"[14] and human beings from Africa were violently reshaped into transatlantic commodities.

This fluid state of retelling, that which presumes at its very center some unchanged primordial truth, or absence of truth, is subsequently bound to the contemporary perspectives of both its narrators and audiences. Constantly interpreted via the outward ripple in the pond, Thomas Sutpen's voyage depends on both his storyteller's and his story listener's capacity for narrative reconstruction: "He went to the West Indies. That's how he said it: not how he managed to find where the West Indies were nor where ships departed from to go there, nor how he got to where the ships were and got in one nor how he liked the sea nor about the hardships of a sailor's life and it must have been hardship indeed for him, a boy of fourteen or fifteen who had never seen the ocean before, going to sea in 1823."[15] The journey, as a projected linear and temporal movement through abstract space, depends entirely on our ascertained historical imperatives and certainties, on our ability to discern what it *must* have been like. Faulkner's history of the Global South and its relative geographies are thus part of a reconstruction project relying on the historical and geographic imaginations of *Absalom, Absalom!*'s many narrators, as well as the dominant readership base for the novel itself, readers who, like Faulkner, were immersed in their own contemporary narratives regarding Haiti and the United States.

Published in 1936, *Absalom, Absalom!* was first read by a US audience at the close of a full-scale military occupation that saw, by official US estimates, more than 3,000 Haitians killed—and, by a more thorough and recent historical accounting, over 6,000.[16] Haiti, as a space for the exercising of violent paternalist discourse and US imperial sensibilities, served both as a stepping stone in what Barbara Ladd refers to as "new nationalism," the shift from a "reunion of North and South after Reconstruction to the ideological rhetoric of Empire building,"[17] and a romanticized backdrop by which these new "nationals" could picture themselves on a modern, imagined map of global circulations and imperial designs. As Mary Renda has documented in her detailed work on the culture of military imperialism in occupied Haiti:

> The United States encouraged not only marines but others as well to see themselves as benefactors helping out a needy, if recalcitrant, child. . . . Popular narratives that sensationalized Haiti and positioned readers as voyeurs in an exotic land made that move all the more appealing. In this sense, sensational narratives reinforced official discourses and strengthened their ability to conscript ordinary citizens into the logic of empire. Together, popular and official discourses invited U.S. Americans to adopt an imperial perspective and fueled public fascination with Haiti as one means to that end.[18]

By the 1930s Haiti had become not only a site of military occupation but an exoticized travel destination that formed a crucial part of US Americans' sense of the global exterior to their home empire. Best-selling texts like William Seabrook's *The Magic Island* (1929), John Vandercook's *Black Majesty* (1928), Blair Nile's *Black Haiti: A Biography of Africa's Eldest Daughter* (1926), and Edna Taft's *A Puritan in Voodoo-Land* (1938) provided pulp accounts of the authors' voyages through a country contextualized by scenes of fetishized abjection and possibilities for new and contrasting definitions of white Northern subjectivity. The subjective agency that came with this new geographic imagination mapped Haiti not only as a "colony" within a wide-reaching US military presence but as a locatable point in the American middle-class formation of a modern, internationalist geography. Haiti, as portrayed by marines, journalists, and bourgeois travelers, was a space of both primordial perversity and capitalist possibility, where white American men and women could depict and embellish representations of the black Haitian Other as both a sexual grotesque and an irrational child in their paternalistic, global family structure.

This self-fashioning of white US identity via the ideological mapping of Haiti as "a theatre for violence"[19] had its roots both in the contemporary anxieties of an early twentieth-century Jim Crow empire and in the former slaveholding society's interpretation of postrevolutionary black nation-states. As Alfred N. Hunt notes, the varying means by which plantation owners distorted and manipulated postindependence Haiti to reaffirm their beliefs regarding distinctions between the races falsified and mythologized an entire century's worth of national history and geopolitical understanding. Hunt claims that "Southerners looked to Haiti more than to the northern states to evaluate what freedom meant to blacks."[20] Indeed, Haiti was not simply a peripheral aberration in the racist narratives of antebellum slave society but a crucial focal point, hotly contested and debated for a symbolic value so significant, according to Hunt, that "the southern interpretation of the Haitian Revolution and the way it was used strongly suggest one of the reasons why it took a civil war to emancipate the slaves."[21]

This interpretation of Haiti as a failed experiment in black liberation persisted throughout the US South and North well into the twentieth century, arguably forming both the ideological roots of the 1915–1934 occupation and, for US African Americans seeking to document and address the violence committed in both the supremacist domestic state and the transnational empire, a point of protest and critical reflection upon the colonialist roots of Woodrow Wilson's so-called noninterventionist state. By the 1920s both US and internationalist newspapers like the *Nation* and *L'Union Patriotique*, as well as major African American organizations like the NAACP, called out actively in opposition to the occupation as a racialized US imperial war, recasting the official state narrative as a continuation of the Jeffersonian response to Haitian liberation. Throughout the 1920s and '30s well-known authors, poets, and playwrights journeyed to Haiti both in political protest against US occupation and in search of ethnographic understandings and cultural connections. James Weldon Johnson's "Self-Determining Haiti" (1920), Zora Neale Hurston's *Tell My Horse: Voodoo and Life in Haiti and Jamaica* (1938), Langston Hughes's "A People without Shoes: The Haitian Masses" (1934), and Eugene O'Neill's *The Emperor Jones* (1920) each voiced, albeit through varying degrees and tactics, a desire to place political concerns of the present in dialogue with a nineteenth-century history highlighting the Haitian Revolution as a nexus in postslavery diasporic struggles.

Central to both the state justifications for the violence committed throughout the US occupation and the subversions and protests against such imperial rhetoric was the construction of historical parallels that situated Haiti neither as an independently locatable nation-state nor as an indistinguishable point in the all-incorporative southern hemisphere but as an ideologically mapped zone of interpolation whose contours were drawn not by the Haitians themselves but by the sociocultural renderings of white and black Americans. Thomas Sutpen's geography lesson is, of course, not exempt from this US project of remapping and rewriting the historical contexts for Haiti. The lesson, in this sense, is not an isolated or passive one, implanted upon the innocence of one young man through schoolteachers and transatlantic journeys, but a transgenerational praxis that Sutpen passes on to Faulkner's readers via the racially inscribed remappings of an emergent American empire.

Absalom, Absalom!'s observational depictions of the Haitian landscape

and the abstract and disorienting violence that leads up to the plantation
revolts and leaves young Thomas Sutpen in a state of confused ambiguity, firing his rifle "at no enemy but at the Haitian night itself,"[22] seem
to allow readers to demap and reconstruct Haiti as an undefined Con-
radian space of timeless American exploitation. This chaotic abstraction
is premised on the presumed "innocence" of its educationally impoverished protagonist. Yet I would argue that the process of geographic and
ecological abstraction is an intricately orchestrated one in which coordinates of both Haiti and the US South are aligned and simultaneously
distinguished along carefully crafted socio-ontological lines.[23] Indeed,
even as the text acknowledges Sutpen's inability to represent appropriately his cultural or ecological landscapes—the inability of Sutpen the
overseer to truly and accurately "see"—he is all the while figuratively
charting such landscapes as ecologically and geopolitically distinct from
Jefferson, Mississippi[24]: "not knowing that what he rode upon was a volcano, hearing the air tremble and throb at night with the drums and
the chanting and not knowing that it was the heart of the earth itself he
heard, who believed . . . that earth was kind and gentle and that darkness
was merely something you saw, or could not see in; overseeing what he
oversaw and not knowing that he was overseeing it, making his daily
expeditions from an armed citadel until the day itself came."[25] Sutpen's
absolution in "not knowing" presupposes that these observations, free
from any knowledge or understanding that would otherwise infect them,
might stand pure and unbiased. And yet the metaphorical language he
uses—while there are volcanoes in Saba, Guadeloupe, Dominica, Martinique, St. Lucia, and Grenada, there are none in Haiti or the Dominican
Republic—situates the island within an abstract and generalized ecological geography additionally mapped by ethnically coded coordinates
apart from US South. Expressed through certain cultural traits—"drums
and chanting"—percussive music in Haiti is disengaged from its historical roots and circumscribed within "the heart of the earth itself,"
an organic, primordial circumscription that privileges moral, theological
renditions of the Haitian Revolution over its importance for modern
politics and Western philosophy. Yet for Sutpen the plantation hand, the
transnational entrepreneur, and the ersatz marine, *seeing* is not about
accurate representations or understanding of the space and culture that
one inhabits. Rather, *seeing*, like overseeing, is a matter of controlling
the situation and the people themselves. It is of no import for Thomas
Sutpen to acknowledge that there are no volcanoes on the island of His-
paniola, that there is a cultural code and historical context rooted in the
percussive chants, that slavery was abolished twenty years prior to his
arrival on the island. Sutpen's responsibility lies not in understanding

the ecologies or communities defining the space he exploits. Rather, he is responsible only for a violent maintenance and control over those conflated communities and spaces when the inherent conflicts make themselves most vividly present. Any contradictions that might arise will be remedied by the racially coded environment, their claims and testimonies removed from the political sphere and contained neatly within that imaginary volcano upon which he rode.

This simultaneous interplay of historical demapping and figurative remapping opens further possibilities for a mythologized portrait of Haiti, subject to white interpolation and the paternalist narrative of implicit US achievement. Just as the chronology and ecological depictions of Sutpen's Haiti are irreconcilable to the actual nation-state, so too do Sutpen's "super-human" feats inherently contradict the historical narrative of independence. In an almost biblical portrayal of white biological divinity, Thomas Sutpen's suppression of the plantation uprising in the West Indies is, I would argue, a racially inscribed rewriting of the Haitian Revolution itself:

> On the eighth night the water gave out and something had to be done so he put the musket down and went out and subdued them. . . . He just put the musket down and had someone unbar the door and then bar it behind him, and walked out into the darkness and subdued them, maybe by yelling louder, maybe by standing, bearing more than they believed any bones and flesh could or should (should, yes: that would be a terrible thing: to find flesh to stand more than flesh should be asked to stand); maybe at last they themselves turning in horror and fleeing from the white arms and legs shaped like theirs and from which blood could be made to spurt and flow as it could from theirs and containing an indomitable spirit which should have come from the same primary fire which theirs came from but which could not have, could not possibly have.[26]

Thomas Sutpen's suppression of the plantation revolt comes not from military technologies, economic privileges, or accessibility to the necessary resources but from an "indomitable spirit" that is given material and historical grounding through the narrative recapitulation of otherwise unbelievable events. The notion that "on the eighth night the water gave out and something had to be done" sets up the premise for a retelling of the biblical Genesis wherein Thomas Sutpen, acting as the Israelite god, makes the Haitian world anew. The paternalist discourse driving the narrative, which Mary Renda suggests "should not be seen in opposition to violence, but rather as one among several cultural vehicles for it,"[27] situates Haiti in a primordial history where white inheritance and black disability constitute the making not only of the social world but of an ontological one in which white subjectivity suppresses blackness for the sustenance and survival of its own excessiveness. Thomas Sutpen's struggle, then, is not a historical one fought against Haitian nationals seeking to drive out foreign plantation owners but a violent forging of the Judeo-Christian narrative in the occupied Caribbean.

This biopolitical cartography, in which the excessiveness of civil society is premised upon the remapping of various "hearts of darkness," calls back to an Enlightenment discourse regarding concepts of the human, where the Cartesian thinking subject was premised upon its asocial Other, the body of the slave. Sylvia Wynter refers to this ontological genealogy as the "coloniality of being," wherein "the West's new master code of rational/irrational nature was now to be mapped onto a projected Chain of Being of organic forms of life, organized about a line drawn between, on the one hand, divinely created-to-be-rational humans, and on the other, no less divinely created-to-be-irrational animals; that is, on what was still adaptively known through the classical discipline of 'natural history' as a still supernaturally determined and created 'objective set of facts.'"[28] As Wynter notes, Western subjectivity, as a conceptual category emerging within eighteenth-century Europe, was always already premised upon an ontological narrative that mythologized the various colonies upon whose goods and resources thinkers like Locke and Voltaire would come to rely. That the Haitian Revolution emerged less than a century after these conversations regarding political man, fundamental rights, and presumed states of nature, revealing the racist contradictions embedded in each, deems it, as Michel-Rolph Trouillot points out, an "unthinkable history" for the West.[29] As Trouillot, Susan Buck-Morrs, Joan (aka Colin) Dayan, and other scholars of nineteenth-century Haiti have noted, the fundamental fact of a successful slave rebellion and anticolonial revolution in Saint Domingue, the wealthiest colony in the Americas, belies the binary narratives of teleological European man and the ahistorical African that have served as the basis of Western philosophical thought from Hobbes to Hegel.[30] Thomas Sutpen's suppression of the plantation revolt and William Faulkner's suppression of the first successful slave revolution in the New World can likewise be subsumed within a larger genealogy of silencing constituting the ideological dimensions for Haiti in 1804, 1824, 1936, and still continuing within our own historical and philosophical discourse today, with the belief that the tenets of liberal Enlightenment thought will be upheld and untainted so long as we forget to mention what was arguably the most important and necessary revolution of the nineteenth century.

By charting a path epistemologically aligned with the jungle-wilderness binaries of colonial cartography, in which particular parts of the globe are deemed inhabitable *only* by bodies void of reason and agency, Thomas Sutpen not only dismisses the Haitian Revolution but remaps it, or *de-maps* it, as a place outside and away from history. Standing as a no place of imperial exploitation, Haiti is not merely determined by the sovereign subjectivities of "civil society" but becomes one of the very foundations upon which they rest. It not only provided and continues to provide the material conditions necessary for the function of countries like the United States (from sugarcane to assembly shops) but stands as an ideological counterpoint to the overdetermined subjectivities present there. It is thus cognitively mapped by US Americans as any and all points resting outside and apart from their own perceived boundaries of sociopolitical community.

And yet, as Thomas Sutpen learns even prior to the inspirations for his journey and design, such ideological technologies of racial violence and ontological coding are not born from the late colonial project alone but have roots in the earlier, more intimate geographies of "civil society" itself. For it was not on his journey to Haiti but during his childhood movement from the mountains of West Virginia to the rural communities of the slave-holding South that young Thomas Sutpen learned of

> a country all divided and fixed and neat with a people living on it all divided and fixed and neat because of what color their skins happened to be and what they happened to own, and where a certain few men not only had the power of life and death and barter and sale over others, they had living human men to perform the endless repetitive personal offices such as pouring the very whiskey from the jug and putting the glass into his hand or pulling off his boots for him to go to bed that all men have had to do for themselves since time began and would have to do until they died and which no man ever has or ever will like to do but which no man that he knew had ever anymore thought of evading than he had thought of evading the effort of chewing and swallowing and breathing.[31]

Here we see most clearly mapped out the intimate contours of Western philosophy: the overdetermined Cartesian subject who cannot help but evade his own biology and all those others, those who must *only* chew, swallow, and breathe, and all the while serve as the very platform of (H)is being. A Global South, one that initiates conversations about hemispheric or national divides, often neglects these intimate geographies that run throughout both the greater Caribbean and the rivers and streams of Yoknapatawpha County, casting forth a topography that requires more complex and critical conversations about race prior to charting and outlining presumed geographic contours. Thomas Sutpen's journey, in this case, is not a new lesson at all but a transatlantic recognition of the very near and close, racialized violence that he and his subsequent narrators have and will continue to negotiate throughout the Global and local South(s).

In his seminal work *The Location of Culture*, Homi Bhabha defines the colonial fetish as that which "represents the simultaneous play between metaphor as substitution (masking absence and difference) and metonymy (which contiguously registers the perceived lack)."[32] For Thomas Sutpen and all those who tell his tale, the young man's journey embeds itself as a lesson wherein geography, that colonial fetish with its ability to dictate, define, and locate the coordinates of certain places, both veils the cartographic process as an unbiased means of observation and simultaneously reveals the hemispheric and intimate technologies of violence and racism inherent to its science. For Faulkner, the "umbilical water-cord"[33] that universally connects histories and hemispheres through its cyclical narrative depictions is both a mask of historical rupture and an acknowledgement of the way in which Western science has used history and cartography to contain this rupture. Quentin Compson and Shrevlin McCannon, two Harvard roommates born in entirely separate parts of the continent distinguished by geographic contours, climates, and cultural attributes, are nonetheless "joined, connected after a fashion in a sort of geographical transubstantiation by that Continental Trough, that River which runs not only through the physical land of which it is the geologic umbilical, not only runs through the spiritual lives of the beings within its scope, but is very Environment itself which laughs at degrees of latitude and temperature."[34] Here the Mississippi River, Faulkner's constantly appearing "umbilical water-cord," sets the contours for an "Environment" that is capable of surpassing specific geographic trademarks and deterministic theories of climate and culture, evoking the possibility of a new map, where primordial contours of spiritual connectivity surpass and supplant the varying degrees of latitude and longitude.

Yet when the universalizing geography of the boys' all-encompassing Eden is confronted with the specter of racial miscegenation, "Environment" quickly becomes the means by which these anxieties are contained, reassuring the boys that space is *always* produced by its sovereign subject[35]: "'I think that in time the Jim Bonds are going to conquer the western hemisphere. Of course it wont quite be in our time and of course as they spread toward the poles they will bleach out again like the rabbits and the birds do, so they wont show up so sharp against the snow.'"[36] Responding to Southern fears of a miscegenation-apocalypse, the "Environment," that "geological umbilical" which "laughs at degrees of latitude and temperature," is simultaneously a source of containment for racial rupture and indeterminism wherein the colder climates can "bleach out" certain races "like the rabbits and the birds do." Seemingly banal and disinterested discourses of geographic and ecological distinction are thus continuously employed in the maintenance of racial hegemonies, revealing the contradictions in the biopolitical project at the same time that they attempt to obscure and dismiss its violence.

What then can we learn from Thomas Sutpen's geography lesson? Certainly not an objective, coordinated account of Haiti, its sociopolitical community, or its history. Indeed, not even a geographic or ecological representation that is mildly aligned with the nation's actual landscapes or historical attributes. Rather, what we witness are the contours of a map defined by technologies of racially specified violence, developed in the antebellum US South and exported to a hemispheric South via the occupation and imperialist domination of formerly independent nations like Haiti. The latitudinal lines of this map are both global and intimate, carving spaces across entire islands in the Caribbean, rivers and fields in the Southern plantation states, and bathrooms and water fountains in the Jim Crow metropolis. It is a map that we continue to witness today, in the form of Third World zones of industry and free trade, as well as the racially coded prison-industrial complexes throughout cities of the Global North. Indeed as US popular response to the 2010 earthquake in Haiti made clear—from the blatantly racist tirades of Pat Robertson to the perhaps equally racist paternalist rhetoric of a historically disengaged news media—"the past is never dead. It's not even past."[37]

I run the risk of some overt and perhaps even irresponsible presentism here, but I cannot help, as a student of Faulkner's works and as a reader of *Absalom, Absalom!*, wanting to engage in the same narrative retellings begun by General Compson, Jason, Quentin, and Shrevlin McCannon. Might I not also imagine Thomas Sutpen's journey from some other time, some other place? Might I not recall him in December of 1929, standing alongside US marines in Les Cayes, Haiti, when ten unarmed farmers were gunned down while protesting against the occupation, bearing more than flesh should be asked to stand?[38] Might I not recall him sitting in many a university history course today, where the Haitian Revolution is still abstracted and obscured, dismissed as an offshoot of the Enlightenment philosophies developed in France, Germany, England, and the United States—and all the while, albeit via new routes of global circulation and exchange, the Caribbean remains a place where poor men go in ships and become rich? I fear that whether we choose to recognize it or not, Thomas Sutpen's journey is a story that continues to be retold in new contexts, by new narrators. The racially inscribed maps charting his route continue to surface, and the lessons learned will continue to haunt us all, so long as we fail to confront and challenge the contradictions left unresolved.

NOTES

1. William Faulkner, *Absalom, Absalom!* The Corrected Text (New York: Vintage International, 1990), 195.

2. Ibid.

3. Ibid., 202.

4. John Muir, *A Thousand-Mile Walk to the Gulf* (New York: Houghton Mifflin Company, 1916), 136–41.

5. Amy Kaplan, "'Left Alone with America': The Absence of Empire in the Study of American Culture," in *Cultures of United States Imperialism*, ed. Kaplan and Donald Pease (Durham: Duke University Press, 1993), 3.

6. I am referring to the US occupation of Haiti by its officially designated dates. However, as embedded in both Hoover's and Roosevelt's disengagement agreements, the United States maintained direct authority over Haiti's transnational economy until 1947. I hope the reader will not consider the 1934 withdrawal of marines from Haiti as a definitive endpoint to the occupation, but recognize, as Faulkner certainly did, that dates are tricky things.

7. Kaplan, 9.

8. Mary A. Renda, *Taking Haiti: Military Occupation and the Culture of U.S. Imperialism, 1915–1940* (Chapel Hill: University of North Carolina Press, 2001), 302.

9. For more on the theories of bio- and necropolitics, see Michel Foucault's *"Society Must Be Defended": Lectures at the Collége de France, 1975–1976*, ed. Mauro Bertani, Arnold I. Davidson, Francois Ewald, and Alessandro Fontana, trans. David Macey (New York: Picador, 2003); Giorgio Agamben's *Remnants of Auschwitz: The Witness and the Archive*, trans. Daniel Heller-Roazen (New York: Zone Books, 2002); and Achille Mbembe's "Necropolitics," trans. Libby Meintjes, *Public Culture* 15.1 (2003): 11–40. I cite Mbembe's necropolitical subject as the more appropriate term here because, unlike Agamben's *homo sacer*, which emerges from extreme historical forms within civil society (such as the European concentration camp), Mbembe's subject exists in a space that is always already coded by extreme historical form (in parts of the world where concentrated violence has become the banal, daily reality).

10. Faulkner, *Absalom, Absalom!*, 201.

11. For more information on postrevolutionary Haitian history, see C. L. R. James, *The Black Jacobins: Toussaint L'Ouverture and the San Domingo Revolution*, 2nd ed. (New York: Vintage, 1989); and Laurent Dubois, *Avengers of the New World: The Story of the Haitian Revolution* (Cambridge: Belknap Press of Harvard University Press, 2005).

12. There are a number of insightful arguments regarding the conveyed dates of Sutpen's Haitian voyage that I do not have the time or space to address in this particular essay. For more information on this topic see Richard Godden, *Fictions of Labor: William Faulkner and the South's Long Revolution* (New York: Cambridge University Press, 1997); and John T. Matthews, "Recalling the West Indies: From Yoknapatawpha to Haiti and Back," *American Literary History* 16.2 (2004): 238–62.

13. Faulkner, *Absalom, Absalom!*, 210; emphasis removed.

14. Ibid., 195.

15. Ibid., 193.

16. For more information on the 1915–1940 US military occupation of Haiti and its reception both within the United States and in Haiti, see Renda.

17. Barbara Ladd, *Nationalism and the Color Line in George W. Cable, Mark Twain, and William Faulkner* (Baton Rouge: Louisiana State University Press, 1996), 148.

18. Renda, 21.

19. Faulkner, *Absalom, Absalom!*, 202.

20. Alfred N. Hunt, *Haiti's Influence on Antebellum America: Slumbering Volcano in the Caribbean* (Baton Rouge: Louisiana State University Press, 1988), 132.

21. Ibid.

22. Faulkner, *Absalom, Absalom!*, 204.

23. I am elaborating on the work begun by Jeff Karem in his essay "Fear of a Black Atlantic? African Passages in *Absalom, Absalom!* and *The Last Slaver*," in *Global Faulkner: Faulkner and Yoknapatawpha, 2006*, ed. Annette Trefzer and Ann J. Abadie (Jackson: University Press of Mississippi, 2009), 162–73.

24. For more information on the ecologies constituting Faulkner's "imagined" map of the Global South, see Matthews.

25. Faulkner, *Absalom, Absalom!*, 202–3.

26. Ibid., 205–6.

27. Renda, 15.

28. Sylvia Wynter, "Unsettling the Coloniality of Being/Power/Truth/Freedom," *CR: The New Centennial Review* 3.3 (2003): 313.

29. Michel Rolph-Trouillot, *Silencing the Past: Power and the Production of History* (Boston: Beacon Press, 1995), 95.

30. See Susan Buck-Morss, *Hegel, Haiti, and Universal History* (Pittsburgh: University of Pittsburgh Press, 2009); Sibylle Fischer, *Modernity Disavowed: Haiti and the Cultures of Slavery in the Age of Revolution* (Durham: Duke University Press, 2004); and Joan (aka Colin) Dayan, *Haiti, History, and the Gods* (Berkeley: University of California Press, 1998).

31. Faulkner, *Absalom, Absalom!*, 179–80.

32. Homi K. Bhabha, *The Location of Culture* (London: Routledge, 2004), 74–75.

33. Faulkner, *Absalom, Absalom!*, 210.

34. Ibid., 208.

35. The phrasing here intentionally signals toward the groundbreaking theoretical paradigms illustrated throughout Henri Lefebvre's *The Production of Space*, trans. David Nicholson-Smith (Oxford: Wiley-Blackwell, 1992).

36. Faulkner, *Absalom, Absalom!*, 302.

37. William Faulkner, *Requiem for a Nun*, in *William Faulkner: Novels 1942–1954*, ed. Noel Polk and Joseph Blotner (New York: Library of America, 1994), 535.

38. For more information on this and other atrocities committed during the occupation, see Benjamin R. Beede, ed., *The War of 1898 and U.S. Interventions, 1898–1934: An Encyclopedia* (Oxford: Routledge, 1994).

Faulkner's Caribbean Geographies in *Absalom, Absalom!*

VALÉRIE LOICHOT

A faraway land is a person as much as a country.[1]

Land of milk and honey, of profit and money, of fear and monstrosity, the West Indies never cease to fascinate the nineteenth-century traveler. In 1887, for instance, the Irish Greek journalist Lafcadio Hearn, living in New Orleans at the time, writes to his friend W. D. O'Connor, "I am going to run away to . . . the West Indies, for a romantic trip—a small literary bee in search of inspiring honey."[2] In 1820 Thomas Sutpen of *Absalom, Absalom!* "[runs] away from home"[3] to go to the West Indies, after learning from his teacher's book that "there was a place called the West Indies to which poor men went in ships and became rich" (195). Hearn and Sutpen's reasons to go to the West Indies could not be more disparate: the romantic Hearn travels there in search of increased emotional experience, literary and sensual, while Sutpen, devoid of all romanticism, goes there for their purely instrumental function, since "they would be most suitable to the expediency of [his] requirements" (194). Nonetheless, Hearn and Sutpen's West Indies have a lot in common. First of all, both men "run away to" them. The West Indies is a place of escape motivated by a lack in the men's current location, whether the problem is boredom for Hearn or poverty for Sutpen. The islands are not worthy for their intrinsic value but used as a remedy or treated as "adjunctive or incremental to [a] design" (194).

In addition, for both men, the archipelago is named, or rather misnamed, by the term "West Indies." The names "Caribbean" or "Antilles" would have been more suitable historically and geographically to refer to the old or former French colonies of Martinique and Haiti, the two main Caribbean sites of *Absalom*. As Barbara Ladd explains, "'West Indies' and 'Caribbean' are used synonymously by many, although for some scholars working in the field, the 'West Indies' properly speaking refers to former British holdings of the region, the 'Caribbean' to areas colonized by France and Spain."[4] In addition, the term "West Indies" is closely linked to Columbus's mistake, since the term was, to quote the French *Grand Larousse Encyclopédique*, "the name given to the New

World by Christopher Columbus who, following his first voyage, thought he had reached the oriental shores of Asia."[5] Thus the term is based on a geographical confusion. The same French encyclopedia specifies that, in French, the translation of West Indies or "Indes occidentales"—which is the term used by Faulkner's French translators—strictly refers to the "French company of the West Indies" (Compagnie française des Indes Occidentales), a trading company founded in 1664 "with a capital of 6 million pounds."[6] In a French colonial context, therefore, "West Indies" or "Indes occidentales" evokes the commercial—not the geographic—region. While the use of the term "West Indies" appears as a geographical misnaming, it is nonetheless faithful to the nature of the islands in Sutpen's mind, which is not geographic but economic. Indeed, as Sutpen specifies to his friend Compson, what he learned from his schoolteacher's book about the West Indies substituted for any formal learning of accounting: "I did not know that in that listening I was equipping myself better for what I should later design to do than if I had learned all the addition and subtraction in the book. That was how I learned of the West Indies. Not where they were" (195).

Sutpen's subsequent stay in Haiti does not reveal anything more about this nonplace called the West Indies. As John T. Matthews has skillfully shown, "Sutpen's famously preserved innocence amounts to the habit of looking without seeing."[7] This overlooking of the Haitian environment translates into a skewed vision of Caribbean geography and history, as many critics argue. Maritza Stanchich shows how Haiti is represented according to an economy of stereotypes, or rather "how it is not represented."[8] Jeff Karem asserts that Faulkner's vision of the Caribbean evades "specific 'historical knowledge,' in favor of a mythic projection of guilt that is symbolically rich but historically impoverished."[9] As Matthews specifies, the reference to Haiti is based on a gross anachronism since Haiti was independent in 1804: "No white French sugar planters remained on Haiti in 1827 [when Sutpen arrives], and all slaves had been freed" (250). Sean Latham comments on the evacuation of the Caribbean on the foldout map published with the 1936 edition of *Absalom:* "Indeed, the spaces most powerfully charged with meaning in the fictional world of *Absalom*—Kentucky [sic], Haiti, and New Orleans—are missing entirely, as if Faulkner were somehow trying to constrain the vast and terrifying reach of the novel within the imaginative lands bound by the Yoknapatawpha and Tallahatchie rivers."[10]

Despite its instrumentalization, evacuation, and misrepresentation, the presence of the Caribbean in *Absalom* has opened up a space of transatlantic dialogue, as Matthews, Ladd, Chris Bongie, George Handley, and Deborah Cohn have shown,[11] a space that J. Michael Dash has called a "New World relationality."[12] My aim in this essay is to provide an extensive view of the multifarious presence of the Caribbean in *Absalom*, not only to demonstrate how Faulkner wrote the Caribbean, but more importantly to address what, in Faulkner's work, has allowed for so many Caribbean writers to adopt the Mississippi man as one of their own.

If Faulkner's novel fails to produce a Caribbean geography as a "description of the surface of the earth" in the strict sense of the term, it nonetheless provides a multiply complex notion of the Caribbean through an incarnation of the landscape in the characters' bodies. In his compelling study of Faulkner's phenomenology, French philosopher Claude Romano argues that Faulknerian texts privilege landscape over geography. While a "geographical space is an already idealized space in which constant points are separated by fixed distances, and in which intermediate spaces are 'empty' in the sense of neutral and indifferent spaces, the space of the landscape is not made of points linked externally by objective data: it deploys itself from a 'here' in its center with a horizon that moves as I move within it."[13] It is precisely this propensity to change with the self, and particularly with the positioning or understanding of the body, that shapes the Caribbean environment in *Absalom*. Sutpen's burned skin, the wild men's mud covering, the French architect's fancy wardrobe, Eulalia Bon's elusive figure, and Charles Bon's composite self bring to the surface of the novel a buried or repressed Caribbean, otherwise skewed or evacuated from geographical representations. In her reflection on space and place in Faulkner, Ladd favors the term "place" over "space." With Edward Casey, she argues that "'place' unlike 'space' . . . 'locates things in regions whose most complete expression is neither geometric nor cartographic.' . . . The proper 'region' of place may well be the body and memory its most complete expression."[14] In this light, the characters' most external interface with the world—skin, mud, or clothing—acts as the embodiment of the Caribbean place.

The Caribbean body landscape, not yet situated geographically, first appears on the second page of the novel with the nightmarish intrusion of Sutpen and his crew abruptly emerging with thunder "upon a scene peaceful and decorous as a schoolprize water color" (4). Hearing and smell, thunder and sulfur, precede visual images, confronting us with what Romano calls "a phenomenology of feelings,"[15] which he uses to describe Benjy's primal perception of the world that precedes knowledge. In the second chapter of *Absalom*, the hellish place gets situated more precisely within a stereotypical geography of the Tropics. Sutpen, its emissary, looks like "a man who had been sick. Not like a man who had been peacefully ill in bed . . . but like a man who had been through some solitary furnace experience which was more than just fever. . . . A man . . . with a short reddish beard . . . in a face whose flesh had the appearance of pottery, of having been colored by that oven's fever either of soul or environment, deeper than sun alone beneath a dead impervious surface as of glazed clay" (24). While they are not yet named as such, we recognize in the description the furnace of the fiery Tropics, associated with both physical and moral disease in the stereotypical economy of eighteenth- and nineteenth-century philosophers and historians such as Buffon, Hegel, or Gobineau. Sutpen's disease causes "more than just fever" since immorality is added to the plain physical illness.

Sutpen is diseased, morally and physically, his skin burned, darkened in a "dishonest suntan" that contrasts with his complexion five years later. As Mr. Compson tells Quentin, "Your grandfather said that some of the faience appearance which the flesh of his face had had when he came to town five years ago was gone now and that his face had an honest sunburn. . . . It was just that the flesh on his bones had become quieter, as though passive after some actual breasting of atmosphere like in running" (36). The immoral tan is therefore dependent upon the tropical environment that acts like a hand fashioning not only skin, skeletal structure, and muscle mass but also morality. Sutpen's face is not just mud but "pottery" and "glazed clay," as if nature had acquired technological agency over the shaping of humanity. In this context, the Mississippi air possesses invigorating, healthy, and morally superior virtues, which is in sharp contrast with the idea of environmental contamination of the body and soul, also commonly attributed to the US South by the US North, as Natalie Ring has shown.[16] In this particular passage of *Absalom*, the Caribbean is instrumentalized to expel south of the South the thickness of the Mississippi air and, with it, the evils projected onto the region.

Sutpen's "wild negroes" serve a similar function of demonizing the Tropics. They appear as a huddled mass devoid of individuality, which one of the narrators terms "the absolute mud" (27). The "wild negroes" are systematically associated with animals: "like beasts half tamed to walk upright like men" (4), "like a pack of hounds" (27), "like a sleeping alligator" (27). However, when we give it a closer look, the "negro clump" is not as deprived of humanity as it seems. As the narrative unfolds, this lack of humanity or individuality is attributed to the failing perception of the town, not to the inherent qualities of Sutpen's men: "The negroes could speak no English yet and doubtless there were more than Akers who did not know that the language in which they and Sutpen communicated was a sort of French and not some dark and fatal tongue of their own" (27). The muddy sight, the ignorance, the clump is thus not that of the men but that of the "coon-hunter" Akers, who, like so many others in town ("and doubtless there were more than Akers who did not know"), fails to perceive the men's tongue as articulated language.[17] Compson—or Faulkner speaking through Compson's narrative—knows best. He describes their language, which we can assume to be Haitian Creole, as "a sort of French," demonstrating an accurate-enough linguistic consciousness for the time.[18] Compson also associates the men with a country, "a much older country than Virginia or Carolina but it wasn't a quiet one" (11). That country, in Compson's speech, acquires a stronger temporal grounding than the Southern states. The much older country is identified as Haiti in the rest of the novel. As I pointed out earlier, there is a clear anachronism in the story of Sutpen acquiring slaves in Haiti in 1827. Instead of attributing this inaccuracy to Faulkner's poor knowledge of the Caribbean,[19] I agree with John Matthews that "Sutpen's material links to the West Indies tend to be obscured by *Absalom's* narrators" (255), and I also tend to think that "a country much older than Virginia" might provide a trace of Faulkner's awareness of Haiti as an old "country" in the sense of state—the first Black Republic—and not just in the sense of land inhabited by a group of people, as in *No Country for Old Men*.[20] Armed with articulated language ("a sort of French") and a country, Sutpen's men are also equipped with survival tactics and technology. Their huddled mass is indeed a survival strategy: "they would sit in a curious quiet clump as though for mutual protection" (28). Similarly, the absolute mud, or absolute undivision, turns into a survival tool: "So [Sutpen] and the twenty negroes worked together, plastered over with mud against the mosquitoes" (28). They thus evolve throughout the narrative from a state of lack to a lack of need for such things as clothes that become superfluous and harmful, as one of the narrators subtly perceives: "during that first summer and fall the negroes did not even have (or did not use) blankets to sleep in" (27). The difference between need and absence of need presents the so-called wild men above a state of depravity and in control of the natural environment, which is not the case with another of Sutpen's Caribbean accessories, the captive French architect.

At first sight, the French architect's body is the polar opposite of the Caribbean wild men's. His first portrait in Mr. Compson's words (chapter 2) points to the complexity of his geographical belonging: "a small, alertly resigned man with a grim, harried Latin face, in a frock coat and a flowered waistcoat and a hat which would have created no furore on a Paris boulevard, all of which he was to wear constantly for the next two years. . . . This was the French architect. Years later the town learned that he had come all the way from Martinique on Sutpen's bare promise and lived for two years on venison cooked over a camp fire" (26). The small man has a Latin face. In Faulkner's novels, the state of being "Latin" in the sense of Spanish-speaking America often marks an ambivalent state at the limit of whiteness and blackness[21] as is the case with Joe Christmas's alleged Mexican father in *Light in August* or with Eulalia Bon's mother of supposed Spanish heritage in *Absalom*. The architect's flowery clothing, which reappears in a strikingly similar way in Charles Bon's wardrobe, also introduces gender ambiguity. Thus, the architect stands at the limits of whiteness and masculinity. Linked to "Latinness" by his face, the architect is attached to Paris by his clothing. The outfit, to which he clings in the ill-adapted plantation and swamp environments, is to him as integral as his own skin. After his capture out of the swamp, it is not his injured leg nor the wounds on his skin that lead to his utter despair but the loss of his hat, a loss that "seemed to gather all misfortune and defeat that the human race ever suffered" (207). More than accessory, the architect's clothing warrants him humanity. After the dismemberment and castration of his outfit, he becomes a vulnerable swamp creature with "little dirty coon-like hands" (207).

After years have passed, the town realizes that the French architect has sprung not from a European boulevard but from the Caribbean island of Martinique. While Martinique and Haiti—formerly Saint-Domingue—were both old French colonies and are thereby historically linked, since the Haitian Revolution, Martinique and Haiti have been represented in popular, literary, and political discourse as polar opposites. While Haiti has been demonized from its revolutionary inception to the recent earthquake (as, for instance, in Pat Robertson's infamous claim about its "pact with the devil"), Martinique has been described as a summit of civilization and sophistication.[22] The city of Saint-Pierre in Martinique was called the "Paris of the Antilles." When the French architect arrived in Mississippi in 1833, Saint-Pierre was at its height. It is likely that Faulkner would have heard of Saint-Pierre and of the massive destruction of the city by volcanic eruption in 1902. It is also likely that he would have encountered Hearn's writings on Martinique, Hearn being his near predecessor in New Orleans and, like him, a regular contributor to the *Times-Picayune*. In his *Two Years in the French West Indies*, published in 1890, Hearn portrays Martinique as a place of utmost sophistication, in contrast, for instance, with the British colony of Barbados: "Compare [the population of Martinique] with the population of black Barbadoes [sic], where the apish grossness of African coast types has been perpetuated unchanged;—and the contrast may well astonish!"[23] For Hearn, Martinique is also a site of linguistic, fashion, and cultural sophistication, and a site of feminization of people and landscape. Thus the choice of Martinique as the place of origin of the

architect seems appropriate and demonstrates Faulkner's literary awareness of the place. Despite this certain recognition, the references to
Haiti and Martinique remain schematic. As Stanchich has argued, for
instance, "Nothing . . . is mentioned or known about Martinique except
in mock descriptions of the architect's fashions [and] a poor imitation of
the French."[24]

The most complex presence of the Caribbean in *Absalom*, outside this
"economy of stereotypes," to use Stanchich's expression (6), is embodied
in the person of Charles Bon. The Caribbean revealed in Bon's body is
not so much the irretrievable site of "that Porto Rico or Haiti or wherever it was he understood vaguely that he had come from" (239) but
the city of New Orleans, which inscribes the presence of the Caribbean within the geographical borders of the US South. In this particular
example, the Caribbean is not so much an accessorial detachable faraway
land but a pervasive presence that shapes humanity within the limits of
this "country all divided and fixed and neat with a people living on it all
divided and fixed and neat because of what color their skins happened
to be and what they happened to own" (179), as young Sutpen imagines
the Plantation South from his childhood West Virginia mountains.

Like his home, the city of New Orleans, Bon is "foreign and paradoxical, with [an] atmosphere at once fatal and languorous, at once feminine
and steel-hard" (86). He is defined precisely by his resistance to stereotypes and multiplies himself in a series of images that resist being
synthesized as a whole. Among these composite images, some do par-
ticipate in an economy of stereotypes based on amalgamation and inter-
changeability. In Rosa's mind, for instance, Bon's New Orleans becomes
interchangeable with the fantasized Arabian Nights of another continent, another time, and another level of reality altogether. Mr. Compson
"like[d] to think" that Henry "looked upon Bon as though he were a
hero out of some adolescent Arabian Nights" (76). Bon is alternately
described as "a catholic of sorts" (75), frenchified, and phoenix-like in
a portrait drawing from nationality, religion, and mythology, conceptual
realms hard to fuse in a single stereotype. In this, Bon represents the
"absolute composite" that, for Martinican thinker Édouard Glissant, is
a defining pattern of Caribbean societies, a Caribbean space in which
Glissant includes Faulkner's Yoknapatawpha as well.[25] For Glissant, this
composite world clashes with "atavistic" societies that ground and legiti-
mize lineage in a land, of which Sutpen's design provides a clear example.
Bon escapes Sutpen's atavistic thinking through his groundlessness: "a
young man . . . with for background the shadowy figure of a legal guard-
ian rather than any parents—a personage who in the remote Mississippi
of that time must have appeared almost phoenix-like, fullsprung from

no childhood, born of no woman" (58). The image of the phoenix, born and reborn of its own ashes, or, more pragmatically, the legal situation of Charles Bon, defines him as a result of the composite world described by Glissant, which gnaws at the "fixed and neat" borders of Yoknapatawpha County. The "fixed and neat" geography is disrupted by the intrusion of blood that sprang from a Caribbean *métissage* or miscegenation, which is particularly why Glissant considers Faulkner as a Caribbean writer: "*Absalom, Absalom!* . . . is precisely about . . . a possibility of incest, a perversion of filiation. But the decisive–fatal—element will be linked to another type of causality: the intrusion of 'black blood.' Undetectable at first in the first Haitian wife of the planter Sutpen . . . it will provide the necessary conditions to forever dissolve the chain of filiation."[26] It is thus this composite, miscegenated genealogy, this mixing, that perverts geography. It is blood that reshapes land. Faulkner's Yoknapatawpha, for Glissant, is not only a perversion of space, an accident due to the intrusion of Caribbean miscegenation, but structurally reproduces the Caribbean family: "In all of Faulkner's works, the clashing mess of names, the forced or willing miscegenations, the double (black and white) lineages, relentlessly reproduce . . . the extended-family style that has contributed for so long to the building of the Caribbean social fabric. It's no accident that Sutpen met his fate in Haiti."[27]

While Glissant includes the world of Yoknapatawpha in his Caribbean, Bon dismisses the Caribbean as a nonplace. As Quentin and Shreve ponder in chapter 8, Bon

> creat[ed] for himself (without help since who to help him) his own notion of that Porto Rico or Haiti or wherever it was he understood vaguely that he had come from like orthodox children do of heaven or the cabbage patch or wherever it was that they came from, except that his was different in that you were not supposed (your mother didn't intend to, anyway) to ever go back there (and maybe when you got as old as she was you would be horrified too every time you found hidden in your thoughts anything that just smelled or tasted like it might be a wish to go back there) . . . and hence no man had a father, no one personal Porto Rico or Haiti, but all mother faces . . . all boy flesh that walked and breathed stemming from that one ambiguous eluded dark fatherhead. (239–40)

The expelling of the Caribbean as origin corresponds to the evacuation of the Haitian mother's body. While other bodies (the French architect's, the wild men's, or Sutpen's) signify and even perform the Caribbean landscape, Eulalia Bon's body remains mute. In this context it is worth noting that the name "Eulalia" comes from the Greek *Eulalos*, one who "speaks well," or one with a good speech ("lalein" referring to speaking or chattering and "eu-" meaning "good" or "bon"). Faulkner's Eulalia ironically remains without speech. The name "Eulalia" also importantly refers to the first written collection of French poetry, "La Séquence de Sainte-Eulalie" (circa 881), a prayer to a twelve-year-old martyr, a text that was also the first transcription of a sacred language—Latin—in secular French. In the Latin version of the sequence we can read, "Spiritus hic erat Eulaliae / Lacteolos, celer, innocuus" (It was the soul of Eulalia / White as milk, quick, innocent).[28] French, at the time of the crumbling Empire of Charlemagne a vernacular entering the written sphere of the dominant Latin language, occupies a similar position to Creole in postrevolutionary Haiti, which gets inscribed as a written language in official documents. In both cases, the feminine and the vernacular gain access to the symbolic dominant masculine writing. As Sutpen named "with his own mouth his own ironic fecundity of dragon's teeth" (48), we can suspect that Faulkner too, named Eulalia with a particular intent. It is not clear whether Faulkner knew about the French and Latin sequences devoted to Eulalia. However, we can at least be certain that he was familiar with the literal meaning of the name, which would have been available in any etymological dictionary, and perhaps with the cult of Eulalia, a saint whose story was well known across the Mediterranean in Portugal, Spain, and France.[29]

Faulkner's naming of Eulalia seems to be in line with this "ironic fecundity." His Eulalia does not have a sequence, does not have a song, nor does she have a body. She is the absent relay that gave birth to Charles Bon and that, through her disappearance, turns the phoenix-like city of New Orleans into a space of parthogenesis or self-birth. On a political level, the evacuation of Eulalia Bon, the Haitian mother, and of her Creole "bon parler," also dismisses Haiti as a crucial cultural and political matrix of New Orleans. As Ned Sublette has shown in *The World That Made New Orleans*, Saint-Domingue, later Haiti, was fundamental to the construction of the city, politically, legally, linguistically, religiously, and culturally.[30] The Caribbean state of Haiti disappears as a nation altogether since it loses its proper name to become a common noun, a phase among others in Bon's development: "the Haiti, the childhood, the lawyer, the woman who was his mother" (250). The Caribbean mumble-jumble, whose names refer to many different political or linguistic realities, merges with religious and childlike tales of origins and originations: "Porto Rico or Haiti . . . or the cabbage patch or wherever it was that they came from" (239). Place of fictional, fictitious, or plain silly origin, the Caribbean further loses its status as geographical space and place to become a taste and smell: "anything that just smelled or tasted like it might be a wish to go back there" (239). Unlike the place of childhood nostalgia that a more orthodox literary child traveled back to through the taste of a madeleine dipped in an herbal tea, the Caribbean site of origin, for Bon, acts as a place of horror that forbids any return of the mind to a memory: the opposite of a Proustian nostalgic journey to a lost past.

Despite its evacuation as a maternal, historical, and political origin through the dismissal of Eulalia Bon, the Caribbean endures in the New Orleans of *Absalom* as a place of miscegenation and compositeness, finding its most compelling manifestation in the practice of *plaçage* that New Orleans, Saint-Domingue, and later Haiti shared.[31] This practice is of course exemplified by Bon's union to the unnamed "octoroon woman." It is no accident that Faulkner expels the word *"plaçage"* from his novel. One could argue that he does so to avoid folklorism. However, he does use the word "lagniappe," clearly marked as New Orleans parlance. Faulkner, or his narrators, opt for the term "morganatic" (80) to describe Bon's relationship to the woman, linking the practice of *plaçage* to Germanic, European, and royal origins, not to the common-law practice of concubinage inherited from Saint-Domingue.

While such practices remain unnamed or silenced—both New Orleanian, Haitian, or Caribbean—they nonetheless invade the "fixed and neat" borders of Yoknapatawpha and ruin Sutpen's atavistic desire. This clash between compositeness and atavism is perhaps nowhere more evident than in the following questions that Charles directs at Henry: "Have you forgot that this woman, this child, are niggers? You, Henry Sutpen of Sutpen's Hundred in Mississippi? You, talking of marriage, a wedding, here?" (94). Charles Bon's irony traps Henry into his own fallacy. Bon presents Henry—Henry Sutpen of Sutpen's Hundred—as the extreme result of atavistic thinking in which the land, in aristocratic fashion, receives the plantation owner's patronymic, which in turn legitimizes the presence of the family on that land in a circular fantasy of reciprocal creation and belonging. The opposition between the words "woman" and "nigger" further reinforces the atavistic world based on "fixed and neat" lineages. This opposition also foreshadows the opposition between the terms "brother" and "nigger" introduced in the dramatic confrontation between Henry and Bon in chapter 8. These oppositions seem to forbid any inclusion of "blackness" within the family. The use of the word "nigger," in the context of antimiscegenation laws, would annul the possibility of a marriage. Despite it all, Henry sees the "morganatic wedding" as an act of bigamy, even if he views this marriage through other cultural norms and laws (for instance Islamic, as when he envisions his sister as "a sort of junior partner in a harem" [94]). The "fixed and neat" bordering between legal citizen and slave, human and nonhuman, Yoknapatawpha and New Orleans, Yoknapatawpha and Haiti has failed. The mess of *métissage* cannot be expelled on a remote island; instead, it is already at work within the continental geographical body of the United States, in New Orleans, no matter how "foreign and paradoxical" a city.

Thus the Yoknapatawpha world has become a Caribbean place through the intrusion of unruly blood into the land. I now want to turn to an unexpected connection between Faulkner and the Caribbean poet Aimé Césaire, who both perform, I argue, a geography of blood. I am using the word "unexpected" because Césaire, a poet and politician born in Martinique in 1913, considered as one of the three founding fathers of the Negritude movement, a voice for the oppressed of the world with a sharp political consciousness, would appear to be an unlikely literary partner for Faulkner. However, in his celebrated 1939 ode to Negritude, *Notebook of a Return to a Native Land*,[32] Césaire develops a geographical consciousness surprisingly similar to General Compson's—or Faulkner's own—vision of the region.[33] To summarize, Césaire's geography is not based on cartographers' maps but shaped by the impression of the blood of slaves and other oppressed people on the land. One verse of his poem, which refers to the similarity between the red earth of Martinique and that of the Southern states of "Tennessee, Georgia, Alabama," encapsulates this vision: "Terres rouges, terres sanguines, terres consanguines" (red earth, sanguine earth, consanguine earth) (46). The red of the earth evolves from a literal geological reference to the blood that the earth has absorbed, to a relation of consanguinity, a cross-fertilization of the earth and the blood of slaves. Compson's geography of the West Indies, in this long and dense passage retold by Quentin to Shreve in the Harvard dorm room, functions in a similar manner:[34]

> . . . a spot of earth which might have been created and set aside by Heaven itself, grandfather said, as a theatre for violence and injustice and bloodshed . . . a little island set in a smiling and fury-lurked and incredible indigo sea, which was the halfway point between what we call the jungle and what we call civilization, halfway between the dark inscrutable continent from which the black blood, the black bones and flesh and thinking and remembering and hopes and desires, was ravished by violence . . . a little lost island in a latitude which would require ten thousand years of equatorial heritage to bear its climate, a soil manured with black blood from two hundred years of oppression and exploitation until it sprang with an incredible paradox of peaceful greenery and crimson flowers and sugar cane sapling size and three times the height of a man . . . but valuable pound for pound almost with silver ore, as if nature held a balance and kept a book and offered a recompense for the torn limbs

and outraged hearts even if man did not. . . . The planting of men too: the yet intact bones and brains in which the old unsleeping blood that had vanished into the earth they trod still cried out for vengeance. And he [Sutpen] oversee-ing it, riding peacefully about on his horse . . . not knowing that what he rode upon was a volcano, hearing the air tremble and throb at night with the drums and the chanting and not knowing that it was the heart of the earth itself he heard. (202)

This is the only evocation of the Caribbean in the novel that performs a true geography as measurement and inventory of the surface of the earth, which provides a sharp contrast with Sutpen's impressionistic sea shanty or with Charles Bon's confused feeling. Terms such as "latitude," "half-way point," and references to the equator clearly situate the pas-sage in geographical thinking. References to indigo sea and volcanoes, precise tropical plants such as crimson flowers and sugarcane, demon-strate an environmental consciousness of geological structures and flora. The most surprising aspect of this geography, however, resides in the fact that the Caribbean landscape is not simply measured mathemati-cally but described by means of an active form of geography or writing of the earth, which intertwines the land with its human presence, in a shared geography of blood. The landscape would be nothing without the cross-fertilization of the presence of its human inhabitants, and more specifically without the "black blood" of the oppressed slaves who have "manured" its "soil," without the sacrifice to the earth of "torn limbs and "outraged hearts," without, in short, the "planting of men." Miles away from the accounting thinking of Sutpen,[35] the West Indian landscape evoked here is based on blood, not on gold. The passage also introduces an idea of justice and ethical thinking. While men—and heaven—fail to pay their moral debt, nature does it for them in a recompense of botanical luxury. Such a thinking of the environment as both shaped and written by human blood, and as avenger, is surprisingly close to Césaire's depiction of the earth. The "planting of men" in Faulkner's text also strongly echoes in Haitian American writer Edwidge Danticat's novel *The Farming of Bones*, in which sugarcane stalks and bones of the buried form one inextricable text.[36]

I will not conclude by saying that Faulkner could be viewed as a thinker of Negritude, which would be far-fetched. However, I will argue that there is a Caribbean geographical consciousness present in at least one of the voices of the rich polyphony or cacophony of the novel. This consciousness is juxtaposed to many other evocations of the region that sharply lack the lucidity of this passage. With this one exception, the novel is indeed full of characters who do not see the Caribbean, beginning with Sutpen, who oversees the plantation and rides the land on his horse not knowing, not knowing (repeated twice in the text) that he is hearing "the heart of the earth" in the drum beats.

Nevertheless, through the variety of its shapes—dreamed, simplified, stereotypical, jumbled up, political, and ethical—the Caribbean speaks in the text and continues to be heard by Caribbean writers, for whom Faulkner is deeply, and paradoxically, an inescapable source. We could name Wilson Harris,[37] Maryse Condé, Vincent Placoly, Suzanne Césaire, and finally Edouard Glissant, who has devoted a monograph to Faulkner's works, *Faulkner, Mississippi*, and who has made countless references to Faulkner from his early writings in the 1960s to his last essays in the 2010s.[38] Having paid close attention to the Faulknerian presence in the entirety of Glissant's corpus, I can say with confidence that Faulkner is Glissant's most important putative father and literary master. I say this with an awareness of the problematic use of the terms "father" and "master" when evoking the relationship of Glissant, a descendant of African slaves, and Faulkner, a member of the white plantocracy.[39]

While reading Glissant's last long critical essay, his *Philosophie de la Relation* published in 2009, I was struck, and moved, by the acute presence of Faulkner in the text of a writer who saw his death approaching.[40] Towards the end of his book, Glissant searches for his mother's birthplace in Martinique and gets lost.[41] He describes the experience of going astray in his native landscape as akin to the experience of being lost in Faulkner: "If you get lost like this in a postage stamp (for example, Faulkner in his Yoknapatawpha), it means you really know it is yours."[42] Glissant's landscape of origin, his mother's birthplace, is inhabited by the Faulknerian landscape that acts as its explanation and its origin. An image of a "postage stamp of native soil" in which one can get lost explains precisely why the Faulknerian landscape evades geography. The contours, while tiny and precise as those of a stamp, can never chart a landscape that becomes yours, that becomes you, because it moves with you.

After spelling out his mother's full name, and after recounting the story of her burial, in the last paragraph of his last book of essays, Glissant leaves the reader in the company of Faulkner: "We pursue the prophetic disorder of the man of the South, who told without telling all the while telling. It's William Faulkner I'm talking about."[43] Why give such a place of honor to a white Southern writer in what appears to be the literary will of a black Caribbean writer? What is there in Faulkner's landscapes that speaks in the Caribbean? Glissant would have answered this question by the notion of *common-place* or "lieu-commun." In *Philosophie de la Relation*, he contrasts what he calls *common-place* (with a hyphen) with the commonplace referring to a cliché. The *common-place* is "a place that always calls upon another world view and sheds light onto it."[44] The propensity of the Faulknerian landscape to act as a *common-place* resides in the potentialities that the landscape contains because its borders (geographic, temporal, bodily, racial) are not "fixed and neat." No other than Glissant's last words can best evoke Faulkner's legacy: "Faulkner's lessons reach much beyond Yoknapatawpha. . . . The landscape of the County has expanded far, far away, in space and in meaning. . . . The 'South' fell asleep, awaiting more changes, whose nature no one can yet predict. In that, it encounters many other regions of the world, erupting or slumbering, chaotic or torpid, Polynesias or Switzerlands, continents or archipelagoes, meandering their way into the enormous Relation of world-totality. It is precisely . . . what endures beyond the County that helps us."[45]

NOTES

1. "Une personne autant qu'un pays, est l'ailleurs" (Édouard Glissant, *Poétique de la Relation* [Paris: Gallimard, 1990], 325). Martinican writer Glissant made that claim in reference to Quentin Compson's Canadian friend Shrevlin McCannon. All translations are mine unless otherwise indicated.

2. Lafcadio Hearn, *The Life and Letters of Lafcadio Hearn*, ed. Elizabeth Bisland, vol. 2 (Boston: Houghton Mifflin, 1922), 3.

3. William Faulkner, *Absalom, Absalom!* (1936; New York: Vintage International, 1990), 305. Hereafter, the abbreviated title *Absalom* will be used to refer to this edition. Page numbers will be indicated parenthetically.

4. Barbara Ladd, "William Faulkner, Édouard Glissant, and a Creole Poetics of History and Body in *Absalom, Absalom!* and *A Fable*," in *Faulkner in the Twenty-First Century: Faulkner and Yoknapatawpha, 2000*, ed. Robert W. Hamblin and Ann J. Abadie (Jackson: University Press of Mississippi, 2003), 47n2.

5. *Grand Larousse Encyclopédique en dix volumes*, vol. 6 (Paris: Larousse, 1960), n.p.

6. Ibid.

7. John T. Matthews, "Recalling the West Indies: From Yoknapatawpha to Haiti and Back," *American Literary History* 16.2 (Summer 2004): 238. Hereafter cited parenthetically in the text.

8. Maritza Stanchich, "The Hidden Caribbean 'Other' in William Faulkner's *Absalom, Absalom!* An Ideological Ancestry of U.S. Imperialism," *Mississippi Quarterly* 49.3 (Summer 1996): 603.

9. Jeff Karem, "Fear of a Black Atlantic? African Passages in *Absalom, Absalom!* and *The Last Slaver*," in *Global Faulkner: Faulkner and Yoknapatawpha, 2006*, ed. Annette Trefzer and Ann J. Abadie (Jackson: University Press of Mississippi, 2009), 162.

10. Sean Latham, "An Impossible Resignation: William Faulkner's Post-Colonial Imagination," in *A Companion to William Faulkner*, ed. Richard C. Moreland (Malden, Mass.: Blackwell Publishing, 2007), 252.

11. See Chris Bongie, *Islands and Exiles: The Creole Identities of Post-Colonial Literatures* (Stanford: Stanford University Press, 1998); George Handley, *Postslavery Literatures in the Americas: Family Portraits in Black and White* (Charlottesville: University of Virginia Press, 2000); Ladd, 31–49; and Deborah Cohn, *History and Memory in the Two Souths: Recent Southern and Spanish American Fiction* (Nashville: Vanderbilt University Press, 1999).

12. "New World relationality is the destabilizing of the inherent meaning of island ground, whether the Plantation South or the Martinican hillside, in favor of an idea of archipelagic space activated by horizontal relations and indirect detours" (J. Michael Dash, "Martinique/Mississippi," in *Look Away! The U.S. South in New World Studies*, ed. Jon Smith and Deborah Cohn [Durham: Duke University Press, 2004], 97).

13. Claude Romano, *Le Chant de la vie: Phénoménologie de Faulkner* (Paris: Gallimard, 2005).

14. Ladd, 46.

15. "[U]ne phénomenologie du sentir" (Romano, 40).

16. Natalie Ring, "Mapping Regional and Imperial Geographies: Tropical Disease in the U.S. South," in *Colonial Crucible: Empire in the Making of the Modern American State*, ed. Alfred W. McCoy and Francisco A. Scarano (Madison: University of Wisconsin Press, 2009), 297–308.

17. On the level of the narration, this would constitute for Glissant an act of "respect-ful opacity," in not trying to project onto the other that which cannot be understood according to one's own cultural parameters. See *Poétique de la Relation*, 203–9.

18. In contrast, in 1895, linguist, tale collector, and Tulane professor Alcée Fortier described the Louisiana Creole used in oral folktales in the following manner: "While singing, [the storyteller] writhes in a horrible manner and gesticulates wildly . . . to the tune of the primitive music" (Fortier, *Louisiana Folktales in French Dialect and English Translation* [Boston: Houghton, Mifflin, and Company, 1895], x).

19. "I assert that Faulkner's vision of the Caribbean and Africa simultaneously evades such specific 'historical knowledge,' in favor of a mythic projection of guilt that is symboli-cally rich but historically impoverished" (Karem, 162).

20. Cormac McCarthy, *No Country for Old Men* (New York: Vintage, 2007).

21. See José Limón's contribution to this volume.

22. "Pat Robertson says Haiti paying for 'pact to the devil,'" *CNN*, January 13, 2010, http://articles.cnn.com/2010-01-13/us/haiti.pat.robertson_1_pat-robertson-disasters-and-terrorist-attacks-devil?_s=PM:US.

23. Lafcadio Hearn, *Two Years in the French West Indies* (1890; New York: Interlinks Books, 2001), 250.

24. Stanchich, 606.

25. See Glissant, *Poétique de la Relation*, 59–75.

26. "Dans *Absalon, Absalon!* . . . il s'agit bien . . . d'un inceste possible, d'une perver-sion de la filiation. Mais l'élément décisif–fatalitaire–sera impliqué à une autre série de causalité: c'est l'intrusion du 'sang nègre'. Il était d'abord indécelable chez la première femme haïtienne du planteur Sutpen. . . . voilà les conditions réunies pour que la chaine de la filiation soit dissoute à jamais dans l'étendue nouvelle" (Glissant, *Poétique de la Relation*, 70).

27. "Dans tout l'œuvre de Faulkner, le carambolage des patronymes, des métissages forcés ou non, des lignées doubles (noire et blanche) reproduit avec acharnement . . . le

style de famille étendue qui a si longtemps contribué à la formation du tissu social dans la Caraïbe. Ce n'est pas par hasard que Sutpen a . . . rencontré son destin en Haïti" (ibid.).

28. Quoted in *Les Séquences de Sainte Eulalie*, ed. Roger Berger and Annette Brasseur (Genève: Droz, 2004), 167.

29. See Berger and Brasseur, *Les Séquences*, 25–34.

30. Ned Sublette, *The World That Made New Orleans: From Spanish Silver to Congo Square* (Chicago: Lawrence Hill Books, 2008). See especially chapters 12 and 13.

31. See Sublette, 150.

32. Aimé Césaire, *Cahier d'un retour au pays natal* (1939; Paris: Présence africaine, 2000).

33. It is unlikely that Césaire would have read *Absalom, Absalom!* in its original English version published in 1936. Rimbault's French translation of the novel was published only in 1955.

34. For compelling analyses of this passage, refer to Farah Jasmine Griffin and Ryan Heryford's respective contributions to this volume.

35. Melanie Benson reflects on Faulkner's obsession—as well as a more general Southern obsession—with this type of mathematical thinking. She explains this fixation by the South's attachment to "an American capitalist economy of limitless opportunity" as well as to "slavery's calculations of worth, value, certainty, and hierarchy." See Benson, *Disturbing Calculations: The Economics of Identity in Postcolonial Southern Literature, 1912–2002* (Athens: University of Georgia Press, 2008), 2.

36. Edwidge Danticat, *The Farming of Bones* (New York: Penguin, 1998). To push the comparison further, the aesthetic of blood, bones, and earth present in Faulkner's description is also very close to that of Wifredo Lam, a Cuban painter who was also Faulkner's contemporary. In Lam's famous painting *The Jungle*, exhibited in New York in 1944, human bodies, sugarcane stalks, and tropical flowers are part of one inextricable tropical mass. A white hand holding the sharp blades of scissors evokes Faulkner's description of the violence inflicted upon the tropical environment. For a reproduction of the painting, see http://www.moma.org/collection/object.php?object_id=34666.

37. See for example Harris's *The Womb of Space: The Cross-Cultural Imagination* (Westport, Conn.: Greenwood Press, 1983) for a reflection on Faulkner and the extended Caribbean.

38. Édouard Glissant, *Faulkner, Mississippi*, trans. Barbara Lewis and Thomas Spear (Chicago: University of Chicago Press, 2000).

39. On this topic, see my *Orphan Narratives: The Postplantation Literature of Faulkner, Glissant, Morrison, and Saint-John Perse* (Charlottesville: University of Virginia Press, 2007), 15–29.

40. Édouard Glissant, *Philosophie de la Relation* (Paris: Gallimard, 2009). Glissant suffered from multiple diabetes-induced ailments at the time of his US visit. He died on February 3, 2011.

41. The cabin in which his mother was born is "swallowed up in a collapsed piece of soil" (engloutie . . . dans un enfoncement de terre) (ibid., 117).

42. "[Vous] vous perdez ainsi dans un timbre-poste (par exemple Faulkner dans son Yoknapatawpha), c'est si vous le connaissez réellement vôtre" (ibid., 142).

43. "Nous poursuivons le désordre prophétique de l'homme du Sud, qui a dit sans dire tout en disant. C'est de William Faulkner qu'il s'agit là" (ibid., 156).

44. "Un lieu où chaque fois une pensée du monde appelle et éclaire une pensée du monde" (ibid., 25).

45. "La leçon de Faulkner dépasse de beaucoup le Yoknapatawpha. . . . [L]e paysage du Comté s'est étendu en loin, d'espace et de signification. . . . Le 'Sud' s'est endormi,

attendant d'autres transformations, dont nul ne peut dire ce qu'elles seront. Il rejoint par
là combien d'autres régions du monde, cahutées ou somnolentes, chaotiques ou torpi-
des, Polynésies ou Suisses, continents ou archipels, qui entrent par tâtonnements dans
l'énorme Relation de la totalité-monde. Mais l'effort épique est cela même . . . qui reste,
et, par delà le Comté, nous aide" (ibid., 262).

A Daughter's Geography: William Faulkner, Zora Neale Hurston, and a New Mapping of "The Black South"

FARAH JASMINE GRIFFIN

This essay is pedagogically driven. What happens, it asks, when you place William Faulkner on what is, for all intents and purposes, an African American literature syllabus? More specifically, what literary insights and geographies emerge when you place Faulkner alongside that other "genius of the South," Zora Neale Hurston? A number of African American and Caribbean writers have engaged Faulkner's oeuvre: among them, Toni Morrison, Ralph Ellison, and Edouard Glissant are the most well known. Consequently, teaching Faulkner alongside any of these canonical writers may yield more complex understandings about race, region, nation, and literary tradition. But Hurston resonates especially because the two share the same historical moment, attention to the American South, and to Haiti and New Orleans as well. Before turning to this pairing, however, let me provide a brief background to the critical context out of which it emerged.

Faulkner and the Black South

In my own earlier work on the black artistic response to the two Great Migrations from the US South to the North, Faulkner helped to give meaning to the region from which so many black folk fled. He, alongside that other literary Mississippian, Richard Wright, portrayed a "provincial" South with a complex and painful racial history: a place where the ongoing legacy of slavery was palatable and where Jim Crow segregation, white supremacy, and racial violence remained all too real. The migration narratives with which I was concerned revealed the South to be an "immediate, identifiable, and oppressive power."[1] A site where power was exercised by people known to its victims, where it relied on the potential victims' fear of the violence that awaits, where it was enacted on black bodies in the spectacle and torture of elaborate lynching and burning rituals and acts of sexual violence. In Amiri Baraka's words, the South was "the scene of the crime."[2] Though he did help me create a conceptual sense of this South as an imagined place, Faulkner's works did not figure prominently in the pages of the project, though they could have. In her essay "Racial Awareness and Racial Development: *The Sound and the Fury* and the Great Migration," Cheryl Lester astutely argues the Great Migration is evident in the migration of black characters in *The Sound and the Fury*. According to Lester, it also appears in Quentin Compson's observation about the absence of segregation in the North, especially on public transportation. Riding on the Cambridge streetcar, Quentin recalls:

> It was full, mostly prosperous looking people reading newspapers. The only vacant seat was beside a nigger. He wore a derby and shined shoes and he was holding a dead cigar stub. I used to think that a Southerner had to be always conscious of niggers. I thought that Northerners would expect him to. When I first came East I kept thinking You've got to remember to think of them as colored people not niggers, and if it hadn't happened that I wasn't thrown with many of them, I'd have wasted a lot of time and trouble before I learned that the best way to take all people, black or white, is to take them for what they think they are, then leave them alone.[3]

This passage didn't find its way into my work on black migration because it better explains the psychic challenges of white Southerners as they navigate Northern spaces. However, the passage does suggest a direction for further study: the spaces of the streetcar, the subway, the passenger train as central tropes in navigating racialized geographies that permit comparison of the way white Southerners and black migrants navigate these mobile spaces in works by Faulkner, Ellison, Charles Chesnutt, and others. This passage exemplifies Lester's contention that "Quentin's migration and development of racial awareness, which led him to experience the dissolution of his racialized identity, represent a geographical and spiritual path not taken by the white South."[4] Lester's essay offers an important analysis of the presence and impact of black migration in *The Sound and the Fury*.

After the publication of *"Who Set You Flowin'?,"* my teaching interests, more so than my scholarship, began to shift. The work on migration narratives had a distinct, well-known trajectory: an escape from a "provincial," racist, violent, circumscribed South to a more "cosmopolitan" though still circumscribed Northern metropolis. I also argued that many post–civil rights texts marked a return migration, back to the South, which was then imagined as a homeland, as the source of black culture, a site of family, community, history, and spirituality—and most especially, as the site of the ancestor. Since that time, informed by the transnational and diasporic turn in American, African American, and Southern literary studies, I have turned my attention to the South, but this time conceived quite differently from the "provincial" space from which black folk fled. For the past several years, I have taught a course titled "Remapping the Black South" that configures a Southern geography beyond national boundaries, that sees the South as a cultural, economic, and political space made up of the United States South, the Caribbean, and parts of Central America. The course always starts with Martin Delany's 1859 serialized novel *Blake; or the Huts of America* and includes writers such as Zora Neale Hurston, Toni Morrison, Katherine Dunham, Nellie Rosario, Marlon Ross, Erna Brodber, and Edwidge Danticat. Charleston, Savannah, New Orleans, Cuba, Jamaica, and Haiti provide the settings for these texts and have come to constitute our map of the Black South. One year, an astute student suggested we include Faulkner in our consideration of the Black South. This made sense. The course wasn't on black Southern writers, but on writers who imagined and reimagined a Black South. I spent the following summer reading and rereading Faulkner and subsequent versions of the course have included *Absalom, Absalom!* It is the third text we read, following *Blake* and Jean Toomer's *Cane.* Faulkner's presence on the syllabus has transformed our readings of the texts that follow. After Faulkner it appears that all subsequent writers are in dialogue with him. His stylistic influence is evident in some instances; in others his concern with the relationship between collective history and individual memory seems to resonate most. The centrality of race for both black and white characters and the original sin of slavery all help shape the fiction we read. In many ways we, my students and I, have come to think of all writers who follow as children of Faulkner and/or Zora Neale Hurston.

Absalom, Absalom! maps a Southern geography that includes Tidewater Virginia, Haiti, Mississippi, and Louisiana. In the figures of Thomas Sutpen and Charles Bon (and to a lesser degree Henry Sutpen) we have characters who migrate between these spaces and whose experiences are narrated throughout. In fact, Thomas Sutpen's story is a kind of migration narrative: a poor white boy in Virginia, scorned by the white elite and their slaves, he goes to the West Indies in search of wealth and in order to create a dynasty that would make him the equal or better of any landed, slave-owning Virginian. By the time he arrives in Mississippi, he has put down a slave uprising in Haiti and married and divorced a mixed-race woman who bears him a son. In Haiti he appears to have acquired the slaves and the means to establish himself in Mississippi. His narrative also takes us to New Orleans, where the vanquished wife and mixed-race son reside. He is the most mobile character in the book, often seen in motion, atop his horse. And, as in the case of many migration narratives, he is a stranger, imagined as someone with no past, no history, no people, and no origins. Significantly, the white female characters of *Absalom, Absalom!* never leave Jefferson and the surrounding areas, but the three mixed-race women, Sutpen's daughter-servant, Clytie, his first wife, Eulalia (ironically meaning "well-spoken"), and Bon's unnamed octoroon mistress, also travel between Black South sites, though the text does not provide narration of their travel. Interestingly, many of the writers who follow Faulkner on my syllabus are women who are either narrating their own mobility (Katherine Dunham and Zora Neale Hurston) or focusing their attention on mobile women characters. I have come to think of the later writers, like Morrison, Gloria Naylor, and Dolen Perkins-Valdez, as Faulkner's black (literary) daughters, artists who give voice, agency, and mobility to Clytie, her anonymous Haitian mother, Eulalia, and the octoroon mistress. Daughters all . . .

A Daughter's Geography

I take the first part of my title, "A Daughter's Geography," from Ntozake Shange's poem "Bocas: A Daughter's Geography." Shange is not the subject of this essay, though in the aforementioned class we do sometimes read the poem and/or her novel *Sassafrass, Cypress, and Indigo*. The writer with whom I am concerned in this consideration of Faulkner's geography is not one of his literary daughters. Zora Neale Hurston, a self-conscious daughter of the South, of the African Diaspora, and especially of the Black South as I have described it, is not a daughter of Faulkner: she is his contemporary. In fact, she is more big sister than daughter: Faulkner was born in New Albany, Mississippi, in 1897, while Hurston was born in Notasulga, Alabama, in 1891. I have not found any evidence that they ever met each other. There is no mention of one in the other's biography. Yet they wrote and published at the same time and both set their most well-known work in the US South. The two writers share more than a historical moment and Southern origins. Both were actively engaged in mapping the South in ways that drew attention to specific sites in Florida or Mississippi, while at the same time drawing our attention to the significance of Haiti and Louisiana, especially New Orleans. And they were engaged in this mapping at the same time. Furthermore, for both authors there is a relationship between New Orleans and Haiti. And for both of them, New Orleans comes to represent a cosmopolitan South, situated even farther south than Mississippi or Alabama or parts of Florida. Both Haiti and New Orleans are spaces raced black or mixed and gendered feminine, if not female. For both writers, Haiti represents an ancient and old race of Africa, while New Orleans is a shiny, glimmering space of new people, a mixed people who carry Africa in their veins, their culture, and their religion. The existence of New Orleans, so close to Mississippi, lends a sense of trepidation and proof that no space is immutable and unchanging. Racial identities are fluid and unmoored in spaces like New Orleans. It is this proximity to one place, where race is not fixed, where racial identities and categories are in flux, that requires a rigid stratification of race, held in place by violence and even murder when necessary, in the places that surround it.

Faulkner and Hurston Imagine Haiti

The United States occupation of Haiti lasted from 1915 to 1934. During this time there was a proliferation of texts and articles about the black nation to its south. In some ways we should see Faulkner's *Absalom, Absalom!* (1936) and Hurston's *Tell My Horse: Voodoo and Life in Haiti and Jamaica* (1938) as products of this moment of heightened interest in and awareness of Haiti.

In *Absalom, Absalom!* Haiti is an imagined space sitting just outside the narrative. It is imagined by Rosa Coldfield and by Mr. Compson as he renders his version of his father's memories of conversations with Sutpen. In all instances, Haiti is a dark place of black violence, mystery, and chaos. In recent years a number of scholars have turned to *Absalom, Absalom!* to demonstrate Faulkner's awareness of "hemispheric connections" between the American South and the Caribbean. Scholars such as John T. Matthews, Jeff Karem, and the writer Eduoard Glissant are but a few of the critics who have considered the place of Haiti in the novel. In "Fear of a Black Atlantic? African Passages in *Absalom, Absalom!* and *The Last Slaver*," Karem notes that Faulkner depoliticizes the revolutionary impulses of Haitian blacks, even though he was aware of them, by revising aspects of the novel that would have "treated the action of black Haitians as political revolt."[5] Karem calls our attention to Faulkner's excision of the sentence where Sutpen shoots "into the Haitian darkness where the *insurrecting* niggers crept and hid and howled and sang" (emphasis added). In subsequent drafts the reference to insurrection disappears. Furthermore, in having Sutpen serve as a plantation manager and having him put down the insurrection of the enslaved in 1827, Faulkner creates a historical impossibility. The Haitian Revolution, a large-scale insurrection, started in 1791. By 1804 the Haitian Constitution outlawed slavery. Haiti came to represent a nation of formerly enslaved blacks who successfully fought their masters and established a republic. This would have different meanings for blacks and whites throughout the Americas. Karem argues that "it is precisely because the region is not locatable as a historical space within the novel, that it can serve as such a capacious symbolic reserve."[6]

We first encounter the Caribbean on the pages of *Absalom, Absalom!* in Rosa Coldfield's section. Haiti is never named. The island nation and its blacks take on the status of otherworldly myth in Rosa's section. In her ghost-haunted voice, she describes Sutpen as a man-horse-demon who arrives with a "band of wild niggers like beasts half tamed to walk upright like men, in attitudes wild and reposed."[7] Both Sutpen and the Caribbean island from which he comes are defined by the fierce strangeness of the blacks that accompany him. The phrase "wild niggers like beasts" will resonate throughout the rest of the novel. Rosa sets the tone by which we judge Sutpen's blacks and Sutpen himself. At one point, the enslaved Haitians are simply referred to as wild beasts. Miss Coldfield describes Sutpen as "a man who rode into town out of nowhere with a horse and two pistols and a herd of wild beasts that he had hunted down singlehanded because he was stronger in fear than even they were in whatever heathen place he had fled from."[8] This is Rosa's description, recollection, and remembrance of a scene she never witnessed. It is her retelling of a tale. And in her mind, Sutpen is himself a monster, a man-horse-demon, he of no past, perhaps not of woman born, from a heathen place with Negro-like beasts, who in Rosa's words "may have come (and probably did) from a much older country than Virginia or Carolina but it wasn't a quiet one."[9] According to Rosa, one could tell this just by looking at Sutpen's Negroes. For Rosa they are significant only in that they reveal something of Sutpen's own demonic nature. He is one with them. He entertains guests by having his Negroes fight for their pleasure and betting, "fighting not like white men fight, with rules and weapons, but like negroes fight to hurt one another quick and bad."[10] Though she is unaware of it, in this instance, Rosa has given a metaphor for white fear of what Haiti itself represents. A revolution, a revolt, where Negroes fight viciously and wildly, without rules or weapons. But Rosa Coldfield ends her section with an evening where Sutpen, bare-chested, enters the ring himself. She recalls her sister, Ellen, Sutpen's wife, "seeing not the two black beasts she had expected to see but instead a white one and a black one, both naked to the waist and gouging at one another's eyes as if their skins should not only have been the same color but should have been covered with fur too."[11] For Rosa, Sutpen is himself othered. Sutpen becomes beast, becomes wild nigger. It is shortly after this that Ellen sees her daughter, Judith, the image of her father, sitting next to another little girl, a Negro girl, who shares the same face. In Rosa Coldfield's story, Haiti remains unnamed; it helps her to establish a sense of the ferocity and viciousness of Sutpen in that he is always worse than his wild Negroes or the place from which they both hail.

"The legend of Sutpen's wild negroes" was brought into town by local men who had spent time in what would become Sutpen's Hundred. They brought with them tales of Negroes who hunted like hounds, Negroes who "could speak no English." Sutpen communicates with them in "a sort of French," though the legend holds it to have been "some dark and fatal tongue of their own."[12] In other words, the legend of Sutpen's Negroes refers not to the actual black bodies he brought to build his plantation but instead to a nightmare fantasy held by the inhabitants of the region to which he brought them.

Haiti, the place, doesn't appear until late in the novel when we finally get Sutpen's story as told to General Compson and relayed to Quentin by his father. In a long, important, and extraordinary passage, we hear a complex description of the island, one that is worth quoting at length here:

> a spot of earth which might have been created and set aside by Heaven itself . . . as a theatre for violence and injustice and bloodshed and all the satanic lusts of human greed and cruelty, for the last despairing fury of all the pariah-interdict and all the doomed—a little island set in a smiling and fury-lurked and incredible indigo sea, which was the halfway point between what we call the jungle and what we call civilization, halfway between the dark inscrutable continent from which the black blood, the black bones and flesh and thinking and remembering and hopes and desires, was ravished by violence, and the cold known land to which it was doomed, the civilised land and people which had expelled some of its own blood and thinking and desires that had become too crass to be faced and borne longer, and set it homeless and desperate on the lonely ocean—a little lost island in a latitude which would require ten thousand years of equatorial heritage to bear its climate, a soil manured with black blood from two hundred years of oppression and exploitation until it sprang with an incredible paradox of peaceful greenery and crimson flowers and sugar cane sapling size and three times the height of a man and a little bulkier of course but valuable pound for pound almost with silver ore, as if nature held a balance and kept a book and offered a recompense for the torn limbs and outraged hearts even if man did not, the planting of nature and man too watered not only by the wasted blood but breathed over by the winds in which the doomed ships had fled in vain, out of which the last tatter of sail had sunk into the blue sea along which the last vain despairing cry of woman or child had blown away—the planting of men too: the yet intact bones and brains in which the old unsleeping blood that had vanished into the earth they trod still cried out for vengeance.[13]

Here, in this Faulknerian sentence, we get the bloody and painful history of Haiti, an island cast between Africa and the New World. An Africa populated by black beings—blood, bone, and flesh, but also thoughts, memories, hopes, and desires—"ravished by violence." An island of contradictory beauty and bounty and exploitation and violence: —"two hundred years" of violence—a blood-soaked land that calls out for vengeance. Later we are told that the African drums and chanting that Sutpen hears are actually "the heart of the earth itself."[14] This geographic space holds and embodies the history to which it has borne witness. The land itself has become the spirit of the people whose blood has watered it. So while Haiti is painted as black and violent, it is a violence born of righteous revenge. And even though Sutpen defeats the uprising on the plantation he manages, he is nonetheless left with a sense of fear. Fear that he does not realize until it is all over, but fear that he carries in his disdain for the taste and smell of sugar. Haiti in *Absalom, Absalom!* exists in the past, but it is a dark and violent past that continues to haunt. In part it haunts because it is remembered, recalled, in a space whose own racial history is as brutal and bloody, a place where the earth is also blood drenched. And yet a place where the enslaved had not yet sought vengeance.

Haiti of *Absalom, Absalom!* exists in memory and narrative. In Zora Neale Hurston's *Tell My Horse*, it very much exists in the present, and its history is the source of religious ritual. Instead of a novel, Hurston writes an ethnography-autobiography, the work of an anthropologist. But as scholars like Barbara Ladd have noted, the "I" of Hurston's ethnographic and autobiographical texts is an "authorial performance."[15] Like Sutpen, Hurston, too, learns to speak Haitian Creole. As with Sutpen, she is the text's protagonist, who migrates from the US South farther south. However, Sutpen "did not know, comprehend, what he must have been seeing every day . . . a pig's bone with a little rotten flesh still clinging to it, a few chicken feathers, a stained dirty rag with a few pebbles tied up in it found on the old man's pillow one morning and none knew . . . how it had come there."[16] Hurston can read these signs of Voodoo ritual; she is the more literate figure. By the time she arrives in Haiti she has already been initiated into the wisdom of African-based religions in New Orleans. She goes to Haiti as a researcher and a seeker to collect material on Voodoo. And, there she learns "the old, old mysticism of the world in African terms."[17] Hurston opens the Haiti portion of *Tell My Horse* with history: "For four hundred years the blacks of Haiti had yearned for peace. For three hundred years the island was spoken of as a paradise of riches and pleasures, but that was in reference to the whites to whom the spirit of the land gave welcome. Haiti has meant spilt blood and tears for blacks. So the Haitians got no answers to their prayers. Even when they had fought and driven out the white oppressors, oppression did not cease."[18] Again, the imagery of blood dominates a description of Haiti. Interestingly, for Hurston the land itself welcomed whites but brought only despair and violence for blacks and does so still. But note that, in Hurston's hands, black Haitians are revolutionary agents: they fought and they drove out their oppressors. This is not a mystical conception of a land that seeks vengeance but a story of human beings in a fight for their own freedom, a fight that is ongoing in the present moment from which she writes. Hurston's Haiti is not a land submerged in the past; it is a nation in the present, one whose black poor continue to be oppressed even after their earlier struggles.

Hurston lived in a suburb of Port-au-Prince, Haiti's capital, and while there, in 1937, she wrote her best-known novel, *Their Eyes Were Watching God*, in seven weeks. Though that novel is set in Florida, the critic Daphne Lamothe notes that Hurston's use of "Vodou imagery enables her to analyze the relationship among migration, culture and identity that lies at the heart of the African Diaspora."[19] Janie resembles the Vodou goddess Erzulie in her physical appearance, relationships, husbands, and ultimate self-realization. In *Tell My Horse* Hurston writes, "Erzulie is said to be a beautiful young woman of lush appearance. She is a mulatto. . . . She is represented as having firm, full breasts and other perfect female attributes. She is a rich young woman and wears a gold ring on her finger."[20] "Erzulie," Hurston adds, "is not the passive queen of heaven and mother of anybody. She is the ideal of the love bed."[21] Most of her devotees are men; "toward womankind, Erzulie is implacable."[22] Erzulie seeks vengeance on all men who betray her. Recall the first description of Janie in *Their Eyes Were Watching God*: "The men noticed her firm buttocks like she had grape fruits in her hip pockets; the great rope of black hair swinging to her waist and unraveling in the wind like a plume; then her pugnacious breasts trying to bore holes in her shirt. They, the men, were saving with the mind what they lost with the eye. The women took the faded shirt and muddy overalls and laid them away for remembrance. It was a weapon against her strength and if it turned out of no significance, still it was a hope that she might fall to their level some day."[23] Janie is Erzulie: a mixed-race woman of means, an object of male desire and female envy.

In *Tell My Horse* Hurston also problematically embraces a form of US nationalism and praises the US occupation of Haiti. Scholars have justifiably criticized what they see as the imperialistic elements of her politics in relation to the Caribbean. Hazel Carby calls *Tell My Horse* "reactionary, blindly patriotic and, consequently, superficial."[24] In her work on Haiti, however, Leigh Anne Duck offers an alternative reading of Hurston's ethnography-travelogue.[25] If in *Absalom, Absalom!* Haiti is important for what it tells us about Sutpen, in many ways in *Tell My Horse* Haiti also sheds light on the relationship between race and democracy in the United States, but that is for a different day.

Even if Hurston is to be critiqued for the book's politics, hers was a respectful treatment of Haitian Voodoo and the culture of the Haitian peasant class. "Voodoo is a religion of creation and life. It is the worship of the sun, the water, and other natural forces, but the symbolism is no better understood than that of other religions and consequently is taken too literally."[26] She devotes the book to exploring, defining, and explaining Voodoo—its history, its practioners, its rituals—in order to demystify it but also to demonstrate its beauty and complexity. In addition, she yearns for Haiti to experience a form of democracy that would ensure access not just to material means but also to literacy that would benefit its black poor. But for our purposes, Hurston sees Haiti as "the Black Daughter of France."[27] So, in Hurston's eyes, this island nation joins the multitude of disinherited black daughters of white fathers within the Diaspora. Haiti is Clytie, not Charles Bon.

Both Faulkner and Hurston recognize the significance and centrality of Haiti. The nation and its history inspire significant parts of their work. For Faulkner, it provides a space-place that helps to explain Thomas Sutpen: his success, his fearlessness, his fear, and his mystery. As place, Haiti plays a significant role in helping Faulkner define the fascinating character who sits at the center of this most complex novel. Haiti, as place, provides Hurston the opportunity to experience Africa in the Americas, and to explore her interests in and concern for black societies that are self-governing. As idea, Haiti helps give shape and meaning to her most beloved character, Janie, of *Their Eyes Were Watching God*. It cannot be insignificant that Haiti shapes both Thomas Sutpen and Janie Crawford, two of American literature's most unforgettable characters, in 1936 and 1937, respectively.

Faulkner and Hurston were each drawn to New Orleans as well. Both authors spent significant time there, and the city is certainly an important part of the Southern geography they mapped in their writings. It is that Deep South city, that northern Caribbean city, that cosmopolitan city, to which I want to turn our attention now.

In her first ethnographic-autobiographical book, *Mules and Men*, Hurston finds New Orleans to be a transitional space in her research on black folk culture, especially Hoodoo and Voodoo. Here, Hoodoo refers to a form of traditional medicine and folk magic practiced by some

African Americans in the United States South and parts of the Caribbean. Voodoo refers to a set of religious practices brought to the New
World by enslaved West Africans. New Orleans is the spiritual gateway
to the Caribbean and the site of Hurston's original initiation into African-
based religious practices. In *Absalom, Absalom!* it is the place where
racial boundaries and borders are transgressed as is made evident in the
city's population of free and affluent mixed-race people. What troubles is
not their existence, but their status. Significantly, in *Absalom, Absalom!*
we are told that spatially this city that challenges racial norms is actually deeper South than Mississippi. Faulkner writes of Charles Bon and
Henry Sutpen, "That spring, they returned *north*, into Mississippi."[28] In
this instance, to travel north is to travel to a less free, more restrictive,
and provincial space. New Orleans is described as "cosmopolitan" while
Mississippi is "bucolic."[29]

Within the narrative New Orleans is the space for the projections
of others' imagination and fantasy. In *Faulkner's Imperialism: Space,
Place, and the Materiality of Myth*, Taylor Hagood writes, "Faulkner's
depiction of New Orleans as Scythia finds its greatest expression in the
person of Charles Bon, in *Absalom, Absalom!* Bon's very body represents amalgamation, ambivalence, and liminality, while he also metaphorically embodies the space of New Orleans as he emerges in the
text's multiple layers of narrative."[30] Mr. Compson astutely calls Bon "a
myth, a phantom: something which they engendered and created whole
themselves; some effluvium of Sutpen blood and character, as though
as a man he did not exist at all."[31] If Haiti serves to tell us something
about Thomas Sutpen, at times it seems Charles Bon exists to tell us
something about New Orleans. He is not just Charles Bon, but "Charles
Bon of New Orleans," who calls that "worldly and even foreign city"
home.[32] Throughout, the city is constantly marked as cosmopolitan. New
Orleans is the place to which Eulalia migrates from Haiti. Shreve and
Quentin assume that it is from this site that she plans what we might call
"Eulalia's Design," her revenge plot against Sutpen. But she is not the
only mixed-race woman there. New Orleans is also the home of Bon's
octoroon mistress and their son. It is the city of *plaçage*, of octoroons,
who are not whores or even courtesans. It is a city of Erzulie's daughters.
It is the place where interracial sexual relationships between white men
and women of African descent, common throughout the South, have
been formalized through ceremony and institution.[33] New Orleans *is*
cultural difference: language, mores, and racial classification. It is other,
an otherness that is female and the feminine, for though Bon is male, he
is always described in sensual, feminine terms. He is an object of desire
for Judith and Henry. Henry has "provincial manners and speech and

clothing," while Bon is "a man a little older than his actual years and enclosed and surrounded by a sort of Scythian glitter, who seems to have seduced the country brother and sister without any effort or particular desire to do so."[34] Note that Bon is older than his years just as, according to Rosa, the Haitian Negroes came from a place much "older" than Virginia. Bon wears "outlandish and almost feminine garments."[35] Again, Mr. Compson imagines him at the University of Mississippi, "reclining in a flowered, almost feminised gown, in a sunny window in his chambers."[36] Similarly, Mr. Compson describes New Orleans as a city where "the architecture [is] a little curious, a little femininely flamboyant and therefore to Henry opulent, sensuous, sinful."[37]

Hurston also gives us a figure who migrates south—not south to New Orleans, but south from New Orleans to Haiti, both literally and textually. The second part of *Mules in Men* documents her Voodoo initiations in New Orleans, the home of Marie Laveau. Through her texts Hurston imagines a broader definition of a Black South, one that is cosmopolitan and shares culture, language, history, people, and interactions with places farther south.

As with Faulkner, Hurston is fascinated with New Orleans as a place of cultural difference. It is a site of spatial otherness for both writers. Historians have noted that blacks from throughout the United States, Europe, and Mexico and throughout the Caribbean settled in New Orleans. Some were brought as slaves. John Blassingame notes that the most distinctive feature of the free black population in New Orleans "was the large number of foreign-born blacks" from places as diverse as Germany, England, France, Spain, and Mexico.[38]

For Hurston, New Orleans is the "hoodoo capital of America," vying with Haiti, in "keep[ing] alive the powers of Africa."[39] Upon arriving in the city in the summer of 1928, she writes to Langston Hughes, "I have landed here in the kingdom of Marie Laveau and expect to wear her crown someday."[40] New Orleans is a Southern city where not just the culture, songs, and folktales of Africa live but the powers of Africa are alive and a black or mixed-race woman can be queen. If Zora is the protagonist of *Mules and Men*, Laveau is the second major figure, and the text's primary ancestor figure. Her nephew, Luke, with whom Hurston studies, narrates her spiritual biography: "She was very pretty, one of the Creole Quadroons and many people said she would never be a hoodoo doctor like her mama and her grandma before her. She like to go to the balls very much where all the young men fell in love with her."[41] Laveau is sister to Bon's octoroon mistress, but she ultimately rejects the life of *plaçage* for spiritual pursuits. She is spiritually precocious and soon her gifts are evident. "The City of New Orleans has a law against fortune tellers, hoodoo doctors and the like," so Marie Laveau practices a subversive art.[42] When the police come to arrest her she uses magic to send them circling away from her home.[43] Laveau, Queen of New Orleans, thus tames the powers of the state. In *Mules and Men* Laveau is a superhero, defying the racist powers that contain, control, exploit, and abuse blacks throughout the South, throughout the nation. She would have to do it through spiritual means, as magic is the only way successful resistance can take place and New Orleans is a place where magic happens. Laveau is a daughter of Erzulie, a mixed-race daughter of the Black South. For both Hurston and Faulkner, then, it is the Creoles of color who embody the difference that is New Orleans. They represent its liminality, its positionality as a close but foreign place.

Considering these two literary figures together allows us to map a Black South centered in New Orleans and radiating out to Mississippi, Florida, and the Caribbean. Together, they forge, give birth to, a body of literature, a set of literary children—mostly, but not only, daughters—who navigate their mapping: from Morrison to Naylor, Allende to Brodber, Perkins-Valdez to Danticat, and the many yet to come.

NOTES

1. Farah Jasmine Griffin, *"Who Set You Flowin'?": The African American Migration Narrative* (Oxford: Oxford University Press, 1995), 4.

2. Leroi Jones, *Blues People: The Negro Experience in White America and the Music That Developed from It* (New York: William Morrow, 1968), 95.

3. William Faulkner, *The Sound and the Fury: The Corrected Text* (New York: Vintage International, 1990), 86.

4. Cheryl Lester, "Racial Awareness and Arrested Development: *The Sound and the Fury* and the Great Migration (1915–1928)," in *The Cambridge Companion to William Faulkner*, ed. Philip M. Weinstein (Cambridge: Cambridge University Press, 1995), 136.

5. Jeff Karem, "Fear of a Black Atlantic? African Passages in *Absalom, Absalom!* and *The Last Slaver*," in *Global Faulkner: Faulkner and Yoknapatawpha, 2006*, ed. Annette Trefzer and Ann J. Abadie (Jackson: University Press of Mississippi, 2009), 163.

6. Ibid.

7. William Faulkner, *Absalom, Absalom!* The Corrected Text (New York: Vintage International, 1991), 4.

8. Ibid., 10.

9. Ibid., 11.

10. Ibid., 20.

11. Ibid., 20–21.

12. Ibid., 27, for all citations from the novel in this paragraph.

13. Ibid., 202.

14. Ibid.

15. Barbara Ladd, *Resisting History: Gender, Modernity, and Authorship in William Faulkner, Zora Neale Hurston, and Eudora Welty* (Baton Rouge: Louisiana State University Press, 2007), 108.

16. Faulkner, *Absalom, Absalom!*, 203.

17. Valerie Boyd, *Wrapped in Rainbows: The Life of Zora Neale Hurston* (New York: Scribner, 2004), 295.

18. Zora Neale Hurston, *Tell My Horse: Voodoo and Life in Haiti and Jamaica* (New York: HarperPerennial, 2008), 65.

19. Daphne Lamothe, *Inventing the New Negro: Narrative, Culture, and Ethnography* (Philadelphia: University of Pennsylvania Press, 2008), 161.

20. Hurston, *Tell My Horse*, 122.

21. Ibid., 121.

22. Ibid., 122

23. Zora Neale Hurston, *Their Eyes Were Watching God* (1937; New York: HarperPerennial, 1998), 2.

24. Hazel V. Carby, *Cultures in Babylon: Black Britain and African America* (London: Verso, 1999), 180.

25. See Leigh Ann Duck, *The Nation's Region: Southern Modernism, Segregation, and U.S. Nationalism* (Athens: University of Georgia Press, 2006), 130–31.

26. Hurston, *Tell My Horse*, 113.

27. Ibid., 93.

28. Faulkner, *Absalom, Absalom!*, 94.

29. Ibid., 252.

30. Taylor Hagood, *Faulkner's Imperialism: Space, Place, and the Materiality of Myth* (Baton Rouge: Louisiana State University Press, 2008), 83.

31. Faulkner, *Absalom, Absalom!*, 82

32. Ibid., 58.

33. See Alecia P. Long, *The Great Southern Babylon: Sex, Race, and Respectability in New Orleans, 1865–1929* (Baton Rouge: Louisiana State University Press, 2004).

34. Faulkner, *Absalom, Absalom!*, 59, 74.

35. Ibid., 76.

36. Ibid.

37. Ibid., 87.

38. John Blassingame quoted in Thadious M. Davis, *Southscapes: Geographies of Race, Region, and Literature* (Chapel Hill: University of North Carolina Press, 2011), 207.

39. Zora Neale Hurston, *Mules and Men* (1935; Bloomington: Indiana University Press, 1978), 193.

40. Carla Kaplan, ed., *Zora Neale Hurston: A Life in Letters* (New York: Anchor Books, 2003), 124.

41. Hurston, *Mules and Men*, 201.

42. Ibid., 200.

43. Ibid., 202.

William Faulkner and the Problem
of Cold War Modernism

HARILAOS STECOPOULOS

"What did you think of the domination of poetics by the CIA?
After all, wasn't Angleton your friend? Didn't he tell you his plans
to revitalize the intellectual structure of the West against the
so-to-speak Stalinists?" . . . "I did, yes, know of Angleton's literary
conspiracies, I thought they were petty—well meant but of no
importance to literature."
        Allen Ginsberg, "T. S. Eliot Entered My Dreams"[1]

Allen Ginsberg's imagined conversation with T. S. Eliot captures an important strain in US literary history. Eliot may not have been an agent working for CIA bureaucrat James Jesus Angleton, but many twentieth-century studies scholars accept as a truism the Cold War state's co-optation of modernism.[2] The evidence is persuasive, particularly in the literary arts. One only has to recall the mid-1960s scandal over the CIA's covert sponsorship of such respected modern literary journals as *Encounter* and the *Kenyon Review* or the State Department's deployment of Robert Frost, Allen Tate, Elizabeth Bishop, and other writers to realize that the US state sought to export US literary modernism as a propaganda tool. To be sure, many contemporary US politicians and citizens still decried modernism's excesses, arguing that avant-garde aesthetics subverted American values. Senator McCarthy's lieutenants burned modernist as well as "left" American works during their notorious tour of US Information Agency (USIA) libraries in 1953. But some of the state's more savvy propagandists recognized that, if properly exploited, maverick writers and texts could both call attention to Communist oppression and highlight the distinct cultural achievements of an individualistic people. Rather than challenging the status quo, the avant-garde would end up serving the state.[3]

For all the importance of this narrative of co-opted modernism, it tends to leave out one valuable aspect of the story, the very aspect that Ginsberg attempted to address in his imagined encounter with Eliot: what did the modernists themselves think of the Cold War state and its relationship to literary culture? That is a relevant question for all writers embroiled in the cultural Cold War, even those who like Allen Tate and John Dos Passos subscribed openly to a conservative political agenda. But that query is particularly germane to those writers who stood in tense relation to the state even as they nonetheless worked intermittently for the State Department or the USIA. What do we make of such liberals as Robert Lowell, a conscientious objector during World War II and a State Department–sponsored literary ambassador during the 1950s? How do we understand the position of Langston Hughes, interrogated by Senator McCarthy and his aides in 1953, and then sent abroad by both the USIA and the State Department in the early 1960s? And, perhaps most challenging of all, where do we place William Faulkner, a Southern political moderate whose longstanding problems with the federal state didn't so much vanish as intensify during a seven-year tenure as a Cold War literary diplomat?

We sometimes forget that the Bard of Oxford served as an unofficial US ambassador during the height of the Cold War. That sort of global assignment seems out of keeping for a regionalist who resisted a trip to Stockholm for the Nobel Prize ceremony and later claimed that the White House was too far to travel for dinner. Yet from 1954, when he traveled to Sao Paulo for the International Writers Congress, to his final trip to Venezuela in 1961, William Faulkner undertook repeated cultural diplomatic missions for the US government. Some of the more important assignments included his month-long stay in Nagano, Japan, in the summer of 1955, a two-week visit to Greece in the spring of 1957, the latter coinciding with an Athens production of *Requiem for a Nun*, and his repeated trips to Latin America. Faulkner also served as a member of the US delegation to the 1952 "Masterpieces of the Twentieth Century" festival in Paris and participated in the 1959 US National Commission for UNESCO conference.[4] No other US writer of the era played so active a role in the cultural Cold War.[5]

Yet for all his willingness to travel the world as an American cultural ambassador, Faulkner didn't allow his affiliation with the US government to dictate his writing or public statements. State Department authorities may have been generally pleased with Faulkner's diplomatic work, but, as David A. Davis, Barbara Ladd, John T. Matthews, and other scholars have taught us, during the 1950s Faulkner frequently expressed his frustration with the American way of life, and he did so at home and abroad.[6] Listening to Faulkner speak in Nagano, scholar Gay Wilson Allen noted how the novelist turned a question about a recent US tragedy into an acerbic commentary on American capital. "In my country," Faulkner proclaimed, "instead of asking the artist what makes children commit suicide, they go to the chairman of General Motors and ask him. . . . If you make a million dollars you know all the answers."[7] That indictment of US capitalism might not have unsettled the readers of the Snopes trilogy, but it may well have shocked the writer's Japanese auditors. Faulkner presented equally vociferous challenges to the authority and structure of the welfare state. In his "Address to the Delta Council" (1952), for example, Faulkner engaged in an impassioned antistatist screed that drew upon his longstanding dislike of New Deal agricultural policy and other forms of state modernization: "The enemy of our freedom . . . no longer threatens us from across an international boundary, let alone across an ocean. He faces us now from beneath the eagle-perched domes of our capitols and from behind the alphabetical splatters on the doors of welfare and other bureaus of economic or industrial regimentation."[8] In such statements, Faulkner appears less "an emissary who said all the right things," as Frederick Karl has described him, than a vociferous critic of the very capitalist polity he represented to the world at large.[9] By the 1950s, the Cold War state might have claimed modernism for its own purposes, but the nation's most acclaimed modern novelist raged against capitalism, social welfare, US foreign policy, and, at times, state-mandated segregation in highly public forums.

That adversarial attitude informed Faulkner's engagement with the diplomatic apparatus he served in the cultural Cold War. To be sure, Faulkner hardly railed against the State Department at every turn. Having unsuccessfully sought to serve in the US military during World War I and World War II, he clearly felt an urge to contribute to the national campaign in this new type of conflict. Faulkner's largely respectful relationship with such low-level State Department figures as Harold E. Howland and Leon Picon reflects this attitude. But when it came to the State Department or any large governmental entity, Faulkner sometimes adopted a different perspective, criticizing not only the urge to regiment writers in a bureaucratic manner, but also the more general attempt to exploit modernist aesthetics for Cold War purposes.

In what follows, I focus on what was by any estimation Faulkner's most difficult experience with US cultural diplomacy: his participation in the People-to-People (PTP) program. An idealistic attempt to connect ordinary Americans to the world without state interference, the PTP program took shape as a series of committees dedicated to particular professions and interests. Faulkner chaired the literary committee, a responsibility that placed the acclaimed modernist in vexed relation to the program's middlebrow internationalism. I first examine the absurd, yet pointed, letter with which Faulkner began his official duties for the PTP program, and then turn to his wry commentary on the very idea of Cold War literary propaganda, included in *The Mansion* (1959).[10]

Through a reading of these two linked texts, I argue that Faulkner's work for the PTP program prompted an attempt to reclaim from the Cold War state the very modernist aesthetic he was meant to wield on behalf of the anti-Communist struggle. That attempt took fragmented and at times incoherent shape, but in its very messiness, Faulkner's riposte to the state made manifest the writer's refusal to surrender his aesthetic to those cold warriors who found in modernism little more than a propagandistic symbol of freedom. For Faulkner, as we shall see, literary modernism had the capacity to bind together different peoples, to underwrite what he might have called an international confederation, but only if its energies exceeded the grasp of any state, East or West.[11]

1

The literary aspects of US cultural diplomacy have not had a long history. While American writers served as US ministers, ambassadors, and consuls from the earliest days of the republic—Benjamin Franklin, Washington Irving, and James Fenimore Cooper come to mind—such figures didn't undertake explicitly cultural missions until well into the twentieth century. With the advent of the Good Neighbor Policy during the 1930s, the state began recruiting US writers to serve specifically as American cultural emissaries.[12] Sinclair Lewis, Thornton Wilder, and other prominent US writers traveled to Latin America to challenge international fascism and win hearts and minds for the United States. In perhaps the most important example, Wilder conducted a three-month-long series of literary readings and public appearances in Colombia, Ecuador, and Peru during the spring of 1941.[13]

That state interest in the writer as ambassador overlapped with and informed another nascent strain in US literary diplomacy: the writer as cultural diplomacy bureaucrat. The Good Neighbor Policy helped inspire the state's creation of new cultural diplomatic institutions in the late 1930s, and various litterateurs were called upon almost immediately to help manage them. The Roosevelt administration appointed playwright Robert Sherwood to serve as the first director of the US Foreign Information Service, director John Houseman to the first directorship of the Voice of America, and poet Archibald MacLeish to the post of assistant secretary of state for cultural affairs. Such filiations of the literary and the bureaucratic continued through the 1940s and expanded considerably during the 1950s with the advent of the cultural Cold War. The US Information Agency (1953) would inadvertently testify all the more to this persistent literary presence when the new government office took as its slogan the tagline "Telling America's Story to the World." For all its surprising investment in innovative writing, the state's conscription of prominent modernists was in many ways a new wrinkle of an ongoing and complicated relationship between literary culture and government propaganda.

When President Eisenhower invited William Faulkner to create a literary committee for the People to People program in 1955, he gestured to the potential importance of writers in a new campaign to shore up the nation's global image. Inspired in large part by public literary figures and backed by the White House, the PTP program attempted to create global community through a private-public network that could both draw on President Eisenhower's support and also deny direct affiliation with the US state.[14] Its nongovernmental status proved particularly important, for the PTP program was designed to encourage an emphatically quotidian version of what international relations scholar Joseph Montville has called "track two diplomacy," a citizens' diplomacy that stands apart from the official version pursued by the state.[15] During the 1950s, the dominant form of US "track two diplomacy" took shape as what Christina Klein has called Cold War integrationism: an eclectic mix of anti-Communism, missionary tradition, New Deal discourse, and sentimentalism that stressed the importance of cultivating benevolent American connections with the world at large. Rather than emphasizing how the United States would contain communism through military and economic means, Cold War integrationism emphasized how ordinary Americans could through global outreach ensure that foreign peoples had a more accurate, which is to say positive, image of the United States. Highlighting the value of international "contact and connection," the PTP program asked and answered what contemporary USIA director Arthur Larson claimed was the pressing question confronting Cold War–era Americans: not "what are we against?" but "what are we for?"[16]

For all his longstanding dislike of bureaucracy, Faulkner well understood the Cold War integrationist goals of the PTP program and how writers might contribute to them. As he explained at one point, his task was to "to organize American writers to see what we can do to give a true picture of our country to other people." Yet having writers "give a true picture of our country" in a largely middlebrow manner created a potentially difficult situation for modernists, Faulkner included. If savvy propagandists in the CIA and the State Department found in modernism a new way of making the West's case against Communism, the PTP program and many of its adherents sought a less aesthetically challenging path that left modernism in an odd position, at once celebrated for its global standing and castigated for its off-putting, if not elitist, aesthetic. For some middlebrow internationalists, modernism seemed more of a liability than a boon inasmuch as it seemed to encourage a rarefied mentality that might clash with the very idea of global community relations. That the proponents of the PTP program included some of the very figures (*Saturday Review* editor Norman Cousins, poet Robert Hillyer) who had seven years earlier vehemently opposed the awarding of the Bollingen Prize to modernist Ezra Pound makes all the more palpable the likely conflict between two competing forms of literary globalism.

Faulkner's first effort at organizing writers speaks to the clash between the middlebrow humanitarianism of the new cultural diplomatic effort and his modernist impulse to *épater le bourgeois*. Having decided to contact potential contributors individually, Faulkner and his cochair (in reality, factotum), journalist Harvey Breit, sent two documents to some of the nation's finest writers, among them Robert Lowell, Marianne Moore, Lewis Mumford, Katherine Anne Porter, John Steinbeck, and William Carlos Williams. The first document was the official PTP program statement drawn from a September 1956 White House conference attended by President Eisenhower, Vice President Nixon, Secretary of State Dulles, and the program committee chairs including Faulkner. Entitled "A Program for People-to-People Partnership," the statement emphasized that the point of the initiative was "to encourage American citizens to develop their contacts with the people of other lands as a means of promoting understanding, peace, and progress." And the statement stressed as well that various forms of public and cultural diplomacy could contribute to this goal: "Friendship between peoples is built on understanding and understanding is nurtured by exchange of information and ideas and by neighborly association." One couldn't ask for a better illustration of the integrationist thrust of the president's new public diplomacy initiative.[17]

Faulkner's accompanying cover letter constituted an example of how one writer might respond to the president's entreaty, but the document also functioned as a provocative riposte to the very idea of enlisting modernists in such a decidedly middlebrow project. I quote the letter here in its entirety:

Dear_____:

The President has asked me to organize American writers to see what we can do to give a true picture of our country to other people. Will you join such an organization?

Pending a convenient meeting, will you send to me in a sentence or a paragraph, or a page, or as many more as you like, your private idea of what might further this project? I am enclosing my ideas as a sample.

1. Anesthetize, for one year, American vocal chords.

2. Abolish, for one year, American passports.

3. Commandeer every American automobile. Secrete Johnson grass seed in the cushions and every other available place. Fill the tanks with gasoline. Leave the switch key in the switch and push the car across the iron curtain.

4. Ask the Government to establish a fund. Choose 10,000 people between eighteen and thirty, preferably Communists. Bring them to this country and let them see America as it is. Let them buy an automobile on the installment plan, if that's what they want. Find them jobs in labor as we run our labor unions. Let them enjoy the right to say whatever they wish about anyone they wish, to go to the corner drugstore for ice cream and all the other privileges of this country which we take for granted. At the end of the year they must go home. Any installment plan automobiles or gadgets which they have undertaken would be impounded. They can have them again if and when they return or their equity in them will go as a down payment on a new model. This is to be done each year at the rate of 10,000 new people.[18]

Several of Faulkner's correspondents commented favorably on the letter, but Faulknerians have generally speaking treated it as a quirky oddity or, to borrow from poet and PTP literature committee participant Donald Hall, an "absurd proposal." Yet Faulkner's ideas are in fact more significant than we have been willing to allow. Faulkner insists on rendering his satire of cultural diplomacy more absurdist than cogent—it almost qualifies as a prank—but this decision doesn't so much eviscerate its critical components as suggest that it is only through avant-garde aesthetics that a writer can offer a proper response to the power of the state, West or East.[19] One might claim in fact that Faulkner's collection of "ideas" is less an insignificant joke than an ad hoc poem prompted by the Cold War state's attempt to harness literature for its own geopolitical ends.

Let us look at Faulkner's suggestions. The first two set an outrageous tone by urging the year-long silencing of Americans ("Anesthetize . . . American vocal chords") and the end to American travel abroad ("Abolish . . . passports"). In this starkly dystopian scenario, the state compels Americans to limit their attempt at either national or international communication; your average American emerges as mute and isolationist. That these suggestions mock the idea of global outreach goes without saying. Rather than affirming the middlebrow internationalism informing the official White House document accompanying his own proposal, Faulkner suggests that the United States would enjoy a much better reputation if Americans suppressed their impulses to connect to others.

To be sure, in those two ideas, Faulkner doesn't comment only on what writers Eugene Burdick and William Lederer would soon dub "the ugly American" in the novel of the same name.[20] Faulkner's reference to silencing and immobilization also recalls the fact of contemporary domestic censorship and oppression during the 1950s. Various film-makers, writers, and artists had been silenced during the ongoing Red Scare, and many others were denied their passports because of charges of un-Americanism. As Caroline Henze-Gongola and Jeb Livingood have argued, many of the writers involved with the literary committee "repeatedly questioned the treatment of artists like Charlie Chaplin and Arthur Miller" and stressed that internal censorship did little to improve the nation's image abroad.[21] Chaplin, Miller, and other leftist modernists would not figure prominently in subsequent committee discussions, however. Thanks largely to an impassioned speech by William Carlos Williams, the poet Ezra Pound, imprisoned in St. Elizabeth's since 1948, would be the only silenced and immobilized US citizen discussed at length by the committee. Indeed, even Faulkner, no great intimate of Pound's, would write in the official PTP's literary committee report that "We should free Ezra Pound. While the chairman of this committee, appointed by the President, was awarded a prize for literature by the Swedish government . . . the American government locks up one of its best poets."[22] The irony is palpable. For Faulkner, the need to reclaim modernism from the US state urged the liberation of a poet notorious for putting at fascist Italy's disposal his own avant-garde voice—a policy recommendation that incensed some members of the PTP committee, most notably Saul Bellow.

The third suggestion in Faulkner's letter continues the theme of American immobilization—"commandeer every American automobile"—but it transforms this theme into a surrealist version of propaganda. To push all American automobiles across the Iron Curtain suggests an attempt to lure Eastern Europeans from the frugality and asceticism of Communism with the temptations of US automotive culture. Americans will deny themselves their beloved cars in order to woo their Communist counterparts over to the side of capitalism and freedom. Yet Faulkner takes what seems to be a propaganda proposal, however extravagant, and renders it outrageous—something closer to a proposal for a massive mobile art installation than an attempt to win Eastern European hearts and minds. The language of sculpture and installation suggests Faulkner's interest in the role of the visual arts in Cold War modernism—a topic he would take up in *The Mansion*. He recognizes as well the ridiculous aspects of Cold War propaganda in his suggestion that Johnson grass seed be secreted throughout each car. As Faulkner well knew, Johnson grass is a species of fast-growing weed found throughout the US Southeast; it is often referred to as the weed that ate the South. To offer Communists millions of cars stocked with this seed suggests an attempt to invade and conquer the Communist bloc not with US troops or ideology or goods, but with plants of a distinctly Southern variety. The Johnson grass would in theory spread throughout Eastern Europe and the Soviet Union, disseminated by the movement of the cars in which the seed had been secreted. The result would be an ironic Americanization of the Eastern bloc, not in terms of politics but rather in pastoral and visual terms. Poland and the Ukraine would now look like the US South even if they remained in thrall to the Communist regime.

This absurdist yet biting approach to the propaganda question informs the next and longest suggestion on the list: the idea that 10,000 young Communists should spend a year in the United States. One might expect such a plan to endorse dominant Cold War values, but in the PTP program letter, Faulkner describes his idea in terms far more critical than they are supportive of the United States. If young Communists are to see "America as it is," much of what they should do is take full advantage of a capitalist economy that locates freedom in one's right to indulge consumer taste. Faulkner does include a reference to freedom of speech ("the right to say whatever they wish about anyone they wish"), thus participating in a typical American act of self-affirmation, if in a manner that recalls his well-known concern over the diminution of privacy in a media-saturated nation. That qualified citation of Americans' freedom of speech then leads to the invocation of a far lesser "privilege": the right "to go to the corner drugstore for ice cream." Faulkner's absurd equation of freedom of speech with the right to buy ice cream is of a piece with his deliberately cynical comment on the situation of the American worker. He suggests that the government find the visiting Communists "jobs in labor as we run our labor unions"—a critique of labor that will resurface in subsequent committee meetings—only to then imply that "jobs in labor" are in the United States nothing more than a way to purchase large commodities "on the installment plan." The list of ideas concludes with a wry reminder that such consumer bliss can be enjoyed only in the land of the free and the home of the brave. Upon leaving the United States, the foreign guests must relinquish their cars and gadgets.

Given this list of ideas, it comes as no surprise that Faulkner grew so frustrated with the People-to-People program that he decided to abjure the very committee "distillate" or overview that he, John Steinbeck, and Donald Hall had signed. Rejecting the document, the PTP program, and all such attempts to organize writers for geopolitical purposes, Faulkner reputedly told Breit, his cochair, that the idea of a literary diplomatic project was unnecessary because "writers all over the world understand each other."[23] Plumbers and lawyers might need such an organization, but writers did not. The only suggestion Faulkner could offer the PTP program was to stamp every US book "True" or "Not True" prior to export. When Breit asked who would determine the veracity of the books, Faulkner replied in a telling way indeed: "a committee of writers."[24] A writers' committee dedicated to middlebrow internationalism becomes in Faulkner's imagination a modernist writers' committee that claims for itself the right to determine and name truth for the world at large. Faulkner's outrageous response to Breit's query gives us a sense of how the novelist viewed the state's attempted co-optation of modern writers. Instead of endorsing or rejecting that co-optation, Faulkner imagines the converse: the writers' co-optation of the state and its functions. Rather than allowing the state to monopolize communication, law, and ideology, the writers assume those duties themselves. Faulkner's closing response to the PTP's literary initiative recalls the absurdist letter with which we began, but it also looks ahead to his more mediated commentary on questions of aesthetics and propaganda in his fiction.

2

Those few scholars who have commented on Faulkner's involvement with the PTP program have tended to focus on its aftermath in the form of a spring 1958 speech Faulkner gave to the University of Virginia English club. That lecture is without a doubt a relevant statement from the author, one that reiterates his longstanding antipathy to statist groupthink and his affirmation of literary individualism. Commenting on the program, Faulkner explained to his auditors, "What doomed it in my opinion was . . . [the assumption that] man himself can hope to continue only by relinquishing and denying his individuality into a regimented group of his arbitrary factional kind, arrayed against an opposite opposed arbitrary factional regimented group."[25] As crucial as that English Club lecture is, it's important as well to consider how Faulkner's vexed experience with the PTP program may have affected his late novels. Faulkner was finishing *The Town* (1957) when he accepted President Eisenhower's invitation, and one finds in that novel language and imagery reminiscent of the writer's scandalous letter. Consider, for example, how Gavin Stevens tries to broaden Linda Snopes's mind by introducing her to poetry over ice cream at the local drugstore.[26] Thanks to Stevens's efforts, the possibilities of free speech as represented by poetry emerge in and through the lowly referent of dessert; the scene stages in narrative terms Faulkner's claim in the letter that freedom of speech ("the right to say whatever they wish") is comparable to going "to the corner drugstore for ice cream." Yet even as *The Town* may have the most compelling temporal claim on Faulkner's PTP experience, *The Mansion*, a novel still in progress when Faulkner delivered the Virginia postmortem, provides the most significant evidence of how the abortive cultural diplomatic project may have incited his imagination and inspired him to comment on the place of modernism, both literary and visual, in the cultural Cold War.

The Mansion makes no direct reference to the People-to-People program or indeed to any other US cultural diplomatic initiative. One will not find references to the USIA or the US State Department in this novel; yet as John T. Matthews has argued, *The Mansion* "engages at every level with the defining geopolitical condition of its era" not only through critical commentary on such contemporary phenomena as blacklisting but also through a complex engagement with themes of imprisonment and freedom.[27] The story of Mink Snopes, exploited, manipulated, driven to violence, and then incarcerated, exemplifies the largest themes of the Cold War moment—as does the life narrative of Mississippi-born Communist and Spanish Republican Linda Snopes Kohl. Moving up and down the scales of Cold War experience, the final chronicle of the avaricious Snopes clan makes manifest how Americans understood the great Manichean conflict as both an ideological clash of sprawling global scope and a national crisis that impacted everyday life.

Perhaps the most significant aspect of *The Mansion*'s historicism is its critique of the aesthetic and political presumptions that underwrote the People-to-People program and other cultural diplomatic initiatives. That critique emerges most vividly in the 1930s New York scenes revolving around Linda Snopes and Barton Kohl's wedding, a historical moment that recalls both the heyday of American Communism and the beginning of the House Un-American Activities Committee (HUAC). From that historical vantage point, the New York section of *The Mansion* responds to some of the issues at stake in Faulkner's vexed relationship to US propaganda, most centrally, the place of modernism in the US state's attempt to win hearts and minds overseas. Faulkner has Linda Snopes Kohl challenge an emerging anti-Communist vision of modernism by telling the young Chick Mallison about the left modernists who fought against Spanish fascism—"Ernest Hemingway and Malraux, and . . . a Russian, a poet that was going to be better than Pushkin only he got himself killed"—but the novelist's main illustration of an alternate and politically subversive modernism is Linda's husband, Barton Kohl.[28] In the words of John T. Matthews, "associating the communist Kohl with experimental nonrepresentational sculpture may be part of Faulkner's resistance to cold war cooptation [sic] of modernist aesthetics."[29]

Sensitive, perhaps, to the important place of abstract expressionism in the Cold War state's attempt to win foreign hearts and minds, Faulkner devotes most of his attention to the visual not the literary arts.

We will attend to Barton Kohl's sculpture as an example Faulkner's "resistance" to Cold War modernism, but we shall also examine that artwork as it figures in the forging of what we might call people-to-people relations in a universalist mode. As we shall see in our analysis of V. K. Ratliff's encounters with both the Communist Kohl and the Russian clothing designer Myra Allanovna, Faulkner's commentary on Cold War modernism proves more than reactive; the novelist's critique also speaks to the place of modernism in precipitating productive intercultural connection, whether in the 1930s or in the 1950s. Ratliff's encounters with Kohl and Allanovna enact a scene in which an ethnic American speaks across a significant divide to two figures whose Communist and Russian identities recall the enemy most hostile to the postwar American way of life. Indeed, we might say that while all the principals involved in these New York scenes are nominally American, significant ethnic and political differences render Ratliff's meetings with first Allanovna and then Kohl a rough approximation of the sort of intercultural communication at the center of the PTP program's integrative vision. Ratliff's ability to communicate and bond with strangers well illustrates the broad goodwill of the American citizenry.

Faulkner seems to endorse in an unironic manner Ratliff's forthright encounters with the Russian Allanovna and the Communist and Jewish Kohl. The satiric conceits of the novelist's PTP program letter don't obtain here. Instead, Faulkner takes up the place of modernism in such encounters by having Ratliff's capacity to engage with these strangers depend on innovative and unsettling visual art—a reminder, perhaps, that a once shocking Beardsley aesthetic played an important role in the novelist's early career. If the People-to-People program tended to envision an unmediated encounter between Americans and "the citizens of other lands," Faulkner focuses on how modernist art provides a third term by and through which Ratliff can find common ground with his Russian and his Communist interlocutors.

Modernism's mediating capacities first come to the fore when Ratliff meets Allanovna, a famous clothing designer of avant-garde sensibilities. One might expect the Russian American Ratliff (the V. K. stands for Vladimir Kyrilytch) to bond easily with a person of Russian birth, but the Cold War demonization of all things Russian suggests otherwise. As Gavin Stevens suggests at one point, Russian names and Russian ancestry prove more a liability than a boon in nativist America, and Ratliff's ethnicity, while indisputably important, seems a largely suppressed sign of his intercultural potential rather than a visible indicator of his urge to forge bonds with the Cold War other.[30] That the Mississipian and Allanovna manage to forge even an aesthetic connection seems an unlikely result at the outset of the encounter. Ratliff first meets the Russian designer at her store, when Stevens takes him there to buy a necktie for the wedding. The elite establishment seems more an art gallery than a haberdashery, with the ties priced accordingly, and circumstances bear out this impression. When Allanovna asks her Mississippi customer for a sense of his taste, Ratliff replies by describing a cravat adorned with an image of a sunflower on a red background, a pleasant image well in keeping with middlebrow art. But Allanovna rejects Ratliff's vision. The designer instead gives the Mississippian a tie that defies such realist expectations and instead forces Ratliff to think acutely about visual perception: "It was jest dusty. No, that was wrong; you had looked at it by that time. It looked like the outside of a peach, that you know that in a minute, providing you can keep from blinking, you will see the first beginning of when it starts to turn peach. Except that it dont do that. It's still jest dusted over with gold, like the back of a sunburned gal" (482). A Southerner eager for pleasant images of home, Ratliff attempts to see peaches and girls in the tie, but Allanovna's art object resists easy figural interpretation. Like the abstract expressionist paintings promoted and sent abroad by the State Department in the late 1940s and 1950s, Allanovna's tie offers the viewer pure color—something like a Rothko on a vastly reduced scale—and thus demands a great deal of the viewer. The Mississippian twice rejects his own perception ("No, that was wrong"; "It dont do that") as he struggles to understand the tie. Ratliff attempts to render the abstract "dust" and "gold" comprehensible by turning color into an anthropomorphized fragment ("the back of a sunburned gal"), but one suspects that in due course this image will give way to yet another interpretation.

Neither Ratliff nor Allanovna offers more commentary on the tie's aesthetic, but we later learn that the sewing-machine salesman comes to prize highly that unusual object; as he tells Chick Mallison much later, the tie "is a private matter"—and thus not available for viewing, let alone use, after the New York trip (539). What might have been a seemingly minor encounter between an avant-garde designer and a sewing-machine salesman from Mississippi, the state at "the lowest rung of culture" (466), takes on singular importance. As Jon Smith has argued, Ratliff recognizes in Allanovna's ties an aesthetic that exceeds both the status consumerism associated with Flem Snopes and the haute bourgeois investment in realistic representation ascribed to Gavin Stevens and Chick Mallison. For Smith, Ratliff takes from this encounter the knowledge that form can convey a sense of "experiential newness."[31] Yet perhaps Faulkner's emphasis on the meaning of abstract form in the Allanovna scenes speaks to more than the tension between country and city, Mississippi and Manhattan, or, in Smith's reading, gemeinschaft and gesellschaft—perhaps Faulkner also expresses through Ratliff's scenes of abstract aesthetic education an openness to hermeneutic possibilities that informs the sewing-machine salesman's willingness to accept and bond with the Cold War other.

In stressing the tie's challenging visual aesthetic and its universalist implications, Faulkner inadvertently comments on the role of interpretation in the Cold War co-optation of modernism. As Lawrence Schwartz, Christina Klein, and other scholars have argued, US propagandists' claim on modernism was in many ways hermeneutic. Rejecting the traditional primacy of social realism in state propaganda, US cultural cold warriors found in the very opacity of modernism an unlikely means of shoring up the West's indictment of Communism.[32] Unlike realist representation and its leftist adherents, the argument went, the formal challenge posed by an Eliot poem or a Faulkner novel or, indeed, a Pollack painting tended to inspire a host of particular aesthetic responses and that very interpretive multiplicity testified to the West's abiding commitment to individual freedom. The freedom enjoyed by the reader or viewer of modernism reflected and drew from the freedom enjoyed by all the fortunate citizens of Western capitalist democracies. That modernism's formal complexity was often of a piece with its deracinated qualities, its distance from national affiliation and thus national propaganda, rendered it an even more valuable tool for the United States in the cultural Cold War.[33] Here was an aesthetic lingua franca that affirmed US values and improved the nation's cultural reputation in one fell swoop.

In Faulkner's version, however, modernism challenges the viewer not only to forge his or her own response to a difficult artwork and thus to assert individualism, but also to use that moment as an opportunity to connect to the Other and recognize the importance of community and collectivity. Indeed, it is their shared investment in the tie's multiple hermeneutic meanings that eventually leads Allanovna and Ratliff to recognize that they both believe in an aesthetic that exceeds everyday "needs" (490). The tie becomes a *tie*—a connection that binds the Mississippian and the Russian together in a collective manner that recalls Faulkner's contemporary investment in the confederation of all peoples.

Faulkner drives that point home by placing this seemingly small *objet d'art* at the intersection of a still more important person-to-person encounter: Ratliff's unlikely bonding not with a Russian, but with a Communist—Linda Snopes's fiancé, Barton Kohl. During the Greenwich

Village party sequence that follows the discussion about sunflowers and abstract aesthetics, Kohl approaches Ratliff and wonders aloud if the tie is indeed an "Allanovna" (486). Ratliff confirms his host's assumption and their conversation soon turns to the art filling the loft, particularly those pieces that are neither "sculpture" nor "pictures . . . hanging on the wall" but some other form "made outen pieces of wood or iron or strips of tin and wires." Faulkner doesn't offer a detailed description of this genre-confounding artwork—*The Mansion* only dabbles in ekphrasis—but Kohl's comments reveal that the pieces are meant to challenge and disturb in predictable modernist manner. "Shocked? Mad?" queries Kohl of Ratliff as the latter gazes upon them (487), the sculptor's comments recalling the many times in which avant-garde visual and literary arts have scandalized the bourgeoisie.

  Kohl's expectations are warranted. Stevens and Mallison later will confirm the disturbing qualities of the artwork as they debate whether one piece depicts an Italian boy engaged in risqué behavior (514). (The fact that the two Harvard men can't determine precisely what it is the boy is doing is part of the scandal.) Yet Ratliff doesn't respond to that artwork in the manner of his more highborn fellow Mississippians. Instead of raging against Kohl and the obscenity of the avant-garde, the sewing-machine salesman responds by telling Kohl, "Do I have to be shocked and mad at something jest because I have never seen it before?" (487). That sensitive riposte to Kohl engenders Ratliff's most important comment on modernism and alterity:

> So he leaned against the wall . . . while I taken my time to look: at some I did recognise and some I almost could recognise and maybe if I had time enough I would, and some I knowed I wouldn't never quite recognise, until all of a sudden I knowed that wouldn't matter neither, not jest to him but to me too. Because anybody can see and hear and smell and feel and taste what he expected to hear and see and feel and smell and taste, and wont nothing much notice your presence nor miss your lack. So maybe when you can see and feel and smell and hear and taste what you never expected to and hadn't never even imagined until that moment, maybe that's why Old Moster picked you out to be one of the ones to be alive.

Ratliff's encounter with the challenge of modernism doesn't provoke a conservative reaction, a hasty retreat to what he knows and thinks. To the contrary, Kohl's nonrepresentational sculptures, like Allanovna's tie, elicit from him a range of aesthetic responses—some figures he recognized, some he did not, some he never would—that testify to his sensory acceptance of the strange and the unknown: "when you can see and feel

and smell and hear and taste what you never expected to and hadn't
never even imagined until that moment." Ratliff's willingness to engage
with aesthetic otherness transmutes into a willingness to accept all sensa-
tions no matter how alien, not because of an obligation or an imperative
(after all "anybody can see and hear and smell and feel and taste") but
because devotion to the full range of experience stands at the center of
a divinely created lifeworld.

By representing such moments in an emphatically phenomenological
manner, Faulkner suggests, if only inadvertently, that the hallmarks of
the People-to-People program—"understanding," "contact," "communication"—never function as transparently and bilaterally as the White
House and the program's middlebrow partisans claimed. For Faulkner,
those commendable international ideals depend upon and work through
a cultural presence that renders the moment of contact a scene of complex and provocative sensation. International exchange succeeds to the
extent that it's mediated, shaped, skewed by discomfiting aesthetics.
And those unsettling aesthetic mediations redound to local and global
politics in complicated ways. Modernism's rich and productive relation to the experiential doesn't only oppose the PTP program's facile
assertion of "contact" and "communication." Modernism also generates
through variegated sensory experience the possibility of new ideological
attachments. For Ratliff to "see and feel and smell and hear and taste
what [he] never expected to and hadn't never even imagined until that
moment" when interacting with Kohl, the "red" modernist, subtends
a potential willingness to approach Communism itself with the same
open spirit. If modernism incited an individual aesthetic response, that
response might potentially contribute to a politics considered subversive
by many Americans of the 1950s.

Unlike the Finns and Linda Snopes Kohl, Ratliff never joins the
Communist Party. No FBI agents come snooping around Ratliff's home
to locate a party card as they do with Linda. And with good reason: such
an investigation would be more likely to discover an enshrined Allanovna
tie and Kohl sculpture in the museum-like parlor than any evidence of
subversive political affiliation (539). Yet even as Faulkner does not have
Ratliff join the card-carrying left, he does have the sewing-machine
salesman play a surprising role in "eliminat[ing]" white segregationist
politician Clarence Egglestone Snopes (595). "Cla'nce," a sort of Mississippi Strom Thurmond, represents the Dixiecrat figures that rose
to prominence in the South during the immediate post–World War II
era. Ratliff doesn't challenge Snopes's political vision or work on behalf
of his competitor's campaign. Instead, the sewing-machine salesman
counters Snopes with a "down-home" prank: he gets two boys to rub

the politician's pants legs with switches taken from trees popular with urinating dogs. The resulting canine assault on "Cla'nce" shames him to the degree that he no longer constitutes a viable candidate and leaves the race. As Ratliff puts it, "He figgered that to convince folks how to vote for him and all the time standing on one foot trying to kick dogs away from his other leg, was a little too much to expect of even Missippi voters" (615). An ordinary white Southerner trumps a Jim Crow politician and in the process suggests newfound willingness to adopt a liberal perspective on politics and American life.

In its ribald humor and folksy appeal, the Clarence Snopes episode suggests a grassroots response to a political problem. Ratliff disciplines a local who has transgressed against community values and good sense. Yet for all its regional qualities, Ratliff's theatrical defeat of the segregationist also recalls both the aesthetic and the political consequences of his New York encounters with modernism. As Jay Watson has noted, the transformation of Clarence—or, more accurately, his leg—into a canine urinal before a crowd of Jefferson citizens recalls the sort of agitprop performance associated with the Dadaists, the surrealists, and other practitioners of a highly public "street" form of modernism.[34] Such argument must remain speculative. However outrageous, Ratliff's spectacle is no Duchampian "readymade" capable of articulating Jefferson to Greenwich Village. At the same time, one cannot doubt that Ratliff's openness to modernist art bears upon his surprising refusal to countenance Clarence's version of Jim Crow—that the sewing–machine salesman's willingness to experience what he's "never expected" and hasn't "even imagined" subtends a new approach to social relations in his native region. Aesthetics have consequences where Ratliff is concerned—and those consequences have the potential to reverberate in the 1950s South.

Modernism played no comparable role in Faulkner's attitude toward white segregationists and segregation itself. The great modernist maintained a moderate stance with respect to the race question that frustrated liberals and infuriated racists. Yet that failure hardly means that Faulkner turned a blind eye to modernism's universalist capacities, particularly in the international frame. Cold warriors might seek to deploy modernist works as aesthetic allegories of the freedom available in the capitalist West and denied in the Communist East, but Faulkner found in modernism a means of expressing another sort of internationalism, one that resisted the middlebrow sentiment of the People-to-People program even as it stressed cultural exchange. Most notably, perhaps, Faulkner's engaged modernism underwrote a commitment to an unusual transnational publishing venture: the Ibero-American Novel Project. An attempt to use Faulkner's reputation as a means of convincing

US presses to promote, translate, and publish Latin American novels, the Ibero-American Project was, as Deborah Cohn has argued, "like Faulkner's overseas missions . . . 'meant to contribute to a better cultural exchange between the two Americas and [to] foment ameliorations in human relation and understanding.'"[35] But if the Ibero-American Novel Project recalled the language and spirit of the People-to-People program, it also stood apart from President Eisenhower's cultural diplomacy initiative in its dedication to literary innovation. Faulkner's novel project may not have fulfilled his desire to have a literary committee declare texts "True" or "Not True," but it did suggest one way in which a writer might attempt his own nonstatist and distinctly literary version of cultural diplomacy. An American novelist promoting Latin American novelists, many of whom tended toward the experimental: with the Ibero-American Novel Project, Faulkner instantiated his vision of modernist internationalism outside the parameters of the Cold War state.

NOTES

Thanks are due Kathy Lavezzo, Jack Matthews, and Jay Watson for their many helpful comments on earlier drafts of this essay.

1. Allen Ginsberg, "T. S. Eliot Entered My Dreams," in *Poems All Over the Place, Mainly Seventies* (Cherry Valley: Cherry Valley Editions, 1978), 46.

2. See, for two representative examples, Alan Nadel, *Containment Culture: American Narratives, Postmodernism, and the Atomic Age* (Durham: Duke University Press, 1995), and Frances Stonor Saunders, *The Cultural Cold War: The CIA and the World of Arts and Letters* (New York: New Press, 2001).

3. I borrow my wording from Greg Barnhisel. See Barnhisel, "*Perspectives USA* and the Cultural Cold War: Modernism in Service of the State," *Modernism/Modernity* 14 (2007): 729–54.

4. The "Masterpieces" festival was sponsored by the Congress for Cultural Freedom (CCF), a CIA "front" that sought to promote anti-Communism among artists and intellectuals throughout the world. Faulkner most likely would not have known about the CIA connection.

5. There isn't much scholarship on Faulkner's cultural diplomatic work. The most important items are Joseph Blotner, "William Faulkner, Roving Ambassador," *International Educational and Cultural Affairs* (Summer 1966): 1–22; Deborah Cohn, "William Faulkner's Ibero-American Novel Project: The Politics of Translation and the Cold War," *Southern Quarterly* 42.1 (Winter 2004): 5–18; Cohn, "Combating Anti-Americanism during the Cold War: Faulkner, the State Department, and Latin America," *Mississippi Quarterly* 59.3–4 (Summer–Fall 2006): 396–413; Catherine Gunther Kodat, "High Art in Low Times," *Boston Review* 29.5 (October–November 2004): 37–39; and Helen Oakley, "William Faulkner and the Cold War: The Politics of Cultural Marketing," in *Look Away! The U.S. South in New World Studies*, ed. Jon Smith and Deborah Cohn (Durham: Duke University Press, 2004), 405–18.

6. See David A. Davis, "A Fable of the Cold War" (unpublished essay); Barbara Ladd, *Resisting History: Gender, Modernity, and Authorship in William Faulkner, Zora Neale Hurston, and Eudora Welty* (Baton Rouge: Louisiana State University Press, 2007), 79–107; and John T. Matthews, "Many Mansions: Faulkner's Cold War Conflicts," in *Global Faulkner: Faulkner and Yoknapatawpha, 2006*, ed. Annette Trefzer and Ann J. Abadie (Jackson: University Press of Mississippi, 2009), 3–23.

7. See Gay Wilson Allen, "With Faulkner in Japan," *American Scholar* 31 (Autumn 1962): 567.

8. See William Faulkner, "To the Delta Council, 1952," in *Essays, Speeches, and Public Letters*, ed. James B. Meriwether (1965; New York: Modern Library, 2004), 132.

9. See Frederick Karl, *William Faulkner: American Writer* (New York: Wiedenfeld and Nicolson, 1989), 891.

10. While most Faulkner biographers chronicle this experience, Joseph Blotner provides the best overview. See "William Faulkner, Committee Chairman," in *Themes and Directions in American Literature*, ed. Ray B. Browne and Donald Pizer (West Lafayette: Purdue University Studies, 1969), 200–19.

11. The fact that Faulkner never undertook a diplomatic mission behind the Iron Curtain suggests a certain unwillingness to play a role at the front lines of the cultural Cold War.

12. It's important to note as well that while the Committee on Public Information didn't send US writers overseas during World War I, the Committee did hire many literary men and women to serve as propagandists for the Division of Syndicated Features.

13. For more information on Wilder's tour, see Amy Spellacy, "Neighbors North and South: Literary Culture, Political Rhetoric, and Inter-American Relations in the Era of the Good Neighbor Policy, 1928–1948" (PhD diss., University of Iowa, 2006), 125–28.

14. Liam Kennedy and Scott Lucas have argued that such private-public hybrids were in certain respects emblematic of Cold War culture's incapacity to respect the division of civil society and the state. See their "Enduring Freedom: Public Diplomacy and U.S. Foreign Policy," *American Quarterly* 57.2 (June 2005): 309–33.

15. The idea of "track two diplomacy" is first defined in W. D. Davidson and J. V. Montville, "Foreign Policy According to Freud," *Foreign Policy* 45 (Winter 1981–82): 145–57.

16. For more information about the People-to-People program, see Christina Klein, *Cold War Orientalism: Asia in the Middlebrow Imagination, 1945–1961* (Berkeley: University of California Press, 2003), 49–60, and Andrew Falk, *Upstaging the Cold War: American Dissent and Cultural Diplomacy* (Amherst: University of Massachusetts Press, 2010).

17. I take these passages from a recently published document collection tracing Faulkner's involvement with the literary committee of the People-to-People program. See "Lost Classic: William Faulkner and the People-to-People Program," *Meridian* 18 (January 2007): 55.

18. Ibid., 54.

19. In certain ways, Faulkner's decision to satirize the very committee he was organizing can be seen as a deliberate way of rendering his literary correspondents comfortable with the idea of serving on such a body. Yet the fact that he proved a recalcitrant chairman who ultimately abandoned the entire project suggests otherwise.

20. See Eugene Burdick and William Lederer, *The Ugly American* (1958; New York: Norton, 1999).

21. See Caroline Henze-Gongol and Jeb Livingood's introduction to "Lost Classics: William Faulkner and the People-to-People Program," *Meridian* 18 (January 2007): 51.

Faulkner himself didn't comment on these examples, but, as David A. Davis has recently reminded us, the novelist disliked Senator McCarthy and the House Un-American Activities Committee and found repulsive the national hysteria over communism. See Davis.

22. Quoted in Blotner, "William Faulkner, Committee Chairman," 212.

23. Ibid., 213.

24. Ibid., 214.

25. Faulkner, *Essays, Speeches, and Public Letters*, 161.

26. See William Faulkner, *The Town* (New York: Vintage, 1957), 189–91. Thanks are due Jack Williams for this reference.

27. Matthews, 4.

28. William Faulkner, *The Mansion* (1959), in *Novels 1957–1962* (New York: Library of America, 1999), 526. Hereafter cited parenthetically in the text.

29. Matthews, 22n30.

30. See Faulkner, *The Mansion*, 473. For an interesting but very different take on Russian ethnicity in *The Mansion*, see Randy Boyagoda, "From Revolutionary through Cold War: The Russian Outlanders of Faulkner's South" (unpublished essay).

31. See Jon Smith, "Faulkner, Metropolitan Fashion, and 'The South,'" in *Faulkner's Inheritance: Faulkner and Yoknapatawpha, 2005*, ed. Joseph R. Urgo and Ann J. Abadie (Jackson: University Press of Mississippi, 2007), 96.

32. See Alan Sinfield, "The Migration of Modernism: Remaking English Studies in the Cold War," *New Formations* 2 (Summer 1987): 107–26; Lawrence H. Schwartz, *Creating Faulkner's Reputation: The Politics of Modern Literary Criticism* (Knoxville: University of Tennessee Press, 1988), 199; and Klein, 66–67.

33. Modernism in this scenario plays an integral role in what we might call the Cold War version of Kantian aesthetics: the cultivation of detachment through aesthetic response doesn't so much produce responsible national citizens as contribute to the making of responsible anti-Communists throughout the world.

34. Personal communication.

35. Cohn, "William Faulkner's Ibero-American Novel Project," 99.

Woman in Motion: Escaping Yoknapatawpha

Lorie Watkins

> *Geography: that paucity of invention, that fatuous faith in*
> *distance of man, who can invent no better means than geography*
> *for escaping; himself of all, to whom, so he believed he believed,*
> *geography had never been merely something to walk upon but was*
> *the very medium which the fetterless to- and fro-going required to*
> *breathe in.*
>
> —*The Hamlet*

Feminist geographers have long considered the effect of geographic differences on gender relations and gender equality. As Linda McDowell writes, "The specific aim of a feminist geography . . . is to investigate, make visible and challenge the relationships between gender divisions and spacial divisions, to uncover their mutual constitution and problematize their apparent naturalness."[1] Quite simply, it's "a social science that puts women back into the equations of understanding and mapping our world."[2] Thus while this branch of geography considers many of the same subjects that other geographers consider, it does so with a focus on gender that involves considerations of spatial constraints, the construction of gender identity through the use of particular spaces, and the lived lives of women in their local geographies.[3] As such, Janet Price and Margrit Shildrick identify a "lived experience, in which 'body and world are mutually constitutive.'"[4] Given the strong link between women, especially Faulknerian women, and the land, the literary application of the tenets of feminist geography to Faulkner's fiction holds promise for a deeper understanding of some of the strongest female characters in his novels.[5]

As Karl Zink first noted, "it is quite possible that the male's ambiguous fear and hatred and love of woman must be explained in terms of his fear and hatred and love of the old Earth itself, to which Woman is so disturbingly related."[6] Subsequent critics have established the central link between woman and land in Faulkner's fiction,[7] but that fiction also shows that women who remove themselves physically from their home environment, their personal geographical area, empower themselves to make life choices in a more typically masculine fashion. After all, my epigraph from *The Hamlet* suggests that escape remains impossible for

Jack Houston specifically and, by extension, for all men; tellingly, it says nothing about women.[8]

Feminist geographers Mona Domosh and Joni Seager note how a patriarchal culture limits female mobility as a spatial/social control: "The control of women's movement has long preoccupied governments, families, households, and individual men. It is hard to maintain patriarchal control over women if they have unfettered freedom of movement through space."[9] They add, "The freedom to roam without fear or accountability has mostly been associated with masculinity. Women on the loose are almost never valorized—in any culture. Indeed geographical 'looseness' in women is assumed to be a universal marker for sexual wantonness—or at least cause for concern about their respectability."[10] Time and time again, though, Faulkner shows us women on the run. Lena Grove perhaps said it best: "My, my. A body does get around."[11] When she climbs from the window of her bedroom in Doane's Mill, Lena may have little idea where she's going, but she knows that she wants to be a "fur piece" from the life choices available in rural Alabama.[12] She may not know what she's running *to*, but she certainly knows what she's running *from*, and her choice is one we see Faulkner's female characters make over and over, with varying degrees of success.[13] *Light in August* ends with Lena still traveling, yet preparing to settle down again, "this time . . . for the rest of her life."[14] Caddy Compson makes good on her childhood promise to "run away and never come back" in *The Sound and the Fury*,[15] and the female Quentin Compson climbs down from the upstairs window of the Compson house to escape to a fate that's as uncertain as her mother's.[16] *As I Lay Dying* highlights the Bundren family members' ulterior motives for making the arduous trip to Jefferson, motives that undercut Addie's final revenge (her posthumous journey home), and her trip ends with her literal commission into Jefferson's soil as the family at long last "get[s] her underground."[17] Temple Drake ventures out with various "town boys" as *Sanctuary* begins, but ends up staring, "vanquished," wrapped "in the embrace of the season of rain and death" at novel's end.[18] Joe Christmas looks back upon the first phase of his affair with Joanna Burden in *Light in August* in geographically gendered terms, seeing "instantaneous as a landscape in a lightningflash, a horizon of physical security and adultery if not pleasure" and recognizing Joanna as "the other the mantrained muscles and the mantrained habit of thinking born of heritage and environment with which he had to fight up to the final instant."[19] Joanna surrenders, albeit with "manlike yielding," and Christmas constructs that submission using geographically gendered language. In *The Unvanquished*, Drusilla Hawk rides with Colonel Sartoris's troops, only later to be vanquished and feminized by Aunt Louisa, a dress, marriage, and perhaps verbena.[20] In that same novel, Granny travels and secures the mules that eventually give her the essence of a plantation owner's power, yet that same power ultimately leads to her death. Miss Habersham makes that fortuitous midnight trip to Beat Four with Chick Mallison and Aleck Sander to exonerate Lucas Beauchamp in *Intruder in the Dust*, yet we last see her "sitting in her own hall now mending the stockings until time to feed the chickens."[21] While all these women do manage brief escapes and gain power by manipulating their personal geographic space, for the most part society either marginalizes them or quickly returns them to their proper positions.

Faulkner's most fully contained natural woman, though, ultimately becomes Eula Varner Snopes. Eula, Faulkner's earth mother extraordinaire with her "ripe peach" of a mouth and "hothouse grapes" for eyes, inspires exactly the male ambivalence Zink points to and feminist geographers chronicle.[22] Ratliff most obviously displays this dualistic attitude in the form of his simultaneous desire for and fear of Eula's sexuality. He connects his fearful desire to the land when he compares Eula to "the unscalable sierra, the rosy virginal mother of barricades for no man to conquer scot-free or even to conquer at all, but on the contrary to be hurled back and down, leaving no scar, no mark of himself."[23] Eula becomes an indomitable mountain Ratliff imagines no man can conquer, perhaps because he fears her too much to attempt such action. In the same passage, Ratliff similarly describes her marriage to Flem as a mythical circumstance in which "the gods themselves had funnelled all the concentrated bright wet-slanted unparadised June onto a dung-heap";[24] while this image obviously illustrates Ratliff's fury at the inherent waste of Eula on Flem, it also connects Eula, as a commodity that her father may "waste," back to the ambivalent relationship between man, woman, and land that Zink first pointed to.

Labove experiences Eula in similar fashion as she enters the classroom like a "moist blast of spring's liquorish corruption" that forces him to worship her in "pagan triumphal prostration before the supreme primal uterus."[25] Through Eula, Labove pays homage to the "supreme primal uterus," which exists for him simultaneously as all of womanhood, life, sexuality, and even the earth itself. Labove more definitively connects Eula to the earth when he likens her to "fine land rich and fecund and foul and eternal and impervious to him who claimed title to it."[26] That imperviousness inspires Labove's desire to "leave some indelible mark of himself" on Eula through sexual domination; essentially, he wants to mark her physically as his territory.[27]

Eula leaves Frenchman's Bend and, upon arriving in Jefferson, has a similar effect on Stevens, inspiring both terror and awe as he longs to "to be swept up as into storm or hurricane or tornado itself and tossed and wrung and wrenched and consumed, the light last final spent insentient husk to float slowing and weightless, for a moment longer during the long vacant rest of life, and then no more."[28] However Eula's journey, like that of so many women before her, ultimately comes to naught when she commits suicide to protect her daughter. Faulkner even describes her death as "her own act of quitting Motion" (*Town* 118). Afterwards Jefferson does remember Eula, yet the town also culturally contains her in death as both a mythic figure and the "virtuous wife" of her epitaph.[29] Moreover, Flem reinscribes her onto the Yoknapatawphan landscape via Eula Acres, the subdivision that he carves out of the old Compson place (*Mansion* 628). As Diane Roberts puts it, "Flem's subdivision would be called Eula Acres, an attempt to control and contain the feminine in ownership: shackled land figuring silenced wife."[30]

Eula's living legacy, Linda Snopes Kohl, embarks on a far more successful journey than her mother and other Faulknerian women before her. Critics have long noted that Linda differs from other Faulknerian women: most notably Hee Kang identifies in Linda a "New Configuration of Faulkner's Feminine," and Keith Louise Fulton quite rightly refers to her as "Faulkner's Radical Woman."[31] Most crucial to my purposes here, as Kang points out, is that "Faulkner, through Linda, changes the landscape of woman's space in his fictional world, tracing a trajectory from the space of victimization, betrayal, and death to a newly configured feminine space of desire, autonomy, and freedom."[32] Kang uses the phrases "woman's space" and "feminine space" metaphorically, but I would suggest that Faulkner's women, especially Linda, quite literally construct new fictionalized geographic spaces through motion. Susan Stanford Friedman speaks to this intersection of new ideas about geography and identity when she writes, "The new geographics figures identity as a historically embedded site, a positionality, a location, a standpoint, a terrain, an intersection, a network, a crossroads of multiply situated knowledges."[33] While I'm not sure that I read Linda's act of second-degree murder quite so positively as does Kang, I would suggest that Faulkner creates a more active, aware, believable female character in part by allowing Linda successful control of her physical environment—and thus her identity—in a way that no woman hailing from Yoknapatawpha has possessed before her.[34] In fact, the crux of Linda's relationships with the men in her life centers in her personal geography. Early on, we see Linda riding in Matt Levitt's "yellow cut-down racer" (*Town* 161), but the law soon runs Matt out of town (174), and Linda's relationship with Stevens and Stevens's conflict with her so-called father

(*Mansion* 711), Flem Snopes, become the narrative focus.[35] Stevens surmises that Flem cannot allow Linda to marry before Will Varner's death;
if she does, Eula will no longer need the respectability of Flem's name
for her illegitimate daughter and will leave Flem and, in doing so, cut
him out of Varner's will. Flem, moreover, will lose control of Varner's
"voting stock" in the bank (*Town* 229).[36] So Flem, like so many fathers
before him, subjugates his daughter to patriarchal control. Stevens sets
out to free Linda from her father's influence and imagines that he can
"save a Snopes from Snopeses" by encouraging Linda to leave Jefferson for an eastern or northern college (160). Stevens imagines Linda
"doomed for marriage with someone beyond his [Flem's] control, either
because of geography or age" and seeks to facilitate that fate by "cor-
rupting her mind, inserting into her mind and her imagination not just
the impractical and dreamy folly in poetry books but the fatal poison
of dissatisfactions's hopes and dreams" (250). As graduation nears, Stevens begins to take more practical steps, having college brochures sent
directly to Linda and buying a traveling case for her as a graduation
present (185, 175).

Ever the shrewd judge of what motivates individuals, Flem uses Stevens's tools to his own advantage, offering Linda the option of a geographic change that he can control. He proposes a summer of travel that
would precede an education at "the University at Oxford," a compromise
between the "Academy" in Jefferson and the schools Stevens proposed.[37]
As Eula tells Stevens of the exchange, "he had her, he had beat her. And
the . . . terrible thing was, she didn't know it, didn't even know there had
been a battle and she had surrendered" (*Town* 285). Flem even talks
Linda into making her own will, a document that gives "her share of
whatever she would inherit from" Eula to Flem (281). Eula elaborates,
"she believes she thought of it, wanted to do it, did it, herself. Nobody
can tell her otherwise" (282), and Ratliff supports her interpretation of
the situation when he thinks of Flem, "He had to make a young girl
(woman now) that wasn't even his child, say 'I humbly thank you, papa,
for being so good to me'" (305). Stevens, however, arranges for Linda
to escape to Greenwich Village after they place Eula's grave marker. He
describes the neighborhood to Ratliff as "a place with a few unimportant
boundaries but no limitations where young people of any age go to seek
dreams." Ratliff replies, "I never knowed before that place had no particular geography. . . . I thought that-ere was a varmint you hunted anywhere" (307). Ratliff thinks that Stevens sends Linda to this geographic
void, the very opposite of Jefferson, so that she can find a husband and
make good his prediction that her "doom would be to love once and lose

him and then to mourn" (*Mansion* 528). Of course Linda does just that, but she doesn't do *only* that.

This geographical change marks the beginning of an equally drastic ideological one. At only nineteen, Linda leaves for New York, meets and marries the communist Jewish sculptor Barton Kohl, and the couple goes to Spain to fight with the Loyalists during the Spanish Civil War. Barton dies when his plane is shot down, and Linda, deafened by a shell that explodes near the ambulance she drove, returns to Jefferson some ten years later in *The Mansion* (492). Back in Mississippi, Linda continues to defy convention as she molds her geographic space to fit her new persona. She may be of (and in) the South, but she hardly plays the role of belle.[38] For example, shortly after arriving, she begins, as Chick puts it, "meddling with the Negroes" (531), inserting herself into the black schools and churches to improve education, and her efforts meet opposition from both the white and black communities. In similar fashion she ventures out to "Jakeleg Wattman's so-called fishing camp at Wylie's Crossing" to buy (and drink) her own bootleg whiskey (528). She even goes so far as to adapt her father's home to suit her new needs when she designs a "mantel," one perhaps deliberately similar to the ledge where Flem so often rests his feet, "at the exact right height and width to support a foolscap pad" for use when she and Stevens "had something to discuss that there must be no mistake about" (545). Fittingly, Stevens utilizes this mantel when he urges Linda to relinquish her communist party card and *"leave Jefferson . . . for good* (544). Linda's response shows just how drastically she has changed in her years away from Jefferson, as she offers to sleep with Stevens even more boldly than did her mother before her (545–46). This change from proper Yoknapatawphan teenager to world traveler and revolutionary woman reflects a marked alteration in Linda's attitude. For example, before leaving Jefferson, Linda believes (or desperately tries to believe) Stevens when he tells her that Flem really is her father (*Town* 304). After meeting her real father, Hoake McCarron, while in New York, Linda says that she loves Stevens "because every time you lie to me I can always know you will stick to it" (*Mansion* 489). Linda goes from depending on Stevens to preserve the safe emotional space that the facade of her paternity provides in *The Town* to telling him in *The Mansion*, "I dont want to be helpless. I wont be helpless. I wont have to depend" (545). With physical and psychological distance she has, it would seem, lost all of the illusions of her childhood, the illusions that Flem and Stevens worked so hard to construct and defend.

After eschewing the dependence that she once feared, Linda proves quite resourceful. After years of observing Flem's and Stevens's manipulations of her own life, she puts what she's learned to good use as she travels to Parchman to orchestrate both Flem's fate and Stevens's. She, of course, arranges for her Uncle Mink's release from jail and in doing so effectively murders her so-called father. As for Stevens, she appears to buy into his vision of chivalric love, encourages him to marry another woman, and then makes him an accomplice to Flem's murder: "By allowing Stevens to discover that she acted with forethought, she forces him to acknowledge her participation in Flem's death. In doing so, she attempts to make him realize his own role as well and admit the danger . . . of his refusal to face the reality of a world in which he continues to take actions that have devastating consequences."[39] Linda certainly blames Flem for manipulating her own life and ending her mother's, but she quite rightly blames Stevens as well and orchestrates Mink's release in hopes of forcing Stevens to accept responsibility for his meddling, destructive ways. Stevens, though, clings to his illusions; indeed, he ludicrously thinks of writing to Linda near the end of *The Mansion*, "*I have everything. You trusted me. You chose to let me find you murdered your so-called father rather than tell me a lie*" (*Mansion* 711). He thinks that he "could" and "perhaps should" write, "*I have everything. Haven't I just finished being accessory before a murder.*" Instead, he chooses the romantic middle ground and simply writes, "*We have had everything*" (711), when, actually, he has nothing save his impossible dreams and a handkerchief stained with the lipstick of Linda's last kiss locked in a drawer in his office (713).

Tellingly, Stevens learns that Linda planned Flem's murder when he discovers that she ordered a Jaguar from a Memphis dealership in July, rather than by phone, as she claims, the day before she buried Flem (*Mansion* 708–9). With her business in Jefferson complete, Linda prepares to leave town yet again and charges Stevens with two tasks that speak to her assumption of Flem's power—returning her father's house to the de Spain family and giving Mink a thousand dollars, perhaps a payment or maybe just money offered to support the man who helped to avenge her mother's death (712).[40] She then kisses Stevens and says, "'Yes. It's time,' and turned and went to the door and stopped and half-turned and only then looked at him: no faint smile, no nothing: just the eyes which even at this distance were not quite black. Then she was gone" (712). Linda's emotionless departure brings to mind what Stevens says of automobiles in *Intruder in the Dust*: "The American really loves nothing but his automobile: not his wife his child nor his country nor even his bank-account first . . . but his motorcar. Because the automobile has become our national sex symbol."[41] Faulkner lets Linda assume that ambiguous seat of power behind the steering wheel and in doing so gives her that "unfettered freedom of movement through space" that Domosh and Seager deem crucial to emancipation from patriarchal control. They write, "Changes in the *mobility* balance of power can disrupt communities and liberate women almost as quickly as any other social transformation. The patriarchal grip slips when women get cars of their own, or bicycles, or wings—which is why those advances are often fiercely resisted."[42] Linda thus becomes one of the few powerful female drivers in Yoknapatawpha. She joins ranks with the likes of Miss Eunice Habersham, who bravely drives her "second-hand vegetable-peddler's pickup" out to Beat Four to help exonerate Lucas Beachamp and later finds herself "snatched up and into the torrent of ballbearing rubber and refinanced pressed steel and hurled pell mell" into traffic after Lucas's near hanging.[43] In addition to Miss Eunice, Linda resembles Caddy Compson, who owns the *"first auto in town"* in *The Sound and the Fury* and surfaces again in the Compson Appendix, in a photo at the side of a "German staffgeneral" with a "powerful expensive chromiumtrimmed sports car."[44] Finally, Linda takes on a power akin to Narcissa Benbow's in *Flags in the Dust*. When young Bayard spots her behind the wheel, he thinks that her image "seemed to have some relation to the instant itself as it culminated in crashing blackness; at the same time it seemed, for all its aloofness, to be part of the whirling ensuing chaos which now enveloped him."[45] A similar catalyst of chaos, Linda, having donned a suit of "freshly-laundered . . . khaki coveralls, her face and mouth heavily made-up against the wind of motion" (*Mansion* 709–10), seems equally prepared to face whatever lies ahead.

At the University of Virginia, Faulkner said of writing about women: "It's much more fun to try to write about women because I think women are marvelous. They're wonderful, and I know very little about them."[46] I would suggest, however, that Faulkner's intricate depiction of the social and spatial strictures trapping the women in his fiction, restrictions that most of his female characters can escape only briefly in flight or totally in death, indicates that he knew quite a bit more about the position of women in the South than he let on, especially towards the end of his career. Noel Polk suggests that "the change in his fictional treatments of gender problems from his earliest books to his latest is undeniable" and adds, "In his late career, Faulkner seems to understand that men cannot claim their own histories until women can claim theirs, too."[47] Theresa Towner points out along those same lines that "Faulkner also knew that any oppressor inhabits his own cage even as he constructs one for another."[48] Accordingly, in Linda, Faulkner creates a tragic, imperfect character, one capable of manipulating her own geographic space to escape from or even to dismantle the various cages Stevens and Flem build to contain her, one capable of constructing cages of her own, and one that we finally find believable, even as she flees the scene of the crime.

NOTES

1. Linda McDowell, *Gender, Identity, and Place: Understanding Feminist Geographies* (Minneapolis: University of Minnesota Press, 1999), 12.

2. Joy Kennedy, "The Edge of the Map: Feminist Geographers and Literature," *Interdisciplinary Literary Studies: A Journal of Criticism and Theory* 6.1 (2004): 80.

3. This definition of feminist geography is necessarily brief. For an excellent, more detailed overview of the discipline, see Marianne DeKoven, ed., *Feminist Locations: Global and Local, Theory and Practice* (New Brunswick: Rutgers University Press, 2001); Mona Domosh and Joni Seager, *Putting Women in Place: Feminist Geographers Make Sense of the World* (New York: Guilford Press, 2001); Kennedy's "Edge of the Map"; Linda McDowell and Joanne P. Sharpe, eds., *Space, Gender, Knowledge: Feminist Readings* (London: Arnold, 1997); McDowell's *Gender, Identity, and Place*; Susan Stanford Friedman, *Mappings: Feminism and the Cultural Geographies of Encounter* (Princeton: Princeton University Press, 1998); and the Women and Geography Study Group of the IBG, *Geography and Gender: An Introduction to Feminist Geography* (London: Hutchinson, 1984). Among the many books available on the subject, as a beginning reader I found these most helpful.

4. Janet Price and Margrit Shildrick, *Feminist Theory and the Body: A Reader* (New York: Routledge, 1999), 337. See Domosh and Seager, 69–71, for a discussion of how the traditional association of the feminine with nature and the masculine with the city traces back to the Renaissance: "This association of the city with the masculine and the rational served to align the power of the new city with men" (69–70). Moreover, they point out that this association is rooted in dominance: "Americans have inherited from the European intellectual tradition a way of conceptualizing the city that dates from the Renaissance. The modern U.S. city is rational, planned, orderly; in other words, it is masculine. The countryside on which the city is imposed is represented as feminine" (71).

5. See Kennedy, 82–87, for a discussion of how feminist geography is useful in literary analysis: "Using feminist geography (and its overlapping partner of ecocriticism) to analyze literature can prove very rewarding" (87). She adds, "Feminist geography (as all feminist theory) uses critical means to question where meaning comes from, and how its origins are posited within the structure of patriarchy. I believe that many of its principles can quite successfully be applied to literature analysis. Doing so would provide a cross-disciplinary approach that may be lacking in many classrooms" (82). I necessarily limit this consideration of Faulknerian women and feminist geography to the most obvious examples in the novels because of constraints of space, but there are many, many other examples in his short stories.

6. Karl Zink, "Faulkner's Garden: Woman and the Immemorial Earth," *Modern Fiction Studies* 2 (1956): 149.

7. See, for instance, Louise Westling, "Thomas Sutpen's Marriage to the Dark Body of the Land," in *Faulkner and the Natural World: Faulkner and Yoknapatawpha, 1996*, ed. Donald M. Kartiganer and Ann J. Abadie (Jackson: University Press of Mississippi, 1999), 126–42.

8. William Faulkner, *The Hamlet*, in *Novels 1936–1940* (New York: Library of America, 1990), 928.

9. Domosh and Seager, 115–16.

10. Ibid., 118.

11. William Faulkner, *Light in August*, in *Novels 1930–1935* (New York: Library of America, 1985), 774.

12. Ibid., 401.

13. Judith Bryant Wittenberg writes of this circumstance in "William Faulkner: A Feminist Consideration," in *American Novelists Revisited: Essays in Feminist Criticism*, ed. Fritz Fleischmann (Boston: G. K. Hall, 1982), 238: "Many of Faulkner's women, however, even the ones ostensibly most confined by the social system, experience a sort of 'liberation' in the crucible of war or severe personal crisis which prompts the discovery and display of qualities of strength, resourcefulness, independence, and even tragic grandeur."

14. Faulkner, *Light in August*, 774.

15. William Faulkner, *The Sound and the Fury*, in *Novels 1926–1929* (New York: Library of America, 2006), 891.

16. Ibid., 1094.

17. William Faulkner, *As I Lay Dying*, in *Novels 1930–1935*, 160.

18. William Faulkner, *Sanctuary*, in *Novels 1930–1935*, 198, 398.

19. Faulkner, *Light in August*, 571–72.

20. See Patricia Yaeger's "Faulkner's 'Greek Amphora Priestess': Verbena and Violence in *The Unvanquished*," in *Faulkner and Gender: Faulkner and Yoknapatawpha, 1994*, ed. Donald M. Kartiganer and Ann J. Abadie (Jackson: University Press of Mississippi, 1996), 222–26, for a discussion of how verbena displaces Drusilla in the text.

21. William Faulkner, *Intruder in the Dust*, in *Novels 1942–1954* (New York: Library of America, 1994), 462.

22. Faulkner, *The Hamlet*, 848, 738. See McDowell's chapter 2 for an excellent discussion of the cultural association of women with uncontained nature and of men with the imposition of planned, urban space on the natural landscape.

23. Faulkner, *The Hamlet*, 877.

24. Ibid., 877–78.

25. Ibid., 835.

26. Ibid., 840. Also see my essay "He's a Bitch: Gender and Nature in *The Hamlet*," *Mississippi Quarterly* 58.3–4 (2005): 441–62, for an extended discussion of the connection between Eula's sexuality and the natural world.

27. Faulkner, *The Hamlet*, 840.

28. William Faulkner, *The Town*, in *Novels 1957–1962* (New York: Library of America, 1999), 81. Further references to this text will be noted parenthetically.

29. Faulkner, *The Mansion*, in *Novels 1957–1962*, 465. Further references to this text will be noted parenthetically. In "Eula's Plot: An Irigararian Reading of Faulkner's Snopes Trilogy," *Mississippi Quarterly* 42.3 (1989): 284, Dawn Trouard describes how Eula's epitaph memorializes "the dark irony of Flem's utter triumph" and adds, "In the discourse of the fathers, inscribed on materials that are intended to last, homage is paid to the qualities that benefit the deceased wife of the new president of the bank. The monument is to Flem." Although some critics, most notably Holli G. Levitsky in "Suicide and Sex: The Cost of Desire (Is Death)," *Southern Quarterly* 41.1 (2002): 29–38, and Diane Roberts in "Eula, Linda, and the Death of Nature," in *Faulkner and the Natural World: Faulkner and Yoknapatawpha, 1996*, ed. Donald M. Kartiganer and Ann J. Abadie (Jackson: University Press of Mississippi, 1999), 159–78, read Eula's suicide as an empowering act of self-definition, as Noel Polk points out in "Faulkner and Respectability," in *Fifty Years*

of Yoknapatawpha: Faulkner and Yoknapatawpha, 1979, ed. Doreen Fowler and Ann J. Abadie (Jackson: University Press of Mississippi, 1980), 131, her act of sacrifice fails to "'take' on Linda, as acts of sacrifice often do not."

30. Roberts, "Eula, Linda, and the Death of Nature," 166. It also seems important to note that, as Domosh and Seager point out, "Just as mobility is not inherently a path to power, so immobility is not always a disadvantage" (120). Several Faulknerian women also use immobility to their advantage, including Dilsey Gibson, Rosa Coldfield, Louisa Hawk, Mrs. Varner, and Maggie Mallison.

31. See Keith Louise Fulton's "Linda Snopes Kohl: Faulkner's Radical Woman," *Modern Fiction Studies* 34.3 (1988): 425–36, and Hee Kang's "A New Configuration of Faulkner's Feminine: Linda Snopes Kohl in *The Mansion*," *Faulkner Journal* 8.1 (1992): 21–41.

32. Kang, 22.

33. Friedman, 19.

34. Ratliff thinks that Linda's avenging her mother's death is justified (*Mansion* 717), but given that he has a shrine to Eula in his parlor (538–39), I note that a definite bias exists. For discussions of Linda as a positive/negative character, see Polk's "Faulkner and Respectability," 130–32; Michael Millgate, *The Achievement of William Faulkner* (New York: Random House, 1966), 246; K. Fulton, 434–35; and Trouard, 292–93.

35. Keith Louise Fulton notes that although Linda and Eula are not the source of the conflict between "Snopes and non-Snopes," they become symbols of the conflict (427).

36, Ratliff supports most of this information on page 200 of *The Town*.

37. When Linda tells Stevens that she plans to attend the Academy because she can't go to the other schools, he reflects, "It wasn't what the Academy was that mattered. It wasn't even that the Academy was in Jefferson that mattered. It was Jefferson itself which was mortal foe since Jefferson was Snopes" (*Town* 191).

38. See Diane Roberts, *Faulkner and Southern Womanhood* (Athens: University of Georgia Press, 1994), 140, for a discussion of Linda as an "anti-Belle."

39. Lorie Watkins Fulton, *William Faulkner, Gavin Stevens, and the Cavalier Tradition* (New York: Peter Lang, 2011), 86.

40. See Kang, 25–26, for a discussion of Linda's repudiation of her father's law.

41. Faulkner, *Intruder*, 463–64.

42. Domosh and Seager, 121. For an interesting discussion of Faulkner, masculinity, and automobiles, see Deborah Clarke's *Driving Women: Fiction and Automobile Culture in Twentieth-Century America* (Baltimore: Johns Hopkins University Press, 2007), 52–58.

43. *Intruder in the Dust*, 425, 426.

44. *The Sound and the Fury*, 948, 1134

45. William Faulkner, *Flags in the Dust* (New York: Random House, 1973), 143.

46. William Faulkner, Remarks to Edward McAleer's Twentieth-Century Literature Class, March 11, 1957, *Faulkner at Virginia*, ed. Stephen Railton, accessed May 23, 2011, http://faulkner.lib.virginia.edu/display/wfaudio04#wfaudio04.2.

47. Noel Polk, *Children of the Dark House* (Jackson: University Press of Mississippi, 1996), 164.

48. Theresa Towner, "The Roster, the Chronicle, and the Critic," in *Faulkner in the Twenty-First Century: Faulkner and Yoknapatawpha, 2000*, ed. Robert W. Hamblin and Ann J. Abadie (Jackson: University Press of Mississippi, 2003), 11. Numerous critics, including David Minter, K. Fulton, and Kang, have suggested that Faulkner learned much from the younger women in his life, relatives and lovers alike. In "William Faulkner: Life and Art," in *Faulkner and Women: Faulkner and Yoknapatawpha, 1985*, ed. Doreen Fowler and Ann J. Abadie (Jackson: University Press of Mississippi, 1986), 7–8, Joseph

Blotner reports that Victoria Johnson (Estelle's granddaughter) even said, "I could see a change over the years in his attitude toward women. The older women in the family—and that would include my mother [Victoria "Cho-Cho" Fielden]—were thought of as fragile but indomitable types and they were on a pedestal in a way and yet they were not considered to think very much or do very much except in the home and they were not really given credit for having much of a brain. Then when Jill and Dean and I came along somehow there seemed to be new respect, perhaps it was only because we went to college. But he seemed to value our thoughts and ideas more and expected us to speak—and he seemed to listen to us."

Contributors

Benjamin S. Child is an assistant professor of English at Colgate University. He has published articles on William Eggleston, Cormac McCarthy, Bob Dylan, and the Cinema Novo movement. He recently completed "Uneven Ground: Figurations of the Rural Modern in the U.S. South, 1890–1945" as part of his doctoral work in English at the University of Mississippi.

Kita Douglas received an MA in English from the University of Victoria in 2012. She wrote her master's essay on the Jimson weed in William Faulkner's *The Sound and the Fury* and, as a doctoral candidate at Duke University, is studying comparative ethnic literatures in the American postwar period.

Farah Jasmine Griffin is William B. Ransford Professor of English and Comparative Literature and African American Studies at Columbia University. She is the author of *"Who Set You Flowin'?": The African American Migration Narrative*; *If You Can't Be Free, Be a Mystery: In Search of Billie Holiday*; *Clawing at the Limits of Cool: Miles Davis, John Coltrane, and the Greatest Jazz Collaboration Ever*; and *Harlem Nocturne: Women Artists and Progressive Politics During World War II*.

Ryan Heryford is a lecturer in the Literature Department at the University of California, San Diego, where he teaches courses in nineteenth- and twentieth-century US literature, cultural studies, and the environmental humanities.

Barbara Ladd, professor of English at Emory University, is the author of *Nationalism and the Color Line in George W. Cable, Mark Twain, and William Faulkner* and *Resisting History: Gender, Modernity, and Authorship in William Faulkner, Zora Neale Hurston, and Eudora Welty*. She is also coediting, with Fred Hobson, *The Oxford Handbook to Southern Literature* and published "Faulkner's Paris: State and Metropole in *A Fable*" in the Spring 2012 *Faulkner Journal*.

José E. Limón is Notre Dame Professor of American Literature, Concurrent Professor of American Studies, and Fellow, Institute for Latino

Studies at the University of Notre Dame. He is the author of *Mexican Ballads, Chicano Poems: History and Influence in Mexican-American Social Poetry, Dancing with the Devil: Society and Cultural Poetics in Mexican-American South Texas*, and *American Encounters: Greater Mexico, the United States, and the Erotics of Culture*.

Valérie Loichot is professor of French and English and a core member of Comparative Literature at Emory University. She is the author of *Orphan Narratives: The Postplantation Literatures of Faulkner, Glissant, Morrison, and Saint-John Perse* and *The Tropics Bite Back: Culinary Coups in Caribbean Literature*. She edited a special volume entitled *Entours d'Edouard Glissant* in honor of the Caribbean poet and philosopher. She has also written numerous journal articles on Caribbean literature and culture, Southern literature, creolization theory, transatlantic studies, feminism and exile, and food studies.

John Shelton Reed is William Rand Kenan Jr. Professor of Sociology Emeritus at the University of North Carolina, Chapel Hill, where he was director of the Howard Odum Institute for Research in Social Science for twelve years. He is the author or editor of nineteen books, primarily about the contemporary American South. Among his publications are *Southerners: The Social Psychology of Sectionalism, Surveying the South: Studies in Regional Sociology*, and *Minding the South*.

Scott Romine, professor of English at the University of North Carolina at Greensboro, is the author of *The Narrative Forms of Southern Community* and *The Real South: Southern Narrative in the Age of Cultural Reproduction*, as well as essays on such Southern writers as Barry Hannah, Thomas Dixon, William Gilmore Simms, Harry Crews, William Alexander Percy, Lillian Smith, and John Crowe Ransom.

Harilaos Stecopoulos is associate professor of English at the University of Iowa and editor of the *Iowa Review*. He is the author of *Reconstructing the World: Southern Fictions and U.S. Imperialisms, 1898–1976* and coeditor of the anthology *Race and the Subject of Masculinities*. He is currently finishing a new monograph, "Telling America's Story to the World: The Literatures of U.S. Diplomacy."

Lorie Watkins is associate professor of English at William Carey University. Her research interests include Southern literature, African American literature, and American modernism. She is the author of *William Faulkner, Gavin Stevens, and the Cavalier Tradition*, edits the annual *Publications of the Mississippi Philological Association* (*POMPA*), and is working on a history of Mississippi's literature, *Writing in the Crooked Letter State*, for the University Press of Mississippi's Heritage Series.

Jay Watson is Howry Professor of Faulkner Studies at the University of Mississippi and the director of Faulkner and Yoknapatawpha. He is the author of *Forensic Fictions: The Lawyer Figure in Faulkner* and *Reading for the Body: The Recalcitrant Materiality of Southern Fiction, 1893–1985*, which received Honorable Mention for the 2013 C. Hugh Holman Award sponsored by the Society for the Study of Southern Literature. He is also the editor of *Faulkner and Whiteness* and *Conversations with Larry Brown*.

Index

www.ingramcontent.com/pod-product-compliance
Lightning Source LLC
Chambersburg PA
CBHW021228020726
47498CB00008B/2751